KAIRAT ZAKIRYANOV

THE TURKIC SAGA OF GENGHIS KHAN AND THE KZ FACTOR

A DOCUMENTARY STUDY

Published in United Kindom
Hertforfshire Press © 2014
(Imprint of Silk Road Media)

Suite 125, 43 Bedford Street
Covent Garden, London
WC2 9HA United Kingdom
www.hertfordshirepress.com

THE TURKIC SAGA OF GENGHIS KHAN AND THE KZ FACTOR
by Kairat Zakiryanov

Typeset by Aleksandra Vlasova
Translated by Robin Thomson

British Library Catalogue in Publication Data
A catalogue record for this book is available from the British Library
Library of Congress in Publication Data
A catalogue record for this book has been requested

ISBN 978-0-9927873-7-0

If I have seen further, it is by standing on the shoulders of giants.

Isaac Newton

Translator's notes:

All citations from The Secret History of the Mongols in English are taken from Urgunge Onon, trans. & ed, *The Secret History of the Mongols*. London: Routledge Curzon, 2001

The citation on pages 134 and 135 by Jack Weatherford is taken from Jack Weatherford: *Genghis Khan and the Making of the Modern World*. 2nd ed. New York: Three Rivers Press, 2005.

The citation on page 138 by John Man is taken from John Man: *Genghis Khan*. London: Bantam, 2005.

All other citations in this work have been translated from the Russian in the original manuscript, with the exception of some of the popular quotes at the beginnings of chapters, where an authentic English version has been found. While much of the academic source material cited would originally have been written in Russian, there are a few cases in which the original would have been a Turkic or a European language.

Kairat Zakiryanov - is a doctor of education and a professor of mathematics. He has been awarded the honours of the Republic of Kazakhstan for his work and is a member of the International Higher Education Academy of Sciences and of the Worldwide Genghis Khan Academy. He was born in the Samara district of Eastern Kazakhstan, said to be the ancestral homeland of the Sumerians, on the Irtysh river.

Dr Zakiryanov is also the author of *Under the Wolf's Nest: A Turkic Rhapsody*.

To my wife Marzia with love and gratitude

PREFACE

How many things, too, are looked upon as quite impossible until
they have actually been effected?
Pliny the Elder

The rapid development of what we have come to call civilisation that is now encroaching on nature's crowning glory, the human being, and the impetuous changes in traditional social and political structures that are permanently reshaping the world, have led to a situation in which the individual has become little more than an apologist for the indiscriminate consumption of all and sundry.

Having by the same token become 'global citizens', as we are told, mankind has also lost many of the traditional values that supported its moral integrity. As Fyodor Dostoyevsky wrote in his notebooks for the novel *The Adolescent*: 'All are separated. Even the children are separated.' Not only national self-identification but also a sense of one's family and genealogical roots have now acquired a distinctly archaic tinge; the result of this, however, has been a weakening of ancestral memory and of a historicistic world view rooted in a sense of one's own time and place. This is so despite the fact that family and homeland were traditionally inseparable elements of the culture and outlook of a given people. As a Kazakh proverb says: *Otan otbasynan bastalady* – 'Homeland starts with the family'.

As regards history, even Karl Marx, with famous polemic but also with full conviction, stated that 'We recognise only one single science, the science of history'. Yet in our own time, history is presented to us for the most part as colourful animations with the freest interpretations and simplified television series created along the lines of American westerns or thrillers, entirely devoid of real content. We need to admit that we have mastered only one of the principles of the Roman empire – that of 'bread and circuses' – while knowing full well that the ability to know the future can only be based on a deep knowledge and consciousness of the past. Clearly, then, the hard work of coming to know one's place in the flow of time, which demands a maximum of physical, intellectual and spirital strength, often turns out to be too heavy a yoke, not only for public awareness but indeed for contemporary historical science, which remains in a state of intellectual numbness before the ruins of the collapsed communist utopias of the 20th century.

All the more valuable, then, are the efforts of individual and original minds at dislodging the immense boulders, so to speak, of the barely-examined past from their accustomed places. Such is the labour of the professor of mathematics Kairat Zakiryanov, who has worked tirelessly and selflessly for many years to dismantle the historical blockages that have formed as a result of years and decades of muteness in historical scholasticism and thanks to the prevailing social and political situation. With his characteristic approach and with a mathematician's unassailable logic, effortlessly linking facts and circumstances that are separated not only by decades but by centuries, he succeeds in penetrating with his thought into the strata of millennia. Zakiryanov is, of course, a universally gifted individual who combines a mathematical precision of analysis with a humanist's depth of synthesis of multiple layers of history. This harmony of intellect and spirit was hinted at in his time by Lomonosov, who proposed that mathematics puts the mind in order, while literature puts in order everything else.

He recalls, not without irony, an utterance of Hilbert: 'He became a historian; mathematics did not contain enough fantasy for him.' More essential however was his heart memory, that had preserved the flickering pulse of tribal traditions. Indeed, *Otan ushin otqa tus, kuymeysing. Aryng ushin arpalas, olmeysing.*

In general terms, what we always strive for is historical truth, a complete picture. Yet we should also bear in mind that from a philosophical point of view, a historical source is fathomless. Moreover, history is more than just the study of sources, that is, of 'dry facts' – it is rather the interpretation of such 'facts', which calls on more than the faculty of reason alone, since a sense of history is perhaps more than anything a belief in one's people and in its moral strengths.

Historical truth is of course relative; each people or nation will pass over certain events and embellish others in its past, and this is simply human nature, because history is also humanity's self-knowledge, which not infrequently results in disappointment and sometimes in curious incidents. For example, one interpretation by modern Ukrainian historians suggests that Troy was founded by Ukrainians. And maybe it was so, if we remember that the Ukrainians themselves are linked to the history of the Turkic peoples. Nor are translators of literature an exception; for example, in certain translations of Gogol from Russian into Ukrainian, the word Russia is replaced everywhere by the word Ukraine.

The authors of a textbook in one of the Baltic countries, however, claimed that one day Aleksandr Suvurov, Generalissimo of the Russian Empire, who never lost a single battle and never retreated under any circumstances, was approaching a village in the Baltic region, saw the fleeing villagers – and turned his army round and left.

The film director Frederico Fellini said that the most fearful situation for an artist (and, I would add, for a scholar) is freedom. Clearly he was not referring to inner freedom, that quality found in outstanding and courageous persons, but rather to an outer insolence, that of a slave who finds himself without his master's supervision and who finds an excuse for his current base behavioiur (or in our case, scholarly slovenliness) in the past.

On this point, perhaps the most important factor is that Zakiryanov's work is guided by the fundamental principle of sculpture, in which the form is moulded from within. He thus grasps the fundamental and essential laws of Being through the internal logic of the historical development of humankind, hidden behind the outer show of dates, names and facts and wholly free of the associated euphoria or any other influence.

A further quality Zakiryanov demonstrates is a rejection of stereotypes of thought. While these may help one to live and survive, they invariably block or restrict the horizon and any real progress. Ultimately, paradoxical as it may seem, by resolutely and consistently cutting away heaps of historical detritus, he is able to move backwards in time – ever deeper into the past of his people – and yet also into the future that is unknown to us all, which can only be made clear, if not explained, by our dimly perceived present.

While examining civilisation, including the Turkic, by the reference point of the era of Genghis Khan, Zakiryanov does not limit himself to the strict historical framework of the 12th century. For one thing, in his reading that period turns out to be consonant with the most burning issues of our own time, and for another, it carries with it the understanding of the key stages in world history overall, taking the author back to the times of the protocivilisation of the proto-nation, and from there to the most ancient mythologems of the peoples of the world.

Clearly he had to take as a reference point the Sumerian period. In essence, this is an attempt to reconstruct the historical edifice of humanity in all its fullness and completeness at a time when world and language were a unity.

Let me give an example of another famous 'non-specialist' historian whose labours were game-changing. In the mid-19th century a man appeared in St Petersburg who was obsessed with the idea of solving the riddles of ancient Troy: Heinrich Schliemann. He was a highly successful businessman who took Russian citizenship, developed his business vigorously and grew wealthy. Wealth did not cool his ardour, however: he was engrossed in the mysteries of Troy. He meticulously studied all available literature and gathered all the facts and information available at that time. Let us note once again that not only was he not a historian or an archaeologist, but he had no involvement with any academic discipline whatsoever. For the sake of achieving his cherished objective, he did not hesitate for a moment to throw all his money into the project for the sake of knowledge and for making known the secrets.

His wife wrote to him from Petersburg: 'When will you come to your senses, all this adventuring at your age? Come home, and for God's sake don't bring Homer with you.' This would have been amusing if it had not ended in drama. The marriage broke up.

From the mound that he considered to be covering the remains of Troy, 250 thousand cubic metres of earth were removed. He himself found 8000 items of pure gold. Schliemann assumed these unique and priceless objects to be jewellery that belonged to Helen herself. He smuggled the treasures out of Turkey and wrote a book. When the Turkish authorities realised what had happened and claimed compensation, he simply paid – and did so generously, five times the amount demanded.

Schliemann wrote ten scholarly books that classified and systmatised his finds and he was awarded a doctorate. But the price of his triumph was heavy. He never saw his children from his first marriage again; and deemed to have broken the laws of the Russian empire twice, the tsar threatened to hang him should he ever dare to enter Russia again. And so Schliemann never saw his adopted country again either. His second wife, who endured with him the hardships and deprivations of many expeditions, finally also gave him up. Such is the lot, sadly, of many or most of those who devote themselves to a cause or an idea.

Many researchers concluded in the 20th century that Schliemann, who discovered seven cities, had been too much carried away, had been too hurried and had in fact missed Troy itself. That may be so, but how important is it in the end? My point is that as far as scholarly daring, creative determination and purely human courage are concerned, Heinrich Schliemann and Kairat Zakiryanov are cousins.

As Francis Bacon is said to have written, referring to the wisdom of the ancients, 'he who fully understands human nature is born to be a ruler'. And therefore for Zakiryanov, Genghis Khan was not a universal tyrant but rather, above all, an outstanding advocate of a strong state, who gathered, in the words of one of the founders of the Eurasianist movement, P.N. Savitsky, vast lands, 'without muddying the purity of national creativity' or the beliefs of the peoples he united, thus preserving national shrines and sacred objects and – most importantly – protecting the peoples of Eurasia from the Catholic West.

There is no doubt that Russian, Soviet and world scholarship have long attempted an objective historical understanding of the period linked to Genghis Khan, that exerted such a decisive influence on the passage of world history thereafter, but the inflexible ideological and political myths that prevailed at those times prevented the task ever being accomplished.

In our own time, when a person is required to constrain himself within a rigid corporate, as they say today, framework in order to succeed, the sheer scale of the philosophical and historical tasks he faces is a source of astonishment. In Professor Zakiryanov's case these tasks are not only set out extremely clearly, but also effectively resolved by a scholar who is already established as a talented mathematician, who has made a notable mark in world mathematical studies by proving one of the classical theorems in modern algebra and who today takes an active part in the formation of educational and state-political institutions in contemporary Kazakhstan.

In my view we are returning in the post-Soviet period to an epoch of individuals who are prepared to shoulder the burden of history without placing their hopes in the now discredited Soviet era of collective undertakings. More than this, having been left without a past, we urgently need to come to know ourselves as a nation, not even in history but in the facelessnes of eternity. Kairat Zakiryanov has meanwhile succeeded in finding within himself the moral strength that allows him, without hiding from the realities of ordinary life, to remain fully himself.

Much of this is owed in turn to Zakiryanov's own teachers, academic and spiritual, among them the head of the school of mathematics at the legendary Akademgorodok near Novosibirsk, Yuri Merzlakov, who among other things translated works by the Czech poet Viktor Dyk. An (admittedly diluted) flavour of this poetry can be found from this English re-translation of Merzlakov's Russian version:

The cables bow and sag
and all is disarray.
Compromises follow one by one
like autumn rain.
The cables bow and sag
and all is disarray.
The aspen leaf is not itself
and all is disarray.
Good and evil tremble as one
faint-hearted shadow –
All is disarray.
Be yourself.

These lines remain even today a kind of beacon for Zakiryanov's life and work.

Speaking generally, it may be said that the availability of archived documents that began in the early 21st century has failed so far to explain what is ultimately the most important thing – the causes of the tragedy. Yet just as the alphabet opens the way for reading, so also this time has opened the way for the individual to come to know himself. This has been the first stage towards an awakening of self-awareness. From here each person has already begun to ask: who am I, who am I with and why am I on this earth?

It has taken a long time for the thirst for documentary evidence to be quenched, and it has still not fully quenched, although even the original document was never a guarantee of anything. Rather, it demanded as a necessary condition at least a subjective honesty and the sincere pursuit by the researcher of the truth.

Sadly, what happens is often different. For example, the Russian philosopher Aleksandr Zinoviev described Aleksandr Sozhenitsyn's

The Gulag Archipelago as 'a grandiose falsification of Soviet history' in which 'each individual fact is correct, but all of them together make a falsification'. And a fact, plucked from its real historical context and allowed to fall into the untouched virgin soul of the chaste Soviet reader, produced a colossal, destructive outcome, the brutal erosion of moral and spiritual values: moral and historical nihilism and consequently a spiritual barrenness...

Such is one of the destructive consequences of the post-communist bacchanalia. Still, the time of rough and primitive, opportunistic factual accounts is now passing and what is now crucial is a conceptual and positive understanding of the past that is capable of comprehending the 'ocean of life'.

By his nature and his moral standing Kairat Zakiryanov is a creator, in any role: official service, scholarship or social and political initiatives.

As Vasily Klyuchevsky wrote, 'the regularity of historical events is inversely proportional to spirituality'. The destructive era that wasted such an enormous number of lives has become a moment of truth for practically every one of us. I believe that for Zakiryanov the Archimedean point has become an immense, primarily moral and spiritual need for each of us to look into and find our place within the tangles of national and world history, not relying on the aid of either official or, obviously, partisan scholarship, nor on popular pseudo-scientific stereotypes and conjectures that are based on phoney discoveries and sensationalism.

In our bustling and precocious time I have always been impressed by his Olympian restraint. To describe him in terms of a genre, one could say that his is the genre of the epic: a deep and often outwardly invisible labour of the mind and soul.

Ivan Turgenev (also a descendant of Genghis Khan) once compared the epic life of his people to a flowing river: while foamy waves play on the surface, deep down at the bottom is complete calm – and yet it is this that determines and directs the course of the river. And so while politicians of all colours work up a frantic storm of imitative activity to froth the smooth surface of the river of life, serious minds grasp its deeper patterns and are guided not by transient gains but by hard work that is directly 'proportional' to spirituality.

To obtain for oneself the Archimedean point, speaking in the manner of Fyodor Tyutchev, the poet, philosopher and diplomat admired by Zakiryanov, that allows one to transform clod-like, stereotypical ideas about life, he never rejected any of the ways pointed to by the wise Confucius: 'By three ways we may learn wisdom. First, by reflection which is noblest; second, by imitation, which is easiest; and third by experience, which is the bitterest.'

It is my view that this triad contains the hidden key to understanding the spiritual and intellectual world of Kairat Zakiryanov himself: an original and independent mind, respect for traditional values proven over the centuries, and also the ability and even courage, as Dostoevsky said, 'to think a thought through to the end', without stopping when confronted with possible difficult consequences or the tragic scenes of real human history. And as for ill-wishers, of which there has not been a shortage in any era, the 7th-century Byzantine John of Damascus commented: 'The storm does not harm small trees, but it destroys the tall, pullling them up by the roots'. A major figure will always find himself in areas of heightened attention and risk, but, happily, Zakiryanov has preserved himself and followed his path, guided by the familiar wisdom attributed to Plato: 'Socrates is my friend, but a much greater friend is the truth.' This is of course the hardest path, because what is right for each person is different, but real truth is the same for all.

It would seem difficult to find a less appropriate yet more thankless time than the present for undertaking fundamental work. Still, as Leo Tolstoy admonished himself and us, 'Carry your cross and believe'. This sacred belief in a necessary rebirth (let us again recall Dostoevsky, whom the eminent Kazakh Shoqan Walikhanov referred to his brother) of a national and simply a human 'belief in oneself' also impels Zakiryanov, with the passion of an Avvakum, to serve this idea that is capable of becoming the unifying force that we all need so urgently.

The scope of his work extends far beyond the problems of the ethnic and historical nature and time of Genghis Khan, acquiring the outlines of questions at the level of humanity in general. It allows us to hope that the reader will be greeted by more than a few brave discoveries and paradoxical hypotheses.

The life and destiny of Genghis Khan are the great secret of the domination by one earthly being of the whole world. He changed the course of all human history. What was it worth to him? We have pondered this secret for a thousand years. And we will find the solution, because we are his successors and we are obliged to be in keeping with him.

Professor Petr Pominov
Candidate of philological sciences

CONTENTS

Preface

PART I: THE TURKIC UNIVERSE   *19*
I. The Great Steppe: birthplace of the Centaurs   *20*
II. From the Andronovo culture to the Turks: unity and a common
ethno-cultural basis. The error of Herodotus   *26*
III. 'Scythian' iron and 'Barbarian' civilisation
IV. Yin, yang and the development of human society. What did *33*
Strabo not mention?
V. At the source of the world religions. The Turkic roots of Jesus *36*
Christ and the Prophet Muhammad   *42*
VI. The KZ Factor and the KZ Postulate   *45*
VII. Confucius   *47*
VIII. Alexander the Great   *53*
IX. King Arthur   *58*

PART II: GENGHIS KHAN
I. He who fully understands human nature is born to be a ruler *63*
II. The eternal people under the eternal blue sky   *90*
III. The genome of Genghis Khan. Is Jochi the son of the Great *104*
Terror of the Universe?
IV. Secrets of birth and death. Crimes and delusions   *110*
V. The Turkic language of Genghis Khan's Mongols   *130*
VI. The Khitan and Jurchen of Manchuria assimilated by the Kazakh
Naiman   *136*
VII. The Turkic union of the Oirat. Why did they become enemies
of the Kazakhs?   *145*
VIII. The unread stone of Kultegin. The Mongols of today and the
Mongols of Genghis Khan   *153*

IX. Turkic Mongolia. The Altaic Ergenekon and the Migration   *167*
Period
X. Genghis Khan in the consciousness of modern Kazakhs   *172*
XI. Mongolia from Modu Chanu to Genghis Khan. The Turkic state
in the lands of Karakorum   *175*
XII. Turkic heraldry and historical memory   *181*
XIII. Under the sign of the trident   *189*
XIV. Genghis Khan and the Kazakh Borjigin. The Kazakh Naiman.
The Kazakh Borjigin. Dacians, Dahai, Aday...   *204*

INSTEAD OF AN EPILOGUE
APPENDICES   *228*
Marco Polo on the Uigurs   *229*
The modern-day Kyrgyz and their ancestors   *231*
The Tatars and the Mongol-Tatar yoke   *236*

PART I
THE TURKIC UNIVERSE

When the barbarian advancing step by step, had discovered the native metals and learned to melt them in the crucible and to cast them in the moulds; when he had alloyed native copper with tin and produced bronze; and finally, when with a still greater effort of thought he had invented the furnace, and produced iron from the ore, nine-tenths of the battle for civilisation was gained.

Lewis Henry Morgan,
American scholar, ethnographer,
sociologist and historian

CHAPTER I
THE GREAT STEPPE: BIRTHPLACE OF THE CENTAURS

You cannot shut out the sun with your hand; however high the eagle flies,
its shadow always remains on the ground.
Saying of the Kazakh Naiman

It would not be difficult in the 21st century to determine the ethnic origin of one or another important person or one or another group of people using the powerful resources of genetic engineering, particularly if the person in question were, say, Genghis Khan. Many direct descendants of the 'Great Terror of the Universes', as he was referred to, may still be counted on the planet today. Sadly, my requests to the competent authorities to permit DNA analysis of the remains of the eldest son of Genghis Khan, laid to rest in the Uly-Tau mountains of central Kazakhstan, have not so far elicited success. Accordingly, I decided to take another approach: to examine the world of the nomads of the Great Steppe from the Hwang Ho river in the east to the Pannonian steppe of the Danube in the west, beginning in the late Neolithic period and the Bronze Age, and also examining the history of their numerous conquests. From two popular encyclopaedias – the *Khronika chelovechestva* by Bodo Harenberg (Moscow: Slovo, 2000, 2nd ed.) and the *Istoria chelovechestva*, specifically the chapter by Brigitte Baier (various authors, Moscow: Ast-Astrel', 2002) I learned that that world held many secrets. For example, Hardenberg writes of the Sumerians as follows: '... It is unclear when they left Central Asia. All that is known is that they became mixed with the local population of this region and then, on the threshold of the 4th-3rd centuries BCE, created the oldest of the known civilisations...'.

So only one thing is known about the Sumerians – that they arrived in Mesopotamia from the steppe of Central Asia. The leading French Egyptologist G. Maspero (*Histoire ancienne des peuples de l'Orient*, Rus. trans. by S. Soldatenkova, Moscow, 1895) considered the Sumerians to be a cattle-breeding people that indeed came from Central Asia, but that the indigenous, autochthonic people of the 'land between the two rivers' were eastern Semitic tribes. In *Götter, Gräber und Gelehrte* (Rus. trans. A.S. Varshavsky, Moscow: Astrel, 2006) the German scholar C.W. Ceram stated that 'The Sumerians brought with them a higher, essentially fully formed culture, which they imposed on the Semites.' According to another scholar, Karlton Kun (Beletsky, M.: *Zabyty mir shumerov*, Moscow: 1980) the Sumerians had already mastered the production of bronze and the techniques for producing objects in precious metals by the time they reached Mesopotamia. And considering the ethnic origin of the Sumerians in terms of their linguistic affiliations, the Kazakh poet, linguist and cultural expert Olzhas Suleimenov (*Tiurki v doistorii*, Almaty: 2002) states that '... a whole series of parallels persuaded me that Turkic writing is fundamentally hieroglyphic and originates in the Ancient Sumerian.'

Moving now to ancient Egypt in the middle of the second millennium BCE (roughly 1650 BCE), Harenberg writes: 'The north of Egypt was captured by the Hyksos – an Asiatic people of probably Semitic origin.' In my book *Pod znakom volka. Tiurkskaia rapsodia* (Almaty: Altyn Baspa, 2012) I considered the fact that this people has no relation to the Semites whatsoever but rather belongs, according to many Western scholars, to the 'Asiatic' Scythians. An English translation of the book (*Under the wolf's nest: a Turkic Rhapsody*, London: Hertfordshire Press, 2012) has subsequently been launched at the UK's Royal Geographical Society, and in March 2013 I gave lectures on the book's basic tenets to staff and students at the universities of Cambridge and Edinburgh. In this case, the conquest of Egyptian territory by Asiatic nomads is again of interest. It was these arrivals that first introduced the Egyptians to the use of war chariots, and the period of rule of the Hyksos, who established the 15th dynasty of the pharaohs, is referred to by historians as a time of flourishing for the country.

As regards the arrival in Asia Minor around 1900 BCE of other mysterious newcomers, the author states: 'The Hittites moved into eastern Anatolia from the north-east in small groups, probably through the Caspian Depression... having mixed with the local population, they established powerful states...' In my book mentioned above I pointed out the similarity of the languages of the Hittites and the later Turkic peoples, making reference to the Academicians Nikolay Marr and S.P. Tolstov.

Bodo Harenberg describes the period of the so-called Mycenaean civilisation of Ancient Greece as follows: 'The origin of the Mycenaeans (Ageans) is unknown, as also is that of the Greek language. It seems that as far back as the 22nd century BCE, conquerors were invading the northern Pelopponese who spoke a language unknown there.' At the same time, Leo Klejn, author of the monograph *Vremya kentavrov. Stepnaia prarodina grekov i ariev* (St Petersburg, 2010), states, for example, that the anthropologist John Lawrence Angel, who examined the dimensions of skulls at Mycenae, ascertained that they belonged to an ancient population of the inner-continental steppes. Referring to the German scholar S. Penner and the Slovakian archaeologists J. Lihardus and J. Vladar, he points out a surprising similarity between the Mycenaean culture and that of the steppes of Ancient Turan. Elsewhere, describing the collapse of the Mycenaean culture, he says: 'Mycenaean culture fell beneath the blows of Dorian conquerors around 1200 BCE who plundered the main Mycenaean centres... The Dorians, who had more advanced iron weapons and cavalry, joined in the fight together with the Aegeans (Achaeans – K.Z.), who were still using bronze weaponry.'

Here we are informed once again that some group of nomads, the Dorians, known in Greek mythology as the Centaurs and who possessed better iron weaponry, and more importantly had replaced the now antiquated war chariots with mounted cavalry, drove out from favourable places the nomads who had earlier arrived there earlier – the Achaeans.

Meanwhile the unknown language spoken by both the first and second waves of these conquerors, as is established below by scholars, is the Scythian language well known to us.

Concerning the Scythians, Klejn, writing now about the middle of the first millennium (roughly 625) BCE, states: 'Around the mid-7th century BCE the Iranian-speaking Scythian nomads penetrated Western Asia. In the 8th century BCE they had settled on the steppes of the northern Black Sea region, forcing out the Cimmerians who lived there. The Scythians continued to the borders of Egypt and participated in the defeat of Assyria.'

In my book I demonstrated that the Scythians were not Iranian-speaking but Turkic-speaking, and as for the Cimmerians, allegedly displaced, in fact the Scythians joined with them in the common task of establishing control over Asia Minor, a land in which Turkic peoples traditionally lived.

Roughly the same version of events is given about the peoples and nations discussed here by the *Istoria chelovechestva*. Describing the period of decline of the Sumerian state, for example, this source states: 'In about 2000 BCE the Elamite tribes, arriving from the east, took and destroyed the city of Ur. Later, the Sumerian kingdom was conquered by another group of nomads – the Amorites.'

Again and again these encyclopaedias tell of various fearless, menacing nomads who arrive from the limitless Asiatic steppes, subjugating with ease the settled peoples and their lands. This was not only in Mesopotamia, Egypt and the Balkans but also on the fringes of Western Europe and Eastern Asia. The conquerors of Western Asia who had arrived from the Eurasian steppes, the Mitanni and Kassites, were joined in the east by the Shang and Zhou that, beginning in the 18th century BCE, created ruling dynasties of Asian nomadic peoples in the Celestial Empire, while in the far west the invaders – Celts, Britons, Saxons, Picts and other cattle-breeding tribes – created what would become the civilisations of Great Britain.

The question arises, of course, of what were the sources of the nomadic peoples' advantages and what was their ethnic origin. In historical studies these peoples, under the single ethnological term of 'Indo-Europeans', are known as the Celts, the Cimmerians, the Scythians (Saka), the Sarmatians, the Alan, the Goths, the Huns, the Turks, the Mongols, the Kipchak, the Pecheneg, the Polovtisans and by other ethnic names, including the Mittani, Hyksos, Hittites, Shang etc. mentioned above. These were the warlike tribes that the encyclopaedias of Bodo Harenberg and Brigitte Baier describe as subjugating, time after time, the settled farming peoples.

Jumping forward in time, I would point out that none of these peoples has disappeared and that today's Kazakhs, Tatars, Kyrgyz, Turks and other related groups are their ethno-cultural descendants, and just as the Turkic world of today is held together by bonds of blood relationship, the various inhabitants of the Great Steppe were also consanguineous, ethno-culturally related brothers.

As regards the term 'Indo-Europeans', this name, used for nomadic and semi-settled peoples, came into use in academic circles because it was believed that their ancestral homeland was on the territories of modern India, Pakistan, Iran and other countries of the Asian continent. They were said to have Caucasoid features and to have achieved Bronze Age technological development. It became an established view among academics that the Indo-Europeans reached what is now Kazakhstan in the 8th century BCE from Western Asia and brought with them the Iron Age and the fruits of technological revolution. Certain scholars even in Kazakhstan itself believed that the Kazakhs were not indigenous to their own territory but rather migrated to the Eurasian steppe in the 5th century BCE from Mongolia and northern China, whereas the aboriginal peoples of the lands of modern-day Kazakhstan were again various Indo-Iranian tribes. Accordingly, all the credit for the conquests of China, India, Mesopotamia, Asia Minor, Greece, Egypt and the European countries described in the above-mentioned encyclopaedias has been given to these mythical Indo-Europeans and the Indo-Iranians. Today, I believe that the situation is changing. Prominent scholars such as the

Irish J.P. Mallory, the Australian V. Gordon Childe, the German E. Walle, the Americans Marija Gimbutas and David Anthony, the Kazakhs Orazak Ismagulov, Amangeldy Narymbaev and Zhumazhan Bayzhumin and others consider that, on the contrary, the active expansion of the peoples of the Eurasian steppe of Scythian-Turkic origin, whose 'visiting cards' were the domesticated horse, wheeled transport, burial mounds, axe-like 'celt' tools and matchless bows and curved sabres, was linked to the emergence of cultural phenomena of the late Stone Age in the Balkans, the Mediterranean, Asia Minor, China and other areas.

Furthermore, J.P. Mallory ('Indoievropeiskaia pradrodina', *Vestnik drevney istorii* (*VDI*), 1997, no. 1) generally considers that there was never a penetration by any type of 'proto-Indo-European' into Central Asia at any time. This viewpoint coincides entirely with the research of the Kazakh professor of history Orazak Ismagulov (*Nasledie Kazakhstana ot epokhi bronzy do sovremennosti*, Alma-Ata: 1970), who believes that the territory of Kazakhstan was never – at least since the Bronze Age – occupied by foreign tribes, and that the Kazakhs and their forebears were always indigenous to the land they presently inhabit.

CHAPTER II
FROM THE ANDRONOVO CULTURE TO THE TURKS: UNITY AND A COMMON ETHNO-CULTURAL BASIS

The Error of Herodotus

To everything there is a season,
and a time to every purpose under heaven;
A time to be born, and a time to die;
a time to plant, and a time to pluck up
that which is planted...
The Bible, Ecclesiastes 3: 1,2

In this section I shall try to substantiate my thesis of the ethno-cultural unity between the modern-day Turkic peoples and their historical ancestors discussed above, including the Celts, Cimmerians, Scythians, Huns and the earlier Andronovo culture of the Bronze Age. In his final work of exceptional originality and depth, *Turan: Vzglyad na istoriu chelovecheskogo obshchestva* (Almaty: Arys, 2012, books I-IV) Zhumazhan Bayzhumin provides findings from the works of numerous scholars that support this point. With the kind permission of the author I will provide some of these arguments here without referring constantly to the source. The Soviet historian and orientalist A.N. Bernshtam stated in his work *Proiskhozhdenie turok. Problemy istorii dokapitalisticheskogo obshchestva* (1935, nos. 5-6): 'The immediate substrate of the Turkish (Turkic) ethnogenesis was Hunnic society, and the direct antecedent of the latter was the Scythian. The Huns, both Asiatic and European, were reared on Scythian ground. The theories that link the Huns with the Turks (the broader Turkic peoples) pave the way towards also calling the Scythians Turks (Turkic).' I shall clarify that the Eastern Huns, or, using

Gumilev's terminology, the 'Hunnu people', are related to the Caucasoid nomads the Zhun, who formed a framework, the ruling class of Shang and Zhou China, and of the earlier kingdom of Sya, and incidentally the Zhun themselves entered the eastern parts of Central Asia as far back as the Eneolithic period, i.e. in the 4th-3rd millennia BCE.

The well-known Greek doctor and thinker Hippocrates of the 5th century BCE wrote in his *On Air, Waters and Places* (Rus. ed. in *VDI*, 1947, no. 1, p. 295) wrote: 'In Europe there is a Scythian race, called Sauromatae, which inhabits the confines of the Palus Maeotis, and is different from all other races'. Thus Hippocrates establishes an affinity between the earlier Scythians (as mentioned, from the 15th century BCE) and the Sauromatians (with whom there is a distance of almost a millennium). An even greater distance in time separates the Scythians and the Goths (who were first mentioned from 214 BCE) but likewise does not prevent their kinship being established. Thus for example the Greek historian Publius Herennius Dexippus wrote in the 3rd century CE: 'The Scythians, called the Goths, who crossed the river Istros in large numbers under Decius, subjected the country, controlled by the Romans, to devastation...' (*VDI*, 1948, no.1, p.308). Further, the Cimmerians and the Huns are separated by a minimum of two millennia. The Byzantine historian Procopius of Caesarea wrote of them: 'In ancient times, the great majority of the Huns, who were then known as the Cimmerians...' (*Voyna s gotami*, Moscow, 1950, p. 386); thus, the continuity can be clearly seen.

The present-day Russian scholar Yuri Drozdov, referring to the Russian historian Andrey Lyzov, who in turn is commenting on the mediaeval Polish chroniclers Strikowsky, Belsky and Wapowsky, writes: 'According to Andrey Lyzov, ... the Polovtsians, Pechenegs, Gepids, Lithuanians and the old Prussians (i.e. non-Teutons) derive from the Turkic-speaking Kimmerians (Cimmerians – K.Z.) and the Goths...' (*Tiurkoiazychny period yevropeiskoi istorii*, Moscow: Litera, 2011, p. 198). Thus we learn that the Polovtsians, Pechenegs, Lithuanians and Prussians that are almost our contemporaries are the ethnocultural descendants of the ancient Cimmerians and Goths. As regards the conquerors of the British Isles, the Celts, creators of the Corded Ware culture, the Greek historian and geographer of the 1st century BCE, Strabo, wrote: 'I confirm, in agreement with the ancient Hellenes, that in the same way as the well-known peoples from the northern lands called themselves by the one name of the Scythians or the nomads, as Homer refers to them, but later, when the western lands also became known, their inhabitants called themselves the Celts and Iberians or mixed Celtiberians and Celto-Scythians...' (*VDI*, 1947, no. 4, pp. 179-180). The name used by this people of itself was the Celts, while the Romans called them the Gauls. The tribe got its ethnonym from the Kazakh word *kelte*, meaning 'short'. The unsurpassed weapon of this tribe was the *balta*, a boat-shaped battle axe with a short haft. The word for the Celtic men's short skirt – the kilt – shares the same semantic. Descendants of the Celts among present-day Kazakhs include, for example, the Naiman Baltaly, whose predecessors lived in the early second millennium BCE on the southern coasts of the Scythian (later named Baltic) Sea and who migrated from there to the British Isles.

In his work *The Aryans: a study of Indo-European origins* (Rus. ed. Moscow, 2010) V. Gordon Childe agrees fully with another scholar, Ellis Hovell Minns, according to whom the Scythians were ethnogenic and cultural predecessors of 'the Huns, the Tatars (read: the Mongols – K.Z.) and the Pechenegs.' The Kurdish mediaeval historian Abu al-Fida speaks unequivocally concerning the predecessors of the Western Huns: 'The Alan are essentially Turks who have adopted Christianity.' (Asadov, F.M.: *Arabskie istochniki o tiurkakh v rannee srednevekov'ye*, Baku, 1993).

Another British scholar, Halford Mackinder, wrote in his work *The geographical pivot of history* (1904): 'Through the steppe... there came from the unknown recesses of Asia, by the gateway between the Ural mountains and the Caspian sea, in all the centuries from the 5th to the 16th, a remarkable succession of Turanian nomadic peoples – Huns, Avars, Bulgarians, Maygars, Khazars, Patzinaks, Cumans, Mongols, Kalmuks. [...] A large part of modern history might be written as a commentary upon the changes directly or indirectly ensuing from these raids.' Earlier – still in the 19th century – another English social history scholar, E.H. Parker, stated clearly in his work *A thousand years of the Tartars*: 'The Scythians, Huns and Turks were different stages in the historical development of the same tribes.'

The work of the Russian authors K.F. Smirnov and E.E. Kuzminskaia (*Proiskhozhdenie indoievropeitsev v svete noveishikh arkheologicheskikh otkrytiy*, Moscow, 1977) discusses the fact that the development of horse breeding in the Nile valley and the highest achievements of Egyptian art are linked to the conquests of Egypt by the Hyksos. When the Hittites took Asia Minor the cult of the horse also became strongly consolidated, while in Greece the arrival of the Achaean nomads, the cult of the horse-drawn military chariot grew analogously.

The authors conclude that these countries were conquered by certain Scythian peoples that were known in Babylon as the Kassites, in Assyria as the Mitanni and in Egypt as the Hyksos. We know, however, that it was in fact the ancestors of the Kazakhs, on the territory of modern Kazakhstan, who first domesticated the horse back in the 4th century BCE, and that it was from the lands of Kazakhstan that the cult of the horse spread, together with the Turanian warriors, to the rest of the continent. In this matter Zhumazhan Bayzhumin reaches the unequivocal conclusion that 'chronological data may testify that the Hittites, Kassites and Mitanni of the ancient East, the Hyksos of Palestine and Egypt, the Achaeans of Greece and the Shang of China were representatives of a single historical wave of cattle-breeders from Turania, who left that land at roughly the same time for the east, the south and the south-east.' To this I would add that today's descendants of these peoples are known in Russian, Arabic, Greek and Latin as 'turk' and in Turkic versions as 'aturgy'; the name literally means 'those who strike down from a horse'. Without suspecting it himself, Yuri Drozdov also revealed the essence of the ethnic term *turk* as meaning the people that had first domesticated the horse, and – using the image of a centaur – that struck down enemies using spears and arrows shot from their unsurpassed bows (*Tiurkoiazychny period yevropeiskoi istorii*, Moscow: Litera, 2011, p. 343). The conquerors of the Eurasian steppe were the

Scythians/Huns/Turks, while the peoples of the occupied countries were called by different names. Some of these have however survived down to our own times. For example, the Hittites of Asia Minor are late Turko-Germanic Geat tribes, the Goths, while in Siberia in the 21st century they are the Ket and in Kazakhstan they are the Kete. There are descendants of the Mitanni, Hyksos and Medes among the Kazakh Matay; of the Achaeans among the Argyn; of the Elamites among tribes of the Kazah Elim uly; there are Shang among the Naiman and, possibly, Sumerians among the Dulat Shymyr, and so on.

The Kazakh scholar Amangeldy Narymbaeva writes in her work *Turan – kolybel' drevnikh tsivilizatsiy* (Almaty, 2009): 'Just as the Sintashta-Arkaim culture once grew, at the end of its evolutionary development, into the Andronovo culture, and this in turn evolved into the Saka culture, in the same way the Saka culture evolved, throughout the entire expanse of the steppes, from the second half of the first millennium BCE into the Hunnic and later into the Turkic culture. These are stages or periods in the cultural development of one and the same people.'

On the same point, Zhumazhan Bayzhumin states: 'The fairly 'gentle' inclusion by various nomadic inhabitants of Turan of congeneric groups of other nomadic 'peoples' can be explained very simply – by their ethnocultural unity. For this reason the main element of the Cimmerian groups fitted relatively easily among the Scythians, and the Scythian groups were included similarly among the Sarmatians and the Sarmatians among the Goths, and subsequently, this whole historical conglomerate of Cimmerian-Scythian-Sarmatian-Gothic nomadic tribes merged smoothly into the composition of the Huns.'

Another thematic example is provided by the Russian historian Dmitry Abramov in his book *Tysiacheletie vokrug Chernogo moria* (Moscow: Algoritm, 2007). 'Researchers link the destruction and partial desolation of Phanagoria and a number of settlements on the Taman Peninsula with the Huns. Yet excavations at Hermonassa have not yielded any data about destruction or fires in the city at the end of the 4th century (the time at which the Huns arrived on the Taman Peninsula – K.Z.).

'Most surprising were the results of excavations at Tanais. It was discovered that this city had been destroyed by barbarians in the middle of the 3rd century and restored to life again only during the period of Hun rule... The example of Tanais demonstrates that it is incorrect to identify the word 'Hun' as a synonym for 'devastation'. That characteristic of this unusual enemy of the Romans was founded on tales told by those defeated by the Huns and escaped Visigoths... On the other hand, written sources give evidence not of eradication but of alignment by the Huns of their conquered peoples and those living beside them as neighbours – the Ostrogoths, the Alan, the eastern Slavs and others.'

We can see from this tale that the Huns were not bloodthirsty, just as their descendants the Mongols of Genghis Khan were not; secondly, we may add that the Huns, having united to themselves their relatives the Alan, the Ostrogoths and others, then moved further westward, conquering Spain, Portugal, Great Britain and other countries. In exactly the same way, Herodotus causes confusion when he speaks of the Scythians, who crossed the Don in the 8th century BCE, attacked the Cimmerians and pursued them as far as Asia Minor as mortal enemies. I have however already pointed out that according to Herodotus, the pursued Cimmerians, about which Herodotus knew nothing, escaped via the eastern side of the Black Sea, while their pursuers the Scythians were moving along the western side of the Caspian. Clearly, something in the reasoning of the 'Father of History' is not quite right here. In fact the Scythians and the Cimmerians, being related, became united and agreed a common objective in establishing control over Asia Minor, the primordial land of the Turkic people.

The claim has also become an axiom in historical studies that the Scythians, having routed the Hittites in Asia Minor in the 8th century BCE, displaced them to the east. What actually happened was that the Scythians and their relations the Hittites extended the hand of assistance to their relatives the Shang of China to keep the local inhabitants of the Celestial Empire obedient. It is generally known that our ancestors in the 18th century BCE established the first ruling Yin dynasty in China, led by nomads of the Shang family, whose descendants in the 21st century CE live among the Kazakh Naiman and Argyn, while the Hittites who went east created the Zhou dynasty in China, the modern-day descendants of whom can be found among the Naiman and the Kete of the Junior *jüz* of the Kazakhs.

Historians all over the world recognise the Migration Period that overtook Europe from the start of the first millennium CE and that literally redrew the entire political and ethnic map of the Old World. A major role in this huge displacement of peoples was played by certain so-called 'Germanic tribes'. Meanwhile Bayzhumin has established that of the some 230 'Germanic' tribes involved in the Migrations, 200 can be traced in modern Kazakh clan names, while the remainder are recorded in Chinese manuscripts as Turanian tribes of Central Asia.

I believe that we have given sufficient arguments to assert that all the nomadic tribes mentioned in the encyclopaedias of Bodo Harenberg and Brigitte Baier that emerged from the Eurasian steppes and conquered the settled populations of Asia Minor, Greece, Mesopotamia, Egypt, China and eastern and western Europe, are related to one another and are the ancestors of today's Turkic peoples.

My office: a museum of the nomads

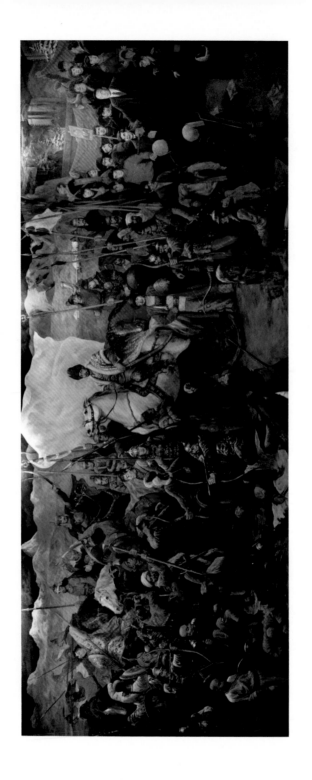

On the path to independence
The khans Abilay and Kensary with Nursultan Nazarbaev, President of Kazakhstan
Composition designed by Kairat Zakiryanov
Artist: Zhomart Ibraev

Davaanyam, the 29th-generation descendant of Genghis Khan, awards a diploma to Kairat Zakiryanov, Academician of the Worldwide Genghis Khan Academy, 2012

Monument to Genghis Khan, London, UK

The triumph of Asia or the decline of Europe: Attila before Rome
Composition designed by Kairat Zakiryanov
Artist: Zhomart Ibraev

The revenge of Queen Tomyris
Composition designed by Kairat Zakiryanov
Artist: Zhomart Ibraev

Genghis Khan: the last blessing of Tengri
Composition designed by Kairat Zakiryanov
Artist: Zhomart Ibraev

The Kazakhs: from the Ergenekon to the Ak Orda
At the centre is Nursultan Nazarbaev, President of Kazakhstan
Composition designed by Kairat Zakiryanov
Artist: Zhomart Ibraev

New icons of the 'Eternal people' and their President

By the 'eternal stones', Stonehenge, UK, 2012

My wife Marzia with the ur-ancestor of the Turkic people. Rome, 2010

In front of the Haghia Sophia, Istanbul with grandchildren Tamerlane, Arslan and Ruslan, 2011

Karakorum: the ancient headquarters of the Turkic khans

Memorial stone at Kok-Nur lake, the place where Genghis Khan was proclaimed khan of all his related tribes in 1186

The famous Kultegin stone near Karakorum, 2006

CHAPTER III
'SCYTHIAN' IRON AND 'BARBARIAN' CIVILISATION

World history was created to the accompaniment
of the tramping of great masses
of the strategic cavalry of the nomads.
Alfred Weber

For what purpose did the nomadic cattle-breeders of the Asiatic steppe conquer the sedentary populations of the peripheral margins? Why did the opposite not occur? Modern scholarship has ascertained the reasons for the cultural and military superiority of some peoples over others as resulting only from fundamental discoveries made by a pioneering ethnos, particularly in the area of weapons, which could then be used for aggressive purposes. In *Under the wolf's nest: a Turkic rhapsody* I noted that the nomads gained a decisive advantage over the settled peoples as a result of their having domesticated the wild horse in the 4th century BCE on the territory of what is now Kazakhstan, and again later with their invention of a method of obtaining iron and implements from it, in particular, weapons. After further inventions – the saddle, the iron stirrup and bit, the curved sabre and iron arrow tips – our ancestors were invincible, and as they conquered the settled populations of warm countries, they brought them the civilisation of the Great Steppe in the image of fearless centaurs.

The American anthropologist Henry Lewis Morgan wrote the following immortal lines about our ancestors in his major work *Ancient society* (Rus. ed. Leningrad, 1954): 'When the barbarian advancing step by step, had discovered the native metals and learned to melt them

33

in the crucible and to cast them in the moulds; when he had alloyed native copper with tin and produced bronze; and finally, when with a still greater effort of thought he had invented the furnace, and produced iron from the ore, nine-tenths of the battle for civilisation was gained'.

The fact that these 'barbarians' were in fact the very Turanian Scythians whose skills and knowledge led to the first use of iron was stated by a number of Greek scholars and thinkers, including Ephorus, who never mentioned iron without prefixing it with the name 'Scythian'. Hellanicus of Mytilene also maintained that the invention of iron weapons was owed to the Scythians (Garkavtsa, A.N. (ed.): *Velikaia step' v antichnykh i vizantiyskikh istochnikakh. Sbornik materialov*, Almaty, 2005).

Iron and the objects made from it gave their possessors an immense advantage over other peoples, if only because iron was then worth more than gold. The Soviet researchers V.M. Masson and Nikolay Merpert concluded that the wheel, and wheeled transport, were first developed by the steppe dwellers ('Voprosy otnositel'noi khronologii Starogo sveta', *Sovr. archeologia*, 1958, no.1). The historian and philosopher Diogenes Laertius attributes the invention of the plough, the potter's wheel and the anchor to the Scythian Anacharsis, while the centaur Chiron, teacher of Heracles, Achilles and other Helladic heroes was the first to compile the celestial globe and to divide the zodiac into constellations. Another Scythian, Abaris the Hyperborean, a friend of the mathematician Pythagorus, invented a method of warfare involving spreading the plague. Herodotus mentioned that Scythia, land of the Hyperboreans, was where the flute, the pipe and the lyre were invented, while V. Gordon Childe ascribed to the Turanian Aryans the discovery of poetic metre.

Why the nomadic way of life in particular facilitated the cultural expansion of its people is explained simply by the 19th-century Russian historian V.V. Grigoriev: (*O skifskom narode sakakh*, St Petersburg, 1871): 'There is no doubt that two conditions are required in order that thinking be intensified: leisure time and social interaction. With respect to both of these factors, nomads are in a far more favourable position than are settled peoples... The nomad's mental horizons are wider than those of the village dweller, his powers of apprehension are more agile and he is quicker witted.'

All the same, however, an answer to the question of why it was precisely the nomadic tribes that captured and dominated the settled peoples remains incomplete unless we add an element of philosophy, a philosophy originating in Asia among the barbarian tribes of the Celestial Empire. In particular this comprises various aspects of the philosophy and world view of Taoism.

CHAPTER IV
YIN, YANG AND THE DEVELOPMENT OF HUMAN SOCIETY

What did Strabo not mention?

For in much wisdom is
much vexation,
and he who increases knowledge
increases sorrow.
The Bible, Ecclesiastes 1:18

It is widely understood that the foundation for the development of the entire material world can be conceived in a study of the interaction of two opposing principles – an approach that was developed by thinkers of Ancient Greece such as Heraclitus, Anaximander and others, and that was given a thorough treatment by Hegel. Credit is due to Zhumazhan Bayzhumin for the brilliant idea of applying this principle of unity and opposition to the development of human societies by dividing the subjects, as it were, of this phenomenon into two fundamental cultural and economic models of human community: mobile cattle-breeders on the one hand and settled agriculturalists on the other. These two social models represent quintessentially opposing principles, which find greatest expression in relation to the material world. The nomad's greatest riches are his cattle, while all his material valuables can be carried on the croup of his horse and in his mobile yurt. He does not build himself palaces, does not fill them with attributes of luxury nor accumulate valuable possessions, and far less would he keep a bank account as understood in 21st-century terms. The Greek historian Ephorus wrote in the 4th century BC of the Saka as follows: 'The Saka, who graze sheep, are Scythian tribes. They live in Asia and are the descendants of just nomads; they do not chase after wealth and are honest in their dealings with one another. They roam with their wagons and they drink milk. They discourage the cultivation of personal property; all property is used communally.' (Garkavtsa, A.N. (ed.): *Velikaia step' v antichnykh i vizantiyskikh istochnikakh. Sbornik materialov,* Almaty, 2005).

The man who works the land turns out to be entirely different, however; without realising it he becomes a slave to his house and property.

The spiritual lives of the nomad and the farmer also differ considerably. While the nomad, according to V.V. Grigoriev (cited above), is likely to reflect on the secrets of how the universe is formed and subsists, on questions of the meaning of earthly life and the constant question of who and what man is and why he is here in the world, the settled landsman is more concerned with his daily bread, and his hard work prevents him having time to consider the meaning of life. The historian of antiquity Strabo, who lived around the time of the birth of Christ, stated: 'The nomads engage more in war than in plundering, and they wage war for the sake of tribute... they are content to receive a provisional, modest tribute, not for profit or gain but simply to satisfy life's everyday needs... The farmers, by contrast, although they are reputed in terms of temperament to be more peaceful and more civilised, are nevertheless self-interested and therefore do not refrain from robbery and other unlawful means of self-enrichment.' (Struve, V.V. (ed.): *Khrestomatia po istorii Drevnego mira.* Moscow, 1951, v. 2). We shall return later to a very precise assessment of the essence of the nomad provided by a major Roman historian and thinker: for him, war is not a method of enrichment or plundering but something quite different, connected to his higher predestination. The Arab historian al-Jahiz wrote: 'The Turks do not know flattery, nor deception, nor arrogance towards those close to them, nor harassment of their colleagues' (Asadov, F.M.: *Arabskie istochniki o tiurkakh v ranee srednevekov'ie.* Baku, 1993). The military prowess of the

Turkic nomads is literally the stuff of legends. Chinese sources speak on this matter: '...Fighting is to the Huns as ploughing is to the ploughman...' (*Poezia epokhi Tan VII-X vv.* Moscow, 1997), while the mediaeval Arabs stated with astonishment: 'For the Turks, to destroy an enemy utterly is to do no more than to re-read a book...' (Asadov, F.M., *op. cit.*).

According to this model, then the nomadic cattle herder and the settled farmer are diametrically contrasting types in both spiritual and material aspects. At the same time, however, they are in a certain sense one, and cannot subsist one without the other. The nomadic type may be personified by 'yang', the masculine principle, while the settled agriculturalist is embodied as its complement, 'yin', the feminine principle.

Let us examine the underlying unity of this complex question. In his time the historian of antiquity Pompeius Trogus coined the phrase 'exules Scytharum' to refer to a tribe or people that had been forced to leave the Eurasian steppe and that had found a new home in the lands of settled farmers – and, importantly, had done so as their new ruler, bringing an advanced territorial and class structure. We mentioned this earlier when discussing the Hyksos of Egypt, the Mitannia and Kassites of Mesopotamia, the Hittites of Asia Minor, the Shang and Zhou of China and others. So why, then, were these tribes 'forced' to leave their old lands and what was behind this?

It is all very simple. As a result of what was known as the 'great division of labour', estimated by specialists to have taken place between four and three millennia BCE, society divided into two broad groups – nomadic cattle breeders and settled farmers. For the former group the habitat was the Eurasian steppe with its cold, harshly continental climate, while for the latter it was lands near to seas and oceans or washed by major rivers, where the climate was mild or tropical. There is little to be gained in discussing national relations between these two social structures, since, in the view of the specialists, it was impossible for an agricultural society to have been created in isolation and likewise impossible for a nomadic structure to have formed by itself

– in the same way that a man and a woman cannot create offspring independently of one another. An economy based on nomadic cattle-breeding was by nature extensive; the only measure of wealth were the animals possessed, while the number of animals depended on the size of grazing land available. To attempt to increase its head of cattle and hence its wealth, therefore, one tribe would seek to seize the pasture of another, weaker tribe; this latter tribe then, to improve its lot or in some cases for bare survival, migrated to the lands of the settled farmers and became 'exules Scytharum'. And while these tribes had been subdued in strength by their kinsmen from the first tribe, these displaced tribes still greatly exceeded in strength and armaments the armies of the settled populations. Having conquered those peoples for the sake of their own survival in new socio-economic conditions, the nomadic tribes set up institutions for government and enforcement – organs of policing, taxation and judiciary, which thereby created the preconditions for the formation of states and civilisations, while the society itself, comprising indigenous agriculturalists and the incoming nomads, remained class-based. The ruling circles and the elite were the incomers, the Turks, while the greater part, the exploited classes that created material wealth were the local natives. This viewpoint is entirely in agreement with the 'aggressive' conception of the formation of class-based societies and states proposed by leading Western scholars such as Friedrich Ratsel, Ludwig Gumplowicz, Franz Oppenheimer, Omeljan Pritsak and others who saw in the nomads a fundamental factor or driving force in historical processes (Khazanov, A.M.: *Kochevniki i vneshny mir*, Almaty, 2002).

Let us also point out that the impulse for a tribe's expansion of its pasturelands at the expense of its neighbours also facilitated another aspect of the cattle-breeding economy as noted by Zhumazhan Bayzhumin. As I.M. D'yakonov (*Nauka i zhizn'*, 1989, no. 9) stated: 'In places where meat and dairy-based diets are widely used, infant mortality falls sharply and population growth begins.' For this reason, at times when there were no droughts, epidemics or wars on the Great Steppe, the number of inhabitants grew rapidly, leading inevitably to territorial disputes and the stealing of grazing lands from neighbours and the presence of 'redundant' hordes of people on the steppe seeking a better way of life, who were well-armed, trained in military actions and who, naturally, succeeded in winning living space over from the settled populations. The arrivals were required to settle close together and to impose a tribute or tax on the local population to support themselves. Where the subordinated population refused to comply, punitive measures were applied by what are understood today as institutions of coercion, as mentioned above – a form of police force, tax inspectorate, courts and the like. Thus, cities, states and civilisations were formed on the lands of the settled agriculturalists – for example in Mesopotamia with the arrival of the Sumerians, in Asia Minor with the Hittites, in China with the Shang and in the British Isles with the Celts (the Britons etc.) and so on. Additionally the nomads' traditions included polygamy, a characteristic noted very precisely by the papal legate Giovanni da Pian del Carpine, who travelled to the Mongol steppe immediately after the rise of Genghis Khan. 'They have as many wives as they can accommodate; some a hundred, some fifty, some ten, some more and some less' (*Puteshestvie v Yevraziiskie stepi*, Almaty, 2003).

Thus, to summarise the above one may state that in the very being of the nomadic mode and in the economic model of nomadic societies there was always a hidden mechanism by which, inevitably, the two fundamentally antagonistic types of society – nomadic and settled – would be brought together. In cases where polygamy was accepted, the steppe-dweller could gain himself additional wives by simply seizing them following victory by his tribe over one or another settled population. Bayzhumin describes an entry in the Chinese chronicle Tangshu: '... in the tale of how the old Turkic leader Chuluo Khan ruled, it is said that in the year 619 his younger brother Buli-She, at the head of two thousand mounted troops, 'took all the women and maidens in the town of Ban-Zhou and departed'. In another Chinese chronicle we read that '... in the course of only one campaign of the 'Syunnu' (the Huns – K.Z.) to Shen-Si (2nd century BCE), fifteen thousand girls and young women were taken away to the steppe..."

For myself I am inclined to believe that the reason for the expansion of the steppe dwellers into the lands of the settled peoples was not primarily economic but rather purely physiological.

I believe that I have managed to give an answer to the complex question of the great contribution made by the nomadic Turks to the formation of many of the world's civilisations and, more specifically, why it was that the nomads were able to conquer the settled populations. In exactly the same way that a man seeks his wife in order to create a family and provide a successor generation, the nomadic society, personified as *yang*, the masculine or celestial principle, pushed out the 'excess' individuals from its centre as part of its normal evolutionary development, these displaced individuals becoming 'exules Scytharum' who, gaining control over their new dwelling lands, now found their *yin* or feminine principle, with which they jointly provided their progeny in the form of new states and civilisations. Here it is appropriate to recall Strabo, who with his own eyes identified the nomads' higher mission, in which war was not a means of gaining wealth but rather a means of execution of a higher will in the evolution of human society.

CHAPTER V
AT THE SOURCE OF THE WORLD RELIGIONS

The Turkic roots of Jesus Christ and the Prophet Muhammad

Man alone together with God forms the majority
attributed to Frank Buchman (1878-1961),
Protestant evangelist, founder of the 'Oxford Group'

It is significant to mention that the Turkic nomads far outstripped their settled counterparts in their spiritual and moral quests. In *Under the wolf's nest: a Turkic rhapsody* I gave a detailed account of the sources of the outlook and religious and philosophical tenets of Tengriism as cultivated among the nomads. Each time they conquered a settled people, they adapted their religion to suit the mind-set of the local inhabitants. This resulted in Zoroastrianism in Persia, Buddhism in India, Islam in Arabia, Judaism in the Middle East and Christianity in Europe. The British scholar of Iranian languages Mary Boyce stated on this point that one should seek the origins of 'the largest of the ancient religions – Zoroastrianism' on the steppes of Kazakhstan situated to the east of the Volga (Mary Boyce: *Zoroastrizm: verovanie i obichai*. Moscow, 1987). According to the information available, Zarathustra was born near to the modern Kazakh city of Uralsk. Moreover, Yuri Drozdov states categorically that the existing historical and linguistic data '... is evidence that early Christianity, as a religion, was formed within the Turkic-speaking world.'

In my book cited above I argued for the Turkic origin of Jesus Christ and also of the Prophet Muhammad. Here I would like to repeat a few points together with some minor additions. Let us begin with

Jesus Christ. In the late 19th century in the region of the Kuban (North Caucasus), in the flood plain of the river Zelenchuk, a gravestone was discovered bearing an inscription in Greek letters and dated from the 11th century. Despite the alphabet, however, the language used was not Greek. Attempts by V.S. Miller and later by the Iranologist Vasily Abaev and others to decipher the text on the basis of Ossetian writing were unsuccessful. At the same time, in 1990 F.Sh. Fattahov was able to read the inscription easily on the basis of Turkic writing (*Na kakom iazyke govorili Alany? Nekotorie itogi i zadachi izuchenia tatarskogo literaturnogo iazyka*. Kazan, 1992, p. 108). The deciphered text reads: 'Jesus Christ, the governor of Nicholas, having been called from the house of the Hobs union (Dulo, Batpay, Adwan, Suvan) by Advant Bakatar Beg himself, who separated from their father's country to that of the Alan (steppes, valleys) is striving, tell of the year of the ox.' (Laypanov, K.T. and Meziev, I.M.: *O proiskhozhdenie tiurkskikh narodov*. Cherkessk, 1993, p. 102). From the text it may be deduced that Christ was a member of the house (union) of Hobs, which consisted of four Kazakh clans: the Dulat, Botbay, Alban and Suan. In addition, Yuri Drozdov (op.cit., p. 556) states that: 'for Jesus the Bible had been translated from Hebrew into Turkic, and Jesus quoted from it in Turkic...'. Jesus had a Semitic origin and spoke Aramaic, which had previously been considered, without foundation, as a western Semitic language. Drozdov takes the Aramaic phrase *maran atha* ('the Lord has come'), which occurs once in the New Testament, and demonstrates that, read as Turkic, it translates as 'father – the instructor of belief'.

As regards the Prophet of the Muslims, Mohammad, the Kazakh scholar Mirzabek Kargabaev suggests: 'The Arabs, and in particular the family of the great Prophet Muhammad always kept a historical chronicle of the lineage of their ancestors... The Quraysh tribe, to which the Prophet belonged, knew a different truth about the nomads... They preserved the name of their great ancestor Khyzyr. When the interests of Islam came into conflict with those of the nomads at the Caspian Gate at Derbent, they recalled where their ancestor, the wandering Khyzyr had come from. According to the historical chronicle they had, the great ancestor of the

Qurayshi (Khidr, Khyzyr or Qydyr – K.Z.) was a wanderer who spread the religion of Tengri about the world that had been conceived by the ancient Sumerians... The Kazakhs still bless their kin, when they are preparing for a long journey, with the words *Zhorytqanda zholdyn bolsyn, zholdasyn Qydyr bolsyn*, i.e. 'May your guardian Qydyr be with you in the unknown lands.' Some scholars suggest that the Qurayshi tribe was a union of Turkic tribes among the Arabs (the Kazakh word *kurama* means a 'union' – K.Z.), while Mecca was a refuge for Arabs of Turkic descent' (Kargabaev, M.: *Atlantida kochevnikov*. Karaganda, 2007). Certainly, the Turks always assimilated their religion of Tengri among the indigenous settled peoples they conquered. This explains how Zoroastrianism appeared in Persia, Islam on the Arabian Peninsula, Buddhism in India and Christianity in Europe, and so on. Meanwhile the ethnonyms of Muhammad's native city, Mecca, certainly have a Turkic character and derive from the word *meken*, which in Kazakh means 'dwelling place', 'residence'. Mirzabek Kargabaev further cites a phrase from the 12th-century Persian poet Nizami addressed to the Prophet: 'Praise to you, son of the Turkic nation! You led the seven tribes. From the seas to the skies, you are glorified in all the world!' There is little more to say!

CHAPTER VI
THE KZ FACTOR AND THE KZ POSTULATE

The greatest wisdom is to know yourself
Galileo Galilei

Before discussing Confucius and his conjectures about his ethnic origin I would like to note the following hypothesis, which arises from my previous discussions. Accepting the basic premise that, as a rule, the well-known civilisations were created as a result of the conquering of settled peoples by nomadic groups from the Eurasian steppe, resulting in a class-based, binary society in which the determining and dominating role was played by the conquerors, the nomads, who were of Turkic origin, then it is reasonable to assume that all the well-known rulers, generals and scholars (thinkers, philosophers, writers and poets) and leading exponents of the arts arose from within this Turkic ruling elite.

Let us call this premise the '**KZ factor**'. Thus, **a certain availability of the KZ factor implies the establishment of the fact of the conquest in time and space of settled agricultural populations by cattle-breeding nomads from the Eurasian steppe and the formation by the latter of class-based states.** If the scholar has established the presence of this 'KZ factor' in time and space, then as a consequence it will follow that the prominent individuals of those binary societies will as a rule belong to the ethnic groups that consist of the conqueror Turks. And so there is probably no need for further demonstration of the fact that it was they who came to be the rulers of states, who were entrusted with the command of armies and who found for themselves the time and opportunities to learn, to create and to reflect on the eternal.

We should note that the conditions of the 'KZ factor' applied up until the end of the era of the great conquests and the start of the Renaissance.

In what follows below, in which the relationship between, say, Confucius, Alexander the Great, King Arthur or his prototype Genghis Khan and other major actors of the past to the representatives of the Turkic ethnos is demonstrated, it will be sufficient for us to establish evidence of the KZ factor in the societies in which they lived.

We have thus established the following 'KZ postulate'. To determine that prominent person X had a Turkic ethnic origin it is sufficient to establish that the KZ factor was present in time and space in the place where that person lived.

CHAPTER VII
CONFUCIUS

By three methods we may learn wisdom.
First, by reflection, which is noblest;
second, by imitation, which is easiest;
and third, by experience, which is the bitterest.
Confucius

The Bronze Age arrived unexpectedly in the basin of the Yellow River (Hwang Ho). 'During the Yin [Shang] dynasty there appeared in China the technology for making bronze, and **it appeared in its finished state** (my emphasis – K.Z.). It was introduced from the developed metallurgical centre of the Tian-Shan and the Altai where, evidently, the method of its production was discovered. Other innovations of the Yin period were chariots' (Yuri Petukhov and Nina Vasilieva: *Yevraziyskaia imperia skifov.* Moscow, 2007). Let us remember that the Yin period in China, with the arrival of nomads from Central Asia of the Shang tribe, began from the middle of the 1700s BCE. Today, members of the Shang are to be found in the Kazakh Argyn and Naiman.

Leonid Vasiliev also discusses the external origin of the Yin-Shang, underlining the fact that the late Stone Age in the Hwang-Ho basin changed unexpectedly into a highly-developed bronze culture, the Shang (*Problemy genezisa kitayskogo gosudarstva*, Moscow, 1988). Chinese sources including the *Shujing* (Book of Documents) and the *Guoyu* (Discourses of the States) also mention the nomadic origin of the incomers to the Yellow River basin.

Zhumazhan Bayzhumin highlights the characteristic features of the ethnocultural origin of these conquerors of China. These include the significant role of animal husbandry, unusual for settled farmers, in the economy of the Shang state, frequent battles between the Shang and their neighbours over pasture lands such as were typical of cattle-breeders, the ritual sacrificing of animals, fortune-telling using their shoulder-blades, their culture of burial in *kurgans* and their pictographic writing, and so forth. According to the findings of the Chinese historian Fan Wen Lan (*Drevniaia istoria Kitaia*, pp. 38-66), it was precisely during this dynasty that the foundations of the ancient Chinese civilisation were formed and the ancient Chinese people came into being. The Shang–Yin was a slave-owning state with hereditary power and a Turkic aristocracy. Lev Gumilev states that 'the most important cultural achievement of this period was the invention of hieroglyphic writing' (*Istoria naroda khunnu*, Moscow: Ast, 2004).

Now we see who was present at the origins of Chinese civilisation. It was the Turkic peoples of the Eurasian steppe, whom later historians contemptuously describe as 'barbarian'.

In the 7th century BCE the conquerors of the Shang were replaced by other conquerors from Central Asia: the tribe of the Zhou. Like the Shang, the Zhou differed strongly from the many indigenous peoples of China with their clear Caucasoid features, for which the Chinese nicknamed them the 'red-haired demons'. The ethnic basis of the Zhou was formed primarily of Turkic-speaking cattle breeders, the Xirong . During the 8th century BCE the Zhou collapsed due to internecine fighting, after which there followed two centuries in which China was ruled by multiple rulers of smaller kingdoms – these rulers again being various clans of Turkic nomads. Gumilev, citing the Russian entomologist Grigory Grumm-Grzhimaylo (*Zapadnaia Mongolia i Uriankhaysky kray*, vol. 2, Leningrad, 1926, p. 69), says: 'At exactly the same time as the Achaeans were ravaging Troy and the Huns were crossing the Gobi, the ruler of the Zhou, King Wen, 'with the forces of blond (and dark-haired) barbarians was completing his conquests between the sea and the Tibetan plateau.' King Wen of Zhou was also known as Wen-wang, and it is worth noting that the title *wang* was conferred by the Turks on their rulers of China.

This was also the case in Korea. Modern Kazakh has a similar word, *zhuan*, which is a synonym of *wang*; it has many shades of meaning, which include 'powerful', 'solid', 'strong', 'powerful' and the like. The phrase *zhuan ata urpagy* literally means 'descendant of a strong and powerful race'. Even today, Kazakh surnames with the root *van, uan* or *zhuan* are common. We may recall that later, the Chinese emperors conferred the title *wang* on the leaders of Turkic tribes that provided various services to the imperial palace. This was also the case with the khan of the Kazakh clan of the Kerey, Togrul, who was awarded the title of *wang khan* by the rulers of the Jin court during the time of Genghis Khan. The Turkic incomers also spread the term *wang* to other countries. Remnants can perhaps be seen in the *pan* of Poland, the *von* of Germany and Austria, the *ban* of Croatia and Hungary and the *don* of Spain, all of which indicate affiliation with the upper echelons of the binary societies of these states. Moreover, the existence of such a title might in a sense form an ethnic marker for the presence of Turanians among those peoples.

Still earlier, before the Shang era, the first Xia dynasty created the Neolithic-era Yangshao culture, about which Yuri Petukhov and Nina Vasilieva suggest that it was created by the same Caucasoid nomads that later formed the Shang and Zhou dynasties.

Commenting on the historical processes that occurred in China after the arrival of the nomadic tribes from the Eurasian steppe, the Chinese historian Wei Juxian (*Issledovania po drevney istorii*, vol. 3, Shanghai, 1937) linked them to the Chinese dualistic model of *yin-yang*. This author proposes that Chinese civilisation developed as a result of the interaction of two opposing principles: the 'feminine', situated in south-eastern China with its indigenous farming population with its Mongoloid features, and the 'masculine', the animal-breeding Caucasoid peoples arriving from the north-west. Another Chinese historian, Wang Tong Ling (*Istoria kitayskoy natsii*, Beynin, 1934) described the origin of his people as a wave-like process that travelled from the west to the east. He outlined four periods of active penetration by the Central Asian nomads into the Celestial Empire: the period of 'Five Emperors', the Xia period, the Zhou period and the Qin period.

Let us now return to Confucius.

The *Shibeng*, the book of genealogy of the great philosopher, gives evidence that he came from a noble line related to the ruling house of the Song under the Zhou dynasty. His contemporaries remembered him by the nickname 'the Xirong', as this was how the nomads were named that, having come from the Eurasian steppe, now formed the ethnic basis of the Zhou empire.

Let us now turn to the lineage of the Xirong tribe.

In *Istoria naroda khunnu* (Moscow: Ast, 2004) the Eurasianist and historian Lev Gumilev states that owing to errors by Sima Qian (the 'Herodotus' of Chinese history – K.Z.), prominent Sinologists such as Nikita Bichurin and A.N. Bernshtam identified the Xirong with the Xiongnu. I would suggest for my part that these scholars are not altogether wrong; even William Montgomery McGovern considered the Xirong to be Xiongnu (McGovern, W.M.: *The early empires of Central Asia*, North Carolina, 1939). Additionally Gumilev, referring to the Greco-Roman writer Claudius Ptolemy, said that south of the Yellow River there lived the Chinese Xing, while north of it dwelt the Turkic Sir. These Sir are mentioned several times on a monument to Tonyukuk situated to the south of Ulan-Bator. The author had occasion to examine this inscription while travelling in Mongolia in 2006. Thus, referring to works by Arrian of Nicomedia (*Periplus of the Erythraean Sea* §39, 49, 64) and J.O. Thomson (*A History of Ancient Geography*, Rus. ed. Moscow, 1953), Gumilev identifies the Sir with another nomadic tribe, the Di. Yet Nikita Bichurin and Grigory Grumm-Grzhimaylo, author of *Zapadnaia Mongolia i Uriankhaysky kray* (Moscow, 1926), believe the Di and the Xirong to be the same people. A.N. Bernshtam writes that 'the Xirong and the Di were, without doubt, Turkic-speaking' (*Ocherki istorii gunnov*, Leningrad, 1951). Current historical thinking identifies the late Xirong with the early Huns.

We have thus established that Confucius, who belonged to the ruling Song house of the Zhou dynasty of nomadic Xirong, was 'Turkic-speaking', to use Bernshtam's expression. In principle this conclusion arises quickly from the '**KZ postulate**', according to which all the eminent military leaders, scholars and philosophers of the binary societies created by the nomads belonged to the ruling class of those nomads and cattle-breeders. In the present case it was only necessary to establish the binary nature of the Zhou and the later so-called 'Warring States', plus the small states created by the Xirong nomads; the remaining arguments, given above, are incidental and only support this thesis. Also incidental is the fact that Confucius may have a Xirong origin.

To support this view let us consider Confucius' lineage on his mother's side. The *Historical Notes* of Sima Qian, mentioned above, include a chapter on the ancestral house of Kong-ji (Confucius) in which he says: 'Confucius was born in the principality of Lu, in the *volost* of Changping and the village of Zuoui. His ancestor was a Song named Kung Fanshu. Fanshu was the father of Bo Xia, who in turn was father of Shuliang He. While still young He broke with custom by marrying a Yan girl. This girl, the wife of He, went to pray on the mountain Niqiushan and later gave birth to a son: Confucius.' The 'breaking with tradition' meant here by Sima Qian was for Confucius' father to have married into a 'barbarian' tribe, that is, to one whose members were Turanian steppe-dwellers. Chinese sources mention the Yan as a Hunnic tribe that migrated to China in the years 337-370.

It follows that if the father of Confucius came from a family of the Turkic ruling elite, then his mother also came a Turkic stock, albeit a less known one.

In fact, much of Confucius' philosophy is based on what amounts to canonical precepts of Tengriism. For example, the earthly ruler appears as the Son of Heaven – in just the same way as, by the hands of the shaman Teb Tengri, Genghis Khan declared himself the chosen one and a son of Heaven. Society, according to Confucius, is divided into two categories – the noble and the commoners – which is exactly what happened in the lands conquered by the nomads. Confucius advocates love and respect towards one's parents and a cult of ancestors (*arwah*). The common people should submit to those in authority, and the dignitary should be honest and respect the ruler. All this amounts in a word to the morals of modern Kazakh society.

Thus it can be seen that the philosophy and outlook of Confucius also reflected his deep connections with the Turkic world.

CHAPTER VIII
ALEXANDER THE GREAT

One may defeat strength with courage and fate with persistence.
attributed to Alexander the Great

In accordance with the '**KZ postulate**' it is sufficient for us, to demonstrate that the Alexander the Great was a Turkic speaker, to determine the class structure of the Macedonian society led by Turkic nomads at the time at which he entered the historical arena. Macedonia, situated north of the Peloponnese, was subjected from the 18th century BCE to a series of invasions by Eurasian nomads – first the Pelasgians, then the Achaeans that created the unique Mycenaean civilisation; and then in the 12th century BCE by tribes of Dorian descent who were known in Greece as the Danai, in Egypt as the Sea Peoples, in Assyria as the Mushki and in Palestine as the Philistines. We know from Homer's *Iliad* that Achilles was a Danai whom Alexander considered his direct ancestor through his mother's line. It is generally known that the Danai were Scythian tribes that lived in the Don (Dana, Tana) basin. As regards Achilles, the Greek historian and philosopher Arrian of Nicomedia (c. 95-175 CE) states that 'Achilles the Scythian was exiled from his homeland in the Azov region by other Scythians and settled in Thessaly' (as cited in *Velikaia step' v antichnykh i vizantiyskikh istochnikakh*, compiled and ed. A.N. Garkavts, Almaty, 2005). Here we see a typical 'exules Scytharum' scenario. We may thus assume the great leader's Scythian roots through his maternal line to be established.

We mentioned earlier that after the collapse of the Zhou empire created by the eastern Scythian Xirong, the Scythians left once more for the territory of what is now Kazakhstan, and then in the 8th century BCE,

53

as they crossed the Don, they encountered the Cimmerian Scythians. According to Herodotus, the Cimmerians in turn moved to Asia Minor where they created the powerful kingdom of Lydia. Another group, however, according to the Italian historian Gaetano de Sanctis, arrived on the Apennine peninsula and created the Etruscan state (*Storia dei Romani*, 4 vols, Rome, 1953–56). As they moved south-west, my data suggests that at this same time (the 8th century BCE) the Cimmerians also created the first state of the Argead dynasty in Macedonia – the descendants of whom today live among the Kazakh Argyn. In his work *Ariy-gunn skvoz'veka i prostranstvo: svidetel'stva, toponimy* (Astana: Foliant, 2001) Shamkhurat Kuanganov describes the archaeological culture area of the Turkic peoples as extending from the river Argun on the Russian Pacific seaboard to the valley of the Aragon in the Pyrenees close to the Atlantic Ocean. It can be seen at once that the Argun river, the Aragon valley and the Argead dynasty share the Turkic root *ar*.

According to a different account, the Turkic-speaking Celts, migrating from the east of the Eurasian steppes to the territory of Macedonia during the early Iron Age (roughly the 8th century BCE) joined forces with the local inhabitants, the Illyrians, to create the highly-developed Hallstatt culture, and it may be that the ancestors of Alexander the Great were drawn from a Celtic union of clans. In such a case we would observe a situation of multiple layers as a sequence of different Turkic tribes rolled up one after another like waves onto the lands of the settled peoples, crowding in upon those of their kin who had arrived previously, and created new state structures. As regards the Peloponnese, it is known that as early as the 18th century BCE Asiatic nomads had arrived – the Pelasgians, who gave the peninsula its name. Herodotus mentioned them: 'What language the Pelasgians speak, I cannot say... they speak a barbarian language' (Herodotus, I, 57, 58). After the Pelasgians came the nomadic Achaeans; then came the Dorians, then again the Scythians, and after that the Celts...

In any case we may consider that the binarity of Macedonian society, in which the ruling class was made up of tribes of Scythian origin from the Eurasian steppe, is thus confirmed and that, as then follows from the **'KZ postulate'**, Alexander, who inherited the throne from his father Philip II of Macedon in 336 BCE, also had Scythian Turkic ancestry through his father's line.

Let us now add a few extra points that add to the main thrust of our deliberations. The Greeks, for example, regarded the Macedonians as 'barbarians', a definition that was applied solely to Scythian tribes, and Herodotus mentions this as well. Moreover, family arrangements in Macedonia were polygamous: Alexander's father Philip had several other wives in addition to Olympias, Alexander's mother. This is in itself a further argument for the great leader being of Scythian descent.

In *Under the wolf's nest: a Turkic rhapsody* I discussed several episodes related to this matter. For example, the 3rd-century Roman historian Justin, who noted in abbreviated form much of Pompeius Trogus' voluminous but now-lost work, *Historiae philippicae et totius mundi origines et terrae situs*, mentions that: 'At that time the Scythian king was Ateus. When he found himself in difficulties during the war with the Istrians, he asked, through the Appolonians, for Philip (Alexander's father – K.Z.) to help him by **adopting him as a son and making him the successor to the Scythian kingdom** (my emphasis – K.Z.). Another episode relates to Alexander at the time of his Indian campaign. The Roman historian Quintus Curtius Rufus, who lived in the 1st century CE and was the author of the *Historiae Alexandri Magni Macedonis*, reported that when his troops refused to go to India, he said: '**I will make those who will go with me, whom you have deserted, into Scythians and Bactrians...**' (my emphasis – K.Z.).

These two moments eloquently and unequivocally highlight the close familial relations between the Macedonian leader and the Scythians.

Additionally, Alexander himself considered Heracles his ancestor by his father's line but, according to Herodotus, it was in fact the Scythians who regarded Heracles as their forefather. Plutarch in his *Parallel Lives* (see *Izbrannye zhizneopisania*, Moscow: Pravda, 1987) noted an interesting detail in the relations between Alexander and the Scythians: 'Generally, Alexander comported himself very proudly before the barbarians (Scythians – K.Z.) – as though he was absolutely certain that his ancestors were gods and he was the son of a god; towards the Greeks, however, he behaved with more restraint and demanded less insistently that they recognise him as a god.' And he is correct in this; a leader who believes in the greatness of his people and himself for having made his people thus, should behave towards those close to him in this way. For example, the Kazakh people of today have elected the president Nursultan Nazarbaev as their leader and this is a matter of great pride for both people and president.

Shamkhurat Kuanganov comments that 'in their legends and traditions the Turkic peoples endow [Alexander] with the divine powers of Tengri. They do not distinguish him from the Turks; the name Iskander or Askandur, composed of syllables of the Turkic parent language, can be translated as follows: *askan* – the one who surpasses, and *dur* – the Great.

'History does not mention any large-scale, bloody battles between Alexander the Great and the Massagetae or the Turanians...', Kuanganov continues. And it could hardly be otherwise; the great leader would not engage in battle against his own people!

As for Alexander's Indian campaign, the historical evidence is highly intricate. In his major work *Metaistoria. Otkuda my rodom? Mify, gipotezy, fakty* (Moscow: Niola-Press, 2010) Nikolay Kikeshev refers to J.O. Thomson, who proposes in his *A History of Ancient Geography* that 'Eratosthenes, drawing up geographical maps on the basis of materials related to Alexander's campaigns, ran into major difficulties', and 'detailed figures about the progress of Alexander in these places is hopelessly contradictory' (in *Metaistoria*, p. 521). Kikeshev shows that Alexander was never in fact in India but rather that he crossed the Zheytsu (Semirechye, 'Seven Rivers') region of modern Kazakhstan and reached what is now Biisk in the Altai, then returned home by way of the Irtysh river catchment in modern Kazakhstan. In this matter Kikeshev mentions that Alexander did reach China, since on mediaeval maps China extended as far as the Teletskoe lake area of the Altai. The hypothesis about the 12th-century Persian thinker and poet Nizami, to which the following memorable lines belong, is thus justified: 'How else did the Turks of the Roman lands take the throne of India and the crown of China?'

Apart from Alexander's journey in the Celestial Kingdom, we shall learn more below about his Turkic origins, which have already been mentioned.

CHAPTER IX
KING ARTHUR

The legends of Arthur have driven the Bible
from the chambers of statesmen.
Attributed to Elizabeth I of England, 1568

Nennius, the 'Herodotus' of the history of Britain, told in his *Historia Brittonum* (see e.g. *Formy istorichestogo soznania ot pozdney antichnosti do epokhi vozrozhdenia*, Ivanovo, 2000) of the settlers of the British Isles from the earliest times. He said that there were four main tribes present: the Britons (Brythons), Saxons, Picts and Scots. The 9th-century *Anglo-Saxon Chronicle*, meanwhile (see translation by James Ingram) states that 'there are in the island five nations; English, Welsh (or British), Scottish, Pictish, and Latin.' There are two views about the origin of the Britons (i.e. the Celtic tribe precursor to the Welsh) and thus of that of the name of the islands. One of these is the tradition peculiar to the Britons and the other is based on Roman records. Looking at the first of these, Nennius states: 'I will try, following my ancestors' tradition, to discover what is known about the British island. The island of Britain was named by the tribe of Brython, who was the son of Alan of the Japheth clan.' According to the Roman version of the settlement of the islands, however, the leader of the tribe was a descendant of the Trojan hero Aeneas. In *Under the wolf's nest* I gave a number of sources, including some from antiquity, that suggested that in either of the two versions, the settlers of the British isles were Turkic-speaking peoples. Here I will say only that all Turkic tribes stem from the line of Japheth, one of the sons of Noah, and that the Alan or Alban are Turkic-speaking peoples that still today live in Transcaucasia and Kazakhstan. I also note that the Alans, led by Alan Gua, who migrated in the 8th century BCE to what are now Mongolia and northern China, laid down the genealogical line of the future 'Great Terror of the Universe', Genghis Khan on his mother's side. As for Aeneas, Yuri Drozdov reaches the unequivocal conclusion that was of Alan (Asi), Turkic extraction. We may note once again that the Asi Alan were a large Turkic-speaking tribe that by the start of the Common Era were living in the Caspian and Black Sea steppe regions.

According to Nennius and the *Anglo-Saxon Chronicles*, before the arrival of the Celtic tribe of the Britons, the islands were uninhabited. At the same time, a number of sources including the archaeologists John Waddell and Barry Cunliffe considered that the migration to Britain of speakers of the Goidelic (Gaelic) languages may have taken place as early as the early Bronze Age, that is at the start of the second millennium BCE. This was the first wave of Celtic expansion. It is vital to point out that the Celts were among these speakers of Goidelic languages. Other scholars suggest that the Celts arrived in Britain at the start of the Iron Age, i.e. in the 8th century BCE. This, clearly, was a different wave of Celtic invasion of the islands. Either way, the views coincide on one matter – that the Britons were of Celtic origin. Plutarch considered that the Celts were members of the Scythian people (see e.g. *Istoria Kazakhstana v proizvedeniakh antichnykh avtorov*, Astana: Foliant, 2005, v.1 p. 289).

It follows that at the time of King Arthur, Britain was populated by Turkic-speaking tribes. In the work cited above Yuri Drozdov proposes that the Anglo-Saxon Chronicles preserved the names of certain ethnic territories that were occupied by the Romans and that all those names were Turkic. This further supports our conclusion that Britain was populated by Turkic speakers at the time of King Arthur.

Let us now turn to Arthur himself, the legendary leader of the Britons who in the 6th century CE routed the invading Saxons, who was the subject of heroic epics that, as noted in 1568 by the secretary to Queen Elizabeth I of England, were said to have surpassed the Bible in popularity among the ruling class. European scholars such as Georges

Dumezil, Helmut Nickel and others consider him to be descended from the Sarmatian tribe of the Iazyges. It is generally known that following the Marcomannic Wars (166–180 CE) between the Romans and the Sarmatians, at the initiative of the Romans their enemy concluded a peace treaty, according to which the Sarmatians were obliged to supply Rome with eight thousand mounted warriors each year to defend Roman domains. After this treaty was agreed, the ancestors of Arthur arrived on the British Isles among one of the Roman legions and, performing their function of occupation, effectively ruled the island nation even once the Romans had departed.

We thus obtain the following picture. To the British Isles, which were already populated by Turkic-speaking tribes that had by now become aboriginal, there came Turkic-speaking Scythians among the ranks of the Roman army, who began to rule the indigenous population. We see a typical binary society with Turkic conquerors. The history of settlement and conquering of Britain is again a complex of multiple layers in which the Celts began to arrive in the early Bronze Age and continued to do so in waves, each in turn then creating its own form of national structure.

It follows that as per the 'KZ postulate', King Arthur, the legendary British statesman (perhaps its prototype) was descended from Turkic stock. Yet even without this we know that he came from the Iazyges tribe of the Sarmatians, who today live among the Kazakh Naiman. The ethnic term *iazyg* is a transformation of the Kazakh word *zhyzyq* or perhaps from *zhasaq*. In the first case this means a plain, the steppe, which in Kazakh is *alan*, while in the latter case the meaning is an army or elite force. The Iazyges and Roxolani formed the main body of the Asi-Alan tribal union of the Sarmatians.

***

In what follows we will discuss Genghis Khan. In prehistoric times the land that is now Mongolia kept China in a state of constant tension;

from time to time nomadic tribes would raid from there and stayed for long periods in its inhabited regions where the living was plentiful. As concerns the close ancestors of Genghis Khan, they came, under the leadership of Borte Chino, to the region that would be the homeland of the 'Great Terror of the Universe', having crossed some sort of interior sea (possibly Baykal – K.Z.) and become the ruling khans of the Borjigin people. The word *borjigin* can be translated – semantically if not literally – from the Kazakh as a part (or tribe) of the People of the Wolf, to which all Turkic peoples considered themselves to belong. Having subdued the inhabitants and then begun to rule in the land of the sources of the three rivers Onon, Kherlen and Tuul, themselves becoming indigenous there, the Turkic predecessors of Genghis and then Genghis himself and his sons created the immense empire of the Mangi El. All the conditions for the **'KZ factor'** are here present and we can quickly obtain proof that this, perhaps the greatest conqueror and statesman of all times and peoples, was Turkic in origin. Meanwhile, my own entirely inexplicable filial love (and the fact that it is indeed filial!) for my great ancestor makes me return to him again and again, to protect him from unjust accusations of misanthropy and to counteract the image of a tyrant that has been created in successive works of history and literature, claiming that he murdered millions of innocent people.

PART II
GENGHIS KHAN

CHAPTER I
HE WHO FULLY UNDERSTANDS HUMAN NATURE
IS BORN TO BE A RULER

In the watercolour *The Fall of Man* by the English artist William Blake, God expels Adam and Eve from the Garden of Eden in accordance with the Biblical legend of Genesis. In the painting, God stands between two trees – the Tree of Life and the Tree of the Knowledge of Good and Evil, which symbolise two temptations that man inescapably faces (see e.g. *Mify narodov mira*, v.1, Moscow: Sovietskaia entsikolpedia, 1980, pp. 406-407).

However, over the centuries of human history the myth of the Fall from Paradise of Adam and Eve, who had tasted the fruit that was forbidden and consequently realised that they were naked, became the most widely known of any. While the basic meaning of the Tree of Knowledge is that knowledge is primarily directed towards and concentrated on the discrimination of good from evil, that is, to a realisation of the essence of Being. It is this, in my view, more significant aspect of the Fall that has not had enough distribution. At the same time, the thirst for knowledge is not only and not so much the primary sin of man as a thinking creature so much as the main, if not the only, purpose of his existence.

Through knowledge the first dwellers in Paradise, firstly, understood their carnal and sinful nature, recognising themselves as man and woman, which, incidentally, became fixed in the human consciousness at, as it were, the ordinary or everyday level. Yet secondly, even this empirical knowledge is conclusive evidence of the fact that they became thinking beings, that is, godlike, because in addition to his mortal and transitory flesh, man received his spirit – the eternal Spirit gifted by God.

Accordingly, through the 'original sin' of Adam and Eve they became thinking beings, though were also evicted from Eden.

I might add that this vital, permanently enduring and probably ineradicable thirst of man for the truth has also been for me the prime motive and substance of my many years of investigations.

My interest in history first grew when I was at school in the Samara region of eastern Kazakhstan. Our teacher Aleksandr Pavlovich Shevchenko would tell us so vividly and with such emotion about one or another event in history that my initial interest in 'days gone by' grew naturally into a love for this fascinating and remarkable discipline. When he spoke, say, about the Napoleonic era, he quoted the sayings of various political figures about the same individual, but in different situations, thus creating an extensive and complex portrait of the person in part and of society overall.

Aleksandr Pavlovich told us, for example, that the newspapers of Paris commented on Napoleon's attempt to return to power following his exile to Corsica. 'A Corsican monster has been washed up on the shore,' the journalists wrote. When Napoleon met with crowds of ecstatic local people, however, and the majority of the male population volunteered for his army, the tone of the publications underwent a radical change: 'Napoleon is on his way to Paris'. And when the emperor's return was evident and inescapable, headlines like the following were all over the evening newspapers: 'Welcome to Paris, sir Bonaparte!' Incidentally, while the principles of the 'KZ factor' cannot be directly applied to the Napoleonic period, I referred in a recent publication (in the newspaper *Megapolis*, 28 May 2012) to the work of French geneticists who took DNA samples of the descendants of one of Napoleon's brothers. My point was that the Napoleon genome had a form of 'registration' in the Transcaucasus, traditionally inhabited by Turkic tribes including the Alan and Alban. We may recall Francis Bacon, who proposed that the person who could fully grasp human nature was fit to be a ruler of men – such a statement could be applied directly and in full to Napoleon. Consider the words he spoke when he established the Legion of Honour: 'And you can rule over people with these trinkets!' Or take his method of ruling the masses, expressed in this phrase, deadly in its accuracy and insight: 'Men are moved by two levers only: fear and self-interest'.

I deliberately used the example here of a historical person from the 19th century since my deliberations will be wholly and completely devoted to a figure no less powerful but far more enigmatic in human history: Genghis Khan, the red-bearded 'Great Terror of the Universe', who lived in the late 12th and early 13th centuries and who was yet recognised eight centuries later by UNESCO as one of the outstanding men of the Second Millennium. And his greatest contribution was perhaps less as a military leader than as an outstanding advocate of a strong state.

It is worth noting the attitude of the West towards Genghis Khan that prevailed until quite recently in historical terms. An example may be found in the Holy Roman Emperor Frederick II, who asserted that the Mongols knew of no other clothing than ox, donkey or horse hides and that they had no arms other than crude, poorly reinforced iron rods. Others claimed that they were short and portly but that their backs and chests were well covered with thick and lavish wool.

In 1242 the Landgrave of Thuringia wrote: 'Within the limits of our abilities we inform you that countless tribes, loathed by other people, roaring and trampling the land with wild animosity, from the east to the very borders of our possession have subjected the whole land to complete ruin, destroying towns, castles and even *municipia*, putting to death not only Christians but also heathens and Jews without mercy, sparing nobody, with the exception of infants, whom their king, glorified by Chinchiton, marks by branding them on the forehead. They do not merely eat people, they devour them...' (Yurchenko, A.G.: *Istoricheskaia geografia politicheskogo mifa. Obraz Chingis-khana v mirovoy literature XIII-XV vv*, St Petersburg: Yevrazia, 2006).

Not only the Europeans but also some in Asia, including the Arabs, also spoke unflatteringly of the Mongols. Abd ar-Rashid al-Bakuwi, for example, wrote: 'It is a Tatar country. They are a large people among the

Turks. They live in the east of the sixth climate. They are like wild animals in the cruelty of their hearts, the rudeness of their temperament, the solidity of their bodies and the coarseness of their nature. They like to quarrel, to spill blood and to torture animals. As for religion, they do not believe in anything whatsoever. Nothing is permitted them and nothing forbidden to them; they eat anything they can catch. They worship the sun. Their language is nothing like other languages or the languages of the Turks, and their writing is different from that of others' (Yurchenko, A.G.: *Istoricheskaia geografia politicheskogo mifa. Obraz Chingis-khana v mirovoy literature XIII-XV vv*, St Petersburg: Yevrazia, 2006). It is clear that the hate and fear of this historian prevents him seeing anything. On the one hand he calls them Turks, yet he denies them a Turkic language. On the other hand he tells about the Mongols while clearly still knowing nothing about them. The Arab historian Ali ibn al-Athir says much the same after witnessing directly the conquest by the Mongols of Mawarannahr (Transoxiana) (see e.g. 'Sbornik materialov, otnosyashchikhsia k Zolotoy Orde' in *Istoria Kazakhstana v arabskikh istochnikakh*, Almaty: Dayk Press, 2005, v.1).

This merely underlines once again that it was Genghis Khan himself who gave the name 'Mongols' to the united clans of Turkic peoples, and this new ethnonym had not yet spread widely outside Mongolia. We will discuss this in more detail below.

No sooner had the Mongols conquered Central Asia and brought China to its knees, however, than attitudes to them shifted greatly. The best European and Asian ruling dynasties fawned on the Mongol leader, competing with one another to send ambassadors, and the most far-sighted of them sought to create kinship relations with them by intermarriage, as was the case with the Jin emperor of China.

After a short time, embassies were sent to Karakorum, Beijing (the last capital of the empire of Genghis Khan) and the Golden Horde by the Pope – a person whom, incidentally, Genghis Khan regarded as ineffective in the world. Later, fulfilling the wishes of his illustrious grandfather, Güyük Khan gathered a large army and set out for the west; he died, however, in mysterious circumstances somewhere near Samarkand.

Unfortunately, history has not preserved for us an original documentary portrait of Genghis Khan. As a consequence of this, Chinese artists endow him with Chinese facial features, while contemporary Mongols give him Mongol features. There is just one of several verbal descriptions of the great leader that has been preserved for us by the Persian chronicler Minhaj al-Siraj Jusjani. According to this, Genghis was tall, with a strong build and a thin grey beard (he was by this time sixty years old), with cat-like eyes in which, commanding respect, shone with the decisiveness and perspicacity of a genius. He was just, inflexible, fearless and cruel! In the words of another chronicler, the eyes of Genghis Khan shone from within with a cold light, and such features could only be possessed by one who was born 'with a clot of baked blood in a clenched fist', as the family chronicle tells us.

From school history lessons we are familiar with expressions like 'the Tatar-Mongol yoke', 'the Mongol invasion' and similar. It was no surprise to us that in historical sources and textbooks, modern-day Kazakh clans were divided on the basis of Mongol or Turkic origin, as though there had existed separate Mongol and Turkic clans in the 13th century. Even then I had an intuition that something about this was wrong. My sixth sense was suggesting that all this was done for political reasons and had little to do with the truth. But back then, in the Soviet period, it was extremely dangerous to even attempt to express doubt in the postulates of Soviet scholarship, never mind to disagree wholesale with the official viewpoint.

Later, once we had become adults, we began to learn that there were direct descendants of Genghis Khan living among the Kazakhs. In wonder we read the works of Japanese researchers who asserted that there was not a single descendant of Genghis among the modern Mongolian people. And, naturally, we asked the question whether Genghis Khan himself was in fact Mongolian as this ethnic term is understood today. And so, wherever had this mythical Mongol people come from? The sources available to us spoke only about the conquests of the Mongols, their bloodthirstiness and incredible cruelty, but there was not a single word about their origins. There were only legends about Genghis' ancestors having appeared by divine will on the earth, as though they were born from miraculous rays of light – in the same way that the Bible describes the arrival on earth of Jesus Christ.

In 1992 I made the acquaintance of people who were present at a meeting between the former US president Jimmy Carter and the staff of one of the private Kazakh TV channels. As the former president congratulated the journalists on their country's newly-found independence, he urged them to give special attention to their own history, which at the time was still far from having been grasped. He made the point explicitly that Genghis Khan had a direct relationship to the Kazakh nation. The former president of Turkey, Turgut Özal, had said the same thing on the eve of his death.

The Secret History of the Mongols is an authoritative source dating from 1240 that gives a detailed family tree of Genghis Khan to up to 22 generations, yet it too skirts the question – who was the father of Bozanshar or Bodonchar Munkhag, the direct ancestor by ten generations of Genghis? He was one of three brothers who were conceived by divine light and were born of Alan Gua of the Kazakh clan of the Koralas, a member of the Alan or Asi tribal union. Genghis Khan and his ancestors were descendants of Bodonchar's 5th son.

Moreover, despite the fact that the main Orientalist scholars consider the above source to be the most trustworthy source from among five or six chronicles from the 13th-15th centuries, from the viewpoint of classical scholarship it still cannot be treated as unfailing in its truthfulness. The original manuscript has still not been found; we are using a text that was written in Chinese characters that was discovered by the head of the Imperial Russian Orthodox mission in Beijing, Palladius Kafarov, in the mid-19th century. The text itself is traced from an example written in Mongolian. The latter example, in turn, was traced from a version written in ancient Kazakh using Naiman writing, evidence of which is given in almost half of the words found in Kafarov's text, that also correlate lexically with the vocabulary of modern Kazakh. In the margins of the Chinese version are words noted down by a translator, the meanings of which he did not understand. And these words were Kazakh!

Naturally, then, the text of *The Secret History of the Mongols*, having undergone several transformations from old Kazakh to modern Mongolian, then to Chinese and then Russian, will have suffered various distortions and changes, as a result of which proper names and clan names will have been drastically altered. For this reason, therefore, we will try in this book, so far as is possible, to restore the aboriginal names, toponyms and ethnonyms used in the original text of this heroic epic of Genghis Khan.

Another source we can use to study the life of Genghis Khan is the *Altan Depter* ('The book of the Golden Dynasty'). This mostly describes the leader's descendants. Again the original is lost, but there are two documents – a Chinese text dated to 1263 titled *Chengwu xin zhenglu* ('An account of the military campaigns of the Holy Emperor Warrior'), and a Persian text from 1305 titled *Jami al-Tawarikh* ('Collected chronicles'), alleged to have been copied from the original by the first vizier of the Ilkhans in Persia, a man known as Rashid ad-Din Hamadani.

The information contained in these sources should be neither disputed nor taken at face value; it is a matter of intuition to place that information in relation to what was possibly the reality.

In the summer of 2006 a festival was held in Ulan-Bator, capital of the modern Mongolian People's Republic, to celebrate 800 years of the Mongol state. As an invited guest, I could not turn down the opportunity to visit sites associated with Genghis Khan. Accompanied by Dr Dzhargalsaykhan, an expert on and admirer of his great compatriot, I travelled some five thousand kilometres across the limitless spaces of Mongolia and took great pleasure in its natural scenery with its fat herds and flocks (35 million head of livestock for a population of two and a half million), its lush meadows and full-flowing rivers.

Let us be objective: largely thanks to school textbooks, our view of our nomad ancestors has long conjured up associations with wild hordes that suddenly appeared before the walls of civilised European cities with the sole objective of looting other people's property, then equally suddenly disappearing for all eternity, like a swarm of voracious locusts. In the words of many Russian and European chroniclers, our ancestors appeared to them as the devil incarnate, going about spreading death and despair. And who were we not called among all this? We were called Polovtsians, Cumans, Pechenegs and Kimeks, the age of whom was reckoned as a year of life of the aforementioned locusts. To sum up, then, they were regarded as wild barbarians who did nothing for civilisation and were capable only of destruction. Yet the poets of the Golden Horde were writing about the rotation of the Earth about the Sun a hundred and fifty years before Copernicus as something that went without saying. This detail alone suggests how progressive was the state founded by our ancestors and how undeserved was the oblivion to which it was consigned. This was discussed in detail in Part I above.

When we reached the lower reach of the Onon river, at the end of our first day of travelling, I stood for a long time at the mound of Del'iun boldoq, where Genghis Khan spent his childhood. It seemed to me as though I was standing on exactly that precipitous bank where the twelve-year-old Temirshin (his childhood name; in Chinese, consonants in the middles of words are weakly pronounced, so Chinese versions often refer to him as Temujin), fighting for leadership, killed Behter, his stepbrother from his father's other wife. As is well known, the two wives of Yesugei, Genghis' father, produced seven young children. Incidentally, Sochigel, Behter's mother, brutally avenged her stepson, firstly by informing the Taichuids of the death of her son at the hand of Temirshin, and secondly by giving the Merkit all details of the location of Temirshin, who by now had already married Börte. As a result, the future leader was avenged twice. First, his fratricide became a humiliating captivity of many days by the Taichuids, and then his favourite wife was handed over for profanation to the warriors of the Merkit.

Sochigel herself suffered humanly for her actions. When Temirshin, along with twenty thousand warriors of his *anda* (childhood friend) Jamukha and twenty thousand Khereid invited by the father of the Wang khan Togrul, suddenly rained down on the Merkit camp, she avoided meeting her son Belegutei, although she knew he was looking for her. 'My sons have been made into khans, they say, but here I am languishing with a peasant. So how can I look my sons in the eye?' she said in the end, then exited the yurt through the left-hand half of the door just as her son was entering through the right.

A note about the names Temirshin and Genghis (Shynggys). As was mentioned earlier, the Turks were the first people in the world to learn to smelt iron (*temir*). Thanks to this they became invincible warriors and many peoples submitted themselves to them. Iron became the object of their veneration and the symbol of their greatness, and so the son of Yesugei was given the name Temirshin, an abbreviated form of the Kazakh *temirdi shyndaushy* or blacksmith. As for Genghis, the root *shyng* coincides semantically with the Kazakh word *shyndagan*, meaning hardened or tempered, while the second part of the word, *gys*, is a reinforcing suffix. Overall, then, *shynggis* (Genghis) would mean 'super-hardened'. Let us note that in his 'Collected chronicles' (see *Sbornik letopisey*, USSR Academy of Sciences, 1952) Rashid ad-Din Hamadani gives the word *chin* the meaning 'powerful', 'strong', while the Khivan khan Abu al-Ghazi Bahadur deciphers the word *shyng* as 'great', 'strong' (*Rodoslovnoe slovo tiurkov*, 'Turkestan', TKISO, 1996).

The Kazakh scholar Hasen Kozha-Ahmet gives a new interpretation of the names of the 'Great Terror of the Universe' in his major work *Zabluzhdenie, dlivsheesia vekami* (Almaty: Bilim, 2013). He suggests: 'When at the *kurultay* [military council] of 1206 the title 'powerful and strong' was conferred upon Temirshin, the people, who venerated iron, expressed this in a word that was familiar to them: *shyndalgan*. It is worth noting that the writer and archivist Amantay Sataev earlier mentioned in his unpublished work *Zhalany mol arkalagan zhihanger*, which was shown to me by his widow Gulzhan Abeldinovna, that Attila ['the Hun'] was known in his childhood by the name Qonzhyq and that he was an unsurpassed master smith. It was for this that he was later given the name Ottyla (Attila), which had the literal meaning of 'fiery'. It is my view that the father of the future 'Great Terror', and the 'Terror' himself, both knew about the acts of their great forebear, and, accordingly, linked the names Temirshin and Genghis to the image of a blacksmith fanning a fire in a furnace.

Later we will give a different interpretation to the name of Attila.

Rashid ad-Din Hamadani and the unknown author of *The Secret History of the Mongols* interpret the reasons for Börte's captivity by the Merkit in different ways. In *The Secret History of the Mongols* Chilger Bökh, the younger brother of Chiledu, from whom Yesugei, Genghis' father, took his wife Hoelun, escaping from Temirshin's sudden attack on the Merkit, exclaimed:

> The black crow,
> though fated to eat [scraps of] skin,
> wished to eat goose and crane.
> I, Chilger, unfortunate and ugly,
> laid hands on the Lady, the qatun,
> and brought calamity on all the Merkits.

[...]

> The bad bird, the buzzard,
> though fated to eat rats and mice,
> wished to eat swan and crane.
> I, Chilger, who am doubly bad,
> became the keeper of the fortunate and mighty Lady,
> and brought calamity on all the Merkits.

Hamadani, on the other hand, suggests that the Merkit handed Börte to the Khereid Wang Khan, and the latter returned her in 'innocence and safety' to Temirshin. How many months Börte spent in captivity by the Merkit is unknown, but the fact that she was pregnant when she was rescued by Temirshin is recorded in all the chronicles of the time.

Genghis Khan named his firstborn Zholshy, i.e. 'wayfarer', because he was born on the return from captivity by the Merkit. His name later mutated to Juchi and then Jochi.

I vividly pictured the Onon in winter, with the boy Temirshin playing on its frozen surface with his *anda* Jamukha, exchanging gifts with him and swearing eternal friendship. Fate would later drive them apart, to face each other across the barricade, prepared for a protracted struggle for power in their country. I stood at the memorial stone close to the confluence of the Orkhon and Selenga rivers, where Temirshin and Jamukha feasted for several days, celebrating the rescue of Börte from the Merkit. And I was saddened when my companion the professor deciphered the petroglyphs on another stone, which said that it was there that the paths of Temirshin and Jamukha separated forever. Why did this happen? Whose fault was it – Temirshin or Jamukha? Many researchers are examining this question. Yet I see the cause of this rupture in their relationship as in the nature of Genghis Khan himself. Attaching itself to the yurt of Jamukha following Börte's rescue, Genghis' family would have found itself in a subordinate role. His fellow-tribesmen had effectively become service personnel, as one might say today, but then – according to the Orientalist Boris Vladimirtsev (author of *Obshchestvenniy stroy mongolov. Mongol'skiy kochevoy feodalizm*, Leningrad, 1934) – they were known as *unagan bogol* or 'slaves in attendance' to the large family of his former friend Jamukha. This in itself went against the nature of the future great leader. He was innately a leader who already knew that he could only reach power by swimming against a turbulent river of blood. In the same way that he killed his stepbrother Behter in order to remain head of his family (since Behter could have become leader of the Borjigin by marrying Temirshin's mother), then, he sacrificed his friendship with his *anda* (the word *ant* in Kazakh means 'oath', 'vow') in order once again to maintain his independence and not to become a vassal of even his closest friend and blood brother. That was the way of Temirshin; any other, and he would never have become Genghis Khan. As John of Damascus said in the 7th century, a storm will not harm small trees, but tall trees it will destroy, pulling them up by the root. In this war between two leaders of the steppe, only one could be victorious. Fate favoured Temirshin, while Jamukha came to a tragic end. Such was the will of fate and heaven...

As I looked at the fast current of the Onon I also imagined the boy Temirshin, hiding himself in the bushes to escape captivity by the Taichuids, his nearest blood relatives.

One afternoon, when we stopped by a Mongol yurt to drink salted tea, I thought that perhaps it was somewhere near here that the young Genghis Khan, also on the run from captivity by the Taichuids, had hidden in a cart packed high with sheep's wool to prevent being spotted by his pursuers. I pictured him in the yurt of his rescuer, Sorkan Shira, where he met his first love Qada'an. It is known that for two nights before escaping from the Taichuids he spent two nights in the house of Sorkan-Shira and it is entirely possible that feelings of affection may have arisen between the young people, as described in *The Secret History of the Mongols*, and Qada'an's father, suspecting this, did not see Temirshin but noticed him hiding in the reeds. And who knows what position Sorkan-Shira might have taken; maybe he dreamed afterwards of becoming related to the offspring of the khan's family. After all, he himself was merely a servant of the Taichuids.

Genghis Khan was no Muslim but nevertheless had four legitimate wives and a large number of concubines, and American geneticists estimate that his descendants from these are of the order of sixteen million people.

As is well known, the mother of Genghis belonged to the Olkhunut, while his elder wife Börte was from the tribe of the Khongirad. According to Rashid ad-Din Hamadani, the Khongirad and Olkhunut derived from two brothers, Quba Shira and Jurluq Mergen. Today the Khongirad are a large Kazakh family that lives primarily in the Southern Kazakhstan and Kyzyl Orda regions of Kazakhstan; this means, then, that the mother of Genghis Khan and the mother of his four sons from his elder wife Börte belonged to families that are today part of the Kazakh people.

Two of his other wives – Yesui and Yesugen – were Tatar, while the beautiful Khulan was of the Merkit. So, not one of them was a Mongol. Moreover, he married all his sons not to Mongols but to girls of what are today Kazakh tribes. Whether this was coincidental or intentional is a rhetorical question.

The senior wife of Genghis' eldest son Jochi was Sartaq Khatun, also of the Khongirad, who bore him the khan Orda Ichen, and his second wife Ukhaa Khatun, also a Khongirad, bore him the great Batu Khan. Chagatay's wife would also be a Khongirad, Sulu khatun. Ögedei, who inherited Genghis' empire, married Töregene, a Naiman. Here the information provided by Rashid ad-Din Hamadani and the Persian historian Ata-Malik Juvayni diverge. The former considers Töregene to be of the Merkit, who bore the khan Güyük, successor to Ögedei. And the wife of the youngest son Tolui was the Khereid Sorghaghtani, who bore him four great khans – Möngke, Kublai, Ariq Böke and Hulagu.

A document survives that gives evidence that Töregene, following the death of her husband Ögedei, was regent of the Mongol Empire for five years; she gave her signature as 'Eke Khatun – Töregene'. The document is dated 10 April 1240 and is bound together by the personal seal of Ögedei Khan. With the following edict she commanded that a certain collection of Taoist texts be printed; the inscription on the seal reads in Turkic: *Mungкe tenqqri – yin Kycen dur* – 'By the power of the Eternal Tengri I command...'.

According to Timur Jumaqan, a researcher of Kazakh history, the all-powerful lady regent of the Mongol Empire was born with an entirely different name, while Töregene was her title. All those families – and this was primarily representatives of the Naiman tribal union – who recognised her power, were moved to a separate social class known as the 'Tore' (the Kazakh word *tör* means 'place of honour'). Jumaqan demonstrates that Genghis Khan was descended from the Kazakh Matai, which in ancient times was thought of as the clan of the grey wolf, in that the *tamga* (emblem, stamp) of this group happens to be a wolf (Kazakh: *böri*).

The familiar legend of the origin of the ancestors of Genghis Khan holds that they were descendants of Borte Chino ('grey wolf') and Gua Maral ('beautiful doe'), who came to the mountain of Burkhan Khaldun in the early 7th century, having crossed one or another landlocked sea. Hasen Kozha-Ahmet, cited above, commenting on the present-day Mongol scholar O. Sükhbaatar (*Zaimstvovannye slova v mongol'skom iazyke*, Ulan-Bator, 1997, p.43) suggests that the word *borte* was borrowed by the Mongols from the Turks, and in modern Mongolian it means 'wolf'. He explains the second part of the name, *chino*, as derived from the old Turkic word *ashnu*, meaning 'earlier', 'before'. Some of the Turks who consider their earliest ancestor to be the wolf call themselves the people of Borte Ashnu, i.e. descendants of the wolf ancestor. The phonetically equivalent words *ashnu*, *ashina*, *shina* and *chino* are origins for the second part of the name of Borte Chino, ancestor of all Darlekin Mongols. Incidentally, Sükhbaatar believes that the word *maral* was also borrowed by contemporary Mongols from the Turks. 'If the names of the original ancestors of Genghis Khan and the Mongols in general, Borte and Maral, are Turkic (as scholars in Mongolia accept), then is it correct to call their descendants 'Mongols'?' asks Kozha-Ahmet rightly.

Sitting for days on end in a jeep, crossing the steppe at speeds of 20-30 kilometres per hour, I reflected with amazement on Genghis Khan, racing across these same spaces on his bay horse for three days and nights without rest or sleep. He was pursuing thieves who had made off with the family's greatest treasure, eight geldings. When we stopped and spent the night in a yurt I imagined that it was here that Genghis Khan met his faithful friend Bo'orchu of the Argyn tribe – whom he later made into one of his closest allies. Such was Genghis' charisma that Bo'orchu, without even telling his father first, joined with his new friend to seek out and rescue the stolen horses.

Among his comrades-in-arms most of all, Genghis Khan valued loyalty and with equal passion hated treachery; those who succumbed to the sin of Judas he had executed. And above all those of them who, trying to curry favour, captured their masters and brought them before him. It was with death that he 'thanked' Jamukha's supporters, who had handed over his former friend, now turned bitter enemy.

The history of the rise of Genghis Khan deserves attention and deep reflection. His father died when he was nine years old, leaving him with his mother and younger brothers; without support from his relatives, who had moved to other grazing lands, he, despite the odds, became a great man. In my view the quality that most helped him to victory was his ability to find others who thought the same way as he. Perhaps also the ability to create his own team, to use a modern phrase, that was capable of solving any problem with which it was confronted.

Genghis Khan divided people into two categories. Into the first of these he placed those who placed the greatest importance on honour and personal dignity. In Genghis' view such people could only come from among nomad stock. The second category contained those who valued material wellbeing and security above all else, and these tended in the main to be from settled cultures. The latter he regarded automatically as potential traitors and turncoats, since they could display treachery for the sake of protecting their own lives or averting threats to their material wealth. He destroyed such persons without regret and did not allow them near him; yet he had a remarkable facility for attracting and finding himself among people of honour. Moreover the subordination of these to him was not a blind reflex action but rather had the character of a sacred belief. With the hands and voice of the shaman Teb Tengri, Genghis achieved such a level that those around him believed that he had been chosen by Heaven. And subservience to the Eternal Blue Sky, Tengri, was regarded at that time as the duty of every nomad born on the earth.

Important evidence of the divine nature of Genghis Khan's power was his introduction of the Great Yassa, a code of laws that acted as a constitution for the populations of his empire, and simultaneously also as a civil and a criminal code. In the view of the Persian Ata-Malik Juvayni, for Genghis Khan's subjects the Yassa became a divine gift of Tengri, a talisman, thanks to which the wars Genghis fought were always accompanied by victory. Capital punishment awaited all – from a rank and file soldier to a 'commander of a thousand' or general – for violations of the laws of the Yassa.

It is probable that the severity of the punishments ensured that the laws were observed with a greater or lesser degree of veracity.

For lying, theft, adultery, false testimony, treason, abandoning a wounded man on the battlefield, use of the belongings of a deceased person by anybody other than his successors, for the carrying of honorary titles by *beks* (equivalent to lords or emirs), for making peace with an enemy, failure to express absolute obedience, keeping a Mongol as a servant, for giving food to a captive without the permission of the captor, for relieving oneself in water or ashes, for becoming bankrupt three times when buying goods and for much else, the penalty was execution. In any event, however, to quote Machiavelli, the ends justified the means: the empire of Genghis Khan, in which an atmosphere of absolute submission to the law prevailed, soon became invincible.

Before every major military campaign Genghis would go up the mountain alone and undo the belt of his caftan and then hang this over his shoulder, kneel and ask the Lord Eternal Blue Sky, Tengri, to grant him victory. His retinue and guard, surrounding the foothills and waiting for his return, might sometimes wait three, four or five days. But when Genghis Khan eventually came down from the mountain, climbed onto his horse and gave orders, they could all be certain that Tengri was on the side of the Mongols and that their khan had been chosen by Heaven.

I thought for a long time about why, before taking the most important decisions, Genghis Khan would climb to the summit of the mountain and did not go, say, into a forest or out onto the nomads' native environment, the steppe. In the end I realised that this was a religious matter, that is, was to do with Tengriism. Rafael Bezertinov suggests that 'the mountains assume the function of the "brain" of the planet... Where once from the depths of the earth an immense energy burst out into space, mountains then appeared. Mountains... provide a link to the Great Mind, while their foundations are submerged in the body of the planet and exert an influence on it... When a person prays, the desires of that person take the form of a subtle energy that extends out to space. When somebody prays on a holy mountain, the subtle energy of their prayer is infused into the column of sacred energy of the mountain itself, and because of this fusion, the power of the prayer is magnified many times... Subtle energy is directly linked to human thinking, and thought energy can be regulated (or directed – K.Z.) both for creative and for destructive purposes. A person who can apply such subtle energy becomes almost all-powerful...' (*Tengrianstvo – religia tiurkov i mongolov*, Kazan: Slovo, 2004).

Genghis Khan possessed this gift.

The number nine had significance for Genghis Khan. He and Börte had nine children – four sons and five daughters, and the famous emblem with a gyrfalcon and nine crescents accompanied him on all his long-distance campaigns. He also kept beside him nine friends and people of like mind who had laid half of the world at his feet: Bo'orchu of the Argyn (Arulat), the first among his friends to believe in the star of Genghis, and who consequently commanded the right flank of his army. In his youth he saved Temirshin's family from starvation by bringing aid and recapturing the family's eight geldings that the Taichuids had seized. Two more were Jelme and his younger brother Subutai from the clan of the Uriankhai, which at some point became part of the Kazakh clan of the Kerey. Rashid ad-Din Hamadani considered that in his times the Kerey were related to: the Sakha (today's Yakut), the Uriankhai (today's Tuvans), the ancestors of the Kazakh Alban, the Tongoit and the Qaraqas. The Tongoit are the Tangut, known in Kazakhstan today as the Dungan. And Jelme saved his friend twice – firstly from captivity by the Merkit, and on a second occasion when Genghis was injured in the shoulder while fighting Jamukha. All the following night Jelme drew off the drying blood from the wound. An incident is known in which Jelme risked his life to fetch some soured milk for his wounded friend from the enemy camp. As for Subutai, who today does not know about this great military leader, a single mention of whose name made all Asia and all Europe tremble, at once loathing him and yet enraptured by the talents of this leader, the likes of which had never been seen before? Of Subutai it is said that he encouraged his troops to exploit the fruits of the civilisations of the countries conquered, to caress their women and to charm their own ears and body with the goods of strangers, but during the battle it was essential to forget all this, indeed to cultivate a loathing of it, so that when the next victory came, they could again restore to themselves the pleasures they had lost.

Regrettably, a tragedy of the militant Turks was always the loss of these instincts in the conquered lands.

Jebe was an outstanding warrior, an archer of unsurpassed skill, to whom Genghis Khan gave this name when he came to him together with Sorkan-Shira after fighting on Jamukha's side. He undertook the most demanding tasks for the khan, including those of physically destroying the Naiman khan Kuchlug, who was already in what is now the Gorno-Badakhshan region of Tajikistan. He was a serf of the Taichuids and was himself of the Suldus, part of the modern Kazakh Aday. In Kazakh the name Jebe means 'arrow'. The *tamga* of the Aday also represents an arrow.

Another of the most important generals was Muqali, of the Kazakh clan of the Jalayir. He was Genghis Khan's representative in northern China once the Mongols had departed westwards to fight Khorezmshah Muhammad. He also commanded the left flank of Genghis Khan's army when Genghis went to punish the Khorezmshaha harshly for killing his messengers.

Borokhul, the adopted son of Genghis' mother Hoelun, of the Wusun, was remembered in *The Secret History of the Mongols* by Genghis Khan as follows:

...on [our] swift expeditions on rainy nights
you never let me hunger

through the night.
While battling the enemy,
you never let me spend the night without broth.

Genghis recalled Borokhul's wife with gratitude for saving his youngest son Tolui from a dagger raised over his head by a Tatar prisoner. Genghis Khan sincerely mourned the loss of his sworn brother Borokhul, who was killed at the hands of forest tribesmen of the Khori-Tumat. It should be mentioned that the greater part of the Wusun left the territory of Mongolia before the start of the Common Era; only an insignificant number remained there, who are today known as the Ushin.

The role of 'minister of defence' was given by Genghis to Kublai of the Barlas – the clan from which Timur would later rise. This is how Genghis Khan spoke of Kublai, Jebe, Subutai and Jelme, affectionately calling them 'my four hounds':

...when I said, "Reach [that place],"
you smashed the ores.
When I said, "Attack!"
you split the rocks.
You broke the shining stones to pieces,
you parted the deep waters.

It is interesting to note that seven generations before Genghis Khan was Hashi Hülüg, but the Barlas drew their lineage from his brother Hashu. It turns out that the descendants of the two great leaders from a single root, Genghis Khan and Timur, are today scattered among various ethnic groups. One of these claims to be Mongol and another Uzbek; but in fact they are both ancestors of today's Kazakhs.

Another of his military marshals, Jirjedai, from the clan of the Manghud, who subsequently formed 95% of the Nogai Horde (read: Kazakh – K.Z.), played an extraordinary role in one of the most precarious moments in the life of Genghis Khan. In a trap set by his sworn father, the Khereid

Wang Khan, Temirshin found himself on the brink of death and only the courage and resourcefulness of Jirjedai saved him. As a sign of his special affection for Jirjedai, Genghis Khan gave him his own wife, the daughter of the brother of Wang Khan, Ibaka-Beki, saying to her: 'I have not said that you are unintelligent, or that your looks and complexion are bad. You have entered my breast and my feet. ... Mindful of the great principle [by which deeds are rewarded], I will favour Jürchedei [because] of his services'. Of course, to give a wife to another man, even one to whom one owes one's life, is an unheard of act, even for an individual as generous in his gifts as Genghis Khan. Still, it seems that following the treachery of his sworn father Togrul (Wang Khan) of the Kerey, Genghis Khan had no desire to build family ties to him by accepting his niece; he thus took advantage of this opportunity to tactfully pass her on to his close comrade. That is the version told in *The Secret History of the Mongols*.

Genghis Khan had the reputation of being a brilliant military leader, but in fact he was not such in the immediate sense. Many battles are recorded in which he lost, for example, with Jamukha and with Wang Khan. He was however a brilliant organiser of military affairs and had grown up among exceptionally bright military leaders.

The ninth military genius available to Genghis may be considered Nay of the Baarin. The Baarin descended from the bondwoman held by Bodonchar. This same woman, already pregnant and now a concubine of Bodonchar, gave birth to a son, Jajiradai, who became the ancestor of the Jamukha clan, and Bodonchar also had a son Baaridai, from whom all the Baarin were descended who lived in the Nogai Horde. As a consequence of *barymta* (cattle theft as an act of revenge), Bodonchar took his bondwoman captive, and hence the etymology of the Baarin. When Genghis Khan punished the Taichuids, the tribe that constituted his closest relatives but that had turned against him, it was Nay with his brother Allakh captured the Taichuid leader Targitay-Kyryldak, whom they served. But, showing wisdom and generosity, they released him as their native khan, while also avowing their allegiance to Genghis Khan. They said to him: 'We captured Tarqutai and were bringing [him to you], but we could not forsake our rightful Qan. How could we kill him? We [therefore] released him and sent him away, [but] we trust you and thought to come and offer you our might.' Genghis Khan replied: 'Had you laid hands on your own Qan, Tarqutai, had you laid hands on your rightful Qan, I should have executed all of you and your clan. [But] you were unable to forsake your rightful Qan; your heart was right.'

He promised to charge Nay with a major task. And when Genghis Khan was proclaimed a great khan in 1206, he appointed Nay to command the forces of the central corps.

However, there had been an event involving Nay earlier, in 1204. When Genghis Khan crushed the warriors of the Merkit Toqtabek, his brother Tair, wanting to become related to Genghis Khan, brought him his daughter Khulan. On the way, they were delayed by none other than Nay and his *nuker* (personal guard), which enraged Genghis Khan, who suspected that he had been having an intimate encounter with Khulan. *The Secret History of the Mongols* recounts his fury with Nay thus:

'Why did you detain them, Naya'a?' He grew very angry and questioned him severely and in detail, intending to make a [matter of] principle of it. While Chinggis Qahan was questioning Naya'a-noyan, Qulan Qatun [interjected]: 'Naya'a said: "I am Chinggis Qahan's great lord. We will travel together to show your daughter to the Qahan, [for] there are disorderly soldiers along the way." That was the warning that he gave us. Had we not been with Naya'a and met soldiers along the way, we might have encountered trouble amid the confusion. Perhaps meeting Naya'a was our good [fortune]. Before asking Naya'a, the Qahan may, if he favours me, ask [my] body, born by the destiny of Heaven to [my] father and mother.' This was the petition that she set before [the Qahan]. While being questioned [by the Qahan], Naya'a said: 'I will never turn my face away from the Qahan and towards [an]other. Whenever I encounter foreign people's girls and women of beautiful complexion or geldings with fine rumps, [each time] I say: "These are the Qahan's." If my desire is other than I indicate, let me die.'

And Genghis Khan granted to each of his nine generals, as a matter of the highest mercy, forgiveness for nine of their misdeeds, each of which would be punishable by death.

Now, a few words about the governors of his state. The first of these was Shigi Qutuqu, who was brought up by his mother. He was Genghis' adopted brother from the Tatar clan of the Alcha, and he was entrusted with directing the court of justice of the empire. Shigi Qutuqu was the living embodiment of 'walls with ears'. Genghis Khan said to him: 'Eradicate theft and crush fraud within all the boundaries of our state', and Shigi Qutuqu fulfilled these instructions in a fitting manner. Additionally, Shigi Qutuqu fulfilled the two roles we today would call Attorney General and Chief Justice simultaneously, in the vast state in which one could travel from the Sea of Japan to the Baltic without incident.

The brilliant advisor, the Naiman-Khitan Yelü Chucai, with whom Genghis Khan became friends during the first campaign to China, created an outstanding system of administration for the empire, thanks to which the state created by Genghis survived for three centuries after his death. The empires of Alexander the Great and Julius Caesar crumbled on the deaths of their founders, while, speaking of the state created by Genghis Khan, Prince Trubetskoy, one of the creators of the Eurasianism movement, asserted that the Russian Empire was the conscious inheritor of and successor to the Empire of Genghis Khan. Meanwhile Yelü Chucai, addressing Genghis Khan after one of his successful conquests, uttered an expression that grew wings of its own: 'One can conquer an empire on horseback, but one cannot govern it on horseback.'

Genghis Khan was a noble-minded man and could pardon even his enemy if he saw in him bravery or a warrior's talent. This was the case with Jebe, mentioned above (whose full name at birth was Zurgadai) when, fighting on the side of Jamukha, he shot an arrow through the neck vertebra of Genghis' white-faced bay horse from a highly unfavourable position, from the top of a hill, which provoked the leader's astonishment. Admitting sincerely to Genghis what had happened, Jebe said (again in *The Secret History of the Mongols*):

'I shot the arrow from the mountain top. If I am to be put to death by the Qahan, then I shall be left to rot on a piece of ground [the size of] the palm [of a hand]. But if I am granted [mercy], then I shall go ahead on behalf of the Qahan.
I will attack for you:
I will slash the deep waters
and erode the shining stone.
At your word, I will go forwards
and smash the blue stones.
If you order me to attack,
I will smash the black stones.
I will attack for you.

And so this is how Genghis Khan formed his team of supporters, with whose aid he was able to enter world history with his reputation expressed as the 'Great Terror of the Universe'.

Breaking with the law of the steppe aristocracy, Genghis Khan placed people in positions of responsibility not according to the attributes of their blood relationships but on the basis of their talent and abilities. With his inherent talent and using his rare gift of insight into the human soul, Genghis Khan only gave tasks to those of his entourage whom he knew could, and who usually did, fulfil that task better than others.

Let us consider a curious fact: when a certain proportion of the population took Temirshin's side in his conflict with Jamukha, the move to the camp of Yesugei's eldest son was not *en masse* – not whole clans, but selectively. Only a certain group of families that took a 'long view', that shared as it were Genghis Khan's political views and his moral outlook and who liked him as a man, took his side. This process is described in *The Secret History of the Mongols*:

'[Temüjin's party] travelled through the night and, at daybreak, saw Qachi'un-toqura'un, Qaraqai-toqura'un, and Qaraldai-toqura'un of the Jalayirs. The three Toqura'un brethren had travelled together through the night... Mönggetü-kiyan's son Önggür and others with their

Changshi'ut and Baya'ut [followers]. From the Barulas came Qubilai and Qudus and their brethren... Bo'orchu's younger brother Ögölen-cherbi left the Arulats and came to join his older brother. [...]'

So we see that those who gathered under the banner of Genghis Khan were people of a particular psycho-physical makeup, and Genghis was highly skilled in finding and selecting such people from among those around him. Jumping forward a little, I note that Ungur or Ongur is identified in the above version as the son of Mungetu-Kiyan, who was the elder brother of Genghis' father Yesugei. Thus Ongur and Genghis Khan were cousins. It follows then that if the Changshi'ut and the Bayad are Ongur's native tribes, then Genghis Khan also belonged to one or the other of them. However, Rashid ad-Din Hamadani did not regard Ongur as the son of Mungetu-Kiyan. Which of the accounts is correct, that of *The Secret History of the Mongols* or that of the illustrious Persian historian, cannot today be determined – although this question determines the bloodline of Genghis Khan himself. From the sources we know only that he was related to the Kiyat, who were as multitudinous as all Turks. In more concrete terms, as we have seen, Genghis Khan's descent is indicated in *The Secret History of the Mongols*. Today the descendants of both the Changshi'ut and the Baya'ut are found among Kazakh clans, but this will be discussed later.

An example quoted by Rashid ad-Din Hamadani produces a sense of astonishment. One time, while examining a worthy candidate for the post of a leader of a thousand, Genghis Khan said: 'There is no *bahadur* [warrior] like Yesunbay and no man can match his talents. But because he has not suffered from the hardships of campaigns and does not know hunger or thirst, he considers all other people, *nuker* [personal guard] and soldiers, similar to himself in their ability to endure hardship, but they are not capable of enduring it. For this reason he is not suitable to be a commander. A man worthy of that position is one who has himself known hunger and thirst and can therefore judge the state of others according to this; a man who calculates his moves and does not allow his men to go hungry or their animals to become emaciated...'

So tell me, reader, on the basis of this, is there anyone else whom one can compare with Genghis Khan for his ability to comprehend that holy grail, the human soul, and to organise military affairs? Another historian of the Mongols, Aleksandr Domanin, said on this matter: 'Hats off, all you who wear shoulder straps, to the military genius of Genghis Khan!' Earlier we mentioned the philosopher Francis Bacon, reputed to have said that he who understands the human nature is born to rule. Genghis Khan understood human nature to a high degree and made full use of what has today become a cliché, the 'human factor', which contains the inexhaustible potential of the human against which even nature is powerless. The Buddha said similarly that there is no fire like desire, no monster like hatred, no net like delusion and no raging river like craving.

So we see that Genghis Khan was familiar with the subtle threads of human psychology. Thanks to his immense talent as a state-builder he created a system of power that rested solely on persons of exceptional psychological resources.

As I took a refreshing swim after our tiring crossing or run (though driving off-road across the endless Mongolian steppe can barely be described as a run) in the cold waters of the Kherlen, not far from where Genghis Khan had his summer headquarters, I visualised the *kurultay* (military assembly) at which the impending Chinese campaign was being discussed down to the last detail – the first major military action outside Mongolia itself.

The history of Genghis Khan includes many obscure pages that are riddled with, as it were, blank spots. The consequence is a degree of verbal juggling. If we take the year of his birth to be the most likely date of 1155 and date his proclamation as khan of his native tribes to 1186 or, as in other sources, 1182, then the question arises of what he did in his twenties and thirties. The available sources do not mention this period of his life. It is known that he married Börte at sixteen and broke his relationship with Jamukha at 18-19, having previously fought with the Merkit, but then he disappears entirely from the field of vision of his contemporaries, which gives reason (according to some scholars such as Gumilev) to assume that he spent a long period in captivity in China. The Russian scholar Aleksandr Domanin, mentioned above, proposes that immediately after he was proclaimed khan of his native tribes in 1186 and the first confrontation with Jamukha, he was captured by his sworn brother and was kept hostage for ten years by the Jin rulers of China. Ten years later, however, as the strength of the Tatars living along the Great Wall of China increased, he was released on bail and given the task of creating a counterbalance to them. Using their favourite principle of 'divide and rule', the Chinese dominated the environments populated by nomadic tribes. These tribes had, accordingly, become disconnected from one another and only Genghis Khan was able to gather them into a single people, to which, along with many others, even tribes of the Celestial Empire submitted (*Mongol'skaia imperia chingizidov. Chingishan i ego preemniki*, Moscow: Tsentropoligraf, 2005).

This hypothesis is also justifiable because, in *The Secret History of the Mongols*, the narrative concerning Genghis Khan leaps from the events of 1186 straight to 1201, when Jamukha was selected as *gurkhan* by other Mongol tribes.

If however we take Genghis Khan's year of birth to be 1167, then the theory of ten years' exile in China no longer stands; on the other hand, however, his lifespan is then shortened to 60 years, which does not concur with the views of many of his biographers. Meanwhile historiography also regards a further date of birth for Genghis Khan. According to the *History of Yuan*, a source on the history of the Mongols of vital importance, and the *Altan Tobchi* ('Golden Summary') of the monk Guush Luvsandanzan, who lived in the 17th century and had access to unique primary sources, 'Temujin was born in the year of the Black Horse (1162) in the first month of summer, at midday on the sixteenth day...'.

We returned home by an ancient route that crossed back into Kazakhstan at Maykapchagay and to the town of Karakorym, the route by which Aleksander Nevsky and other Russian princes travelled to visit the great khan to obtain a *yarlyk* or edict confirming their position as rulers. I was overcome by conflicting feelings: on the one hand my investigations had confirmed my view that Genghis Khan was born and grew up among a milieu of Kazakh peoples, but I felt uncomfortable before my welcoming Mongol hosts, whom with my studies I had effectively deprived of their great ancestor. Still, I believe that Mongolia, with its immense natural beauty and its talented people, has a promising future, and that the spirit of Genghis Khan, which moves over this land and these people, will help make that future great.

Well known in the field of mathematical logic, which I have studied in some depth, are Gödel's incompleteness theories, the basic sense of which is that any theory is consistent if and only if there exists a corresponding model. The argument I will give in what follows about Genghis Khan being descended from a clan that includes my own ancestors (the Sumerians, Cimmerians, Scythians, Sarmatians, Sir, Huns, Alans, Qiyad and possible descendants of the Kazakh clans of the Baganal, Matai, Sirgeli, Tarakt, Tabyn, Tama, Merkit, Aday and Shanyshkyly) is based on the available sources together with some of my own proposals about the formation of the Kazakh ethnos. At the same time this hypothesis does not contradict, in my view, the voluminous existing, unsystematised material and facts from our own history, and therefore the model we are proposing, without claiming to be the final truth, may fill in some gaps in our historical knowledge with regard to the problem of the formation of the Kazakh ethnos and Kazakh statehood. And this includes specific historical figures from among the Kazakh people.

The Scottish philosopher Thomas Carlyle once said: 'Happy the people whose annals are blank in history books!' Nevertheless I hope that my 'amateur' investigations (from the point of view of professional historians) will uncover a new page in the history of the Kazakh people.

CHAPTER II
THE ETERNAL PEOPLE UNDER THE ETERNAL BLUE SKY

*They [the ten thousand things] grow and
flourish and then return to the source.
Returning to the source is stillness, which is the way of nature.
The way of nature is unchanging.*
Lao Tsu

Once I witnessed a curious event. As a third-year university student I worked in my free time in a students' construction gang in the Almaty (then Alma-Ata) region. One day a local *aksakal* (bearded elder) came up and asked me in Kazakh: 'Ruyng kim?' Unaware at the time that the word *ru* meant 'clan', I could not answer and said I did not understand him. He then said, 'Well, where are you from? I come from Narynkol, and there are Albans living there. What about you?'

I remembered that when we were children there had been talk of us being so-called 'shala-Kazakh' or half Kazakh – not fully Kazakh – because, while my father was a Kazakh, my mother's ancestors were from both Kazakhs and Kazakh Tatars. The latter had once migrated to Kazakhstan from Kazan when the Russian tsar issued a decree that Tatars should be conscripted into the regular army. The decree did not apply to Kazakhs, even though the Kazakhs were by this time subjects of the Russian Empire.

Many Tatars moved to Kazakhstan to dodge the draft. A diaspora of 20-30 families settled near our village of Karaotkel, twelve kilometres from the Irtysh river; in time they became intermixed with the local Kazakh population. My mother was a descendant of this diaspora of migrants.

So when I told the *aksakal* that I was a 'shala-Kazakh' he burst out laughing and said that there was no such clan among the Kazakhs. This gave me a sense of shame, and when I got home I asked my grandfather at length about who we were and where we were from.

That was when I first learned that I am from the Naiman. Naturally there was much that my grandfather did not know, but he explained that within the broad Naiman tribe we were part of the Matay, and among the Matay we were the Shang, and among these we were the Qarauyl-jasak and so on. This group was mainly settled in what is today the Samara district of the East Kazakhstan region. But then he unexpectedly came up with some deeper knowledge after all and quoted me a popular saying with undisguised pride: 'Alshyn bolsang – Aday bol, Wusun bolsang – Botbay bol, Argyn bolsang – Altai bol, Naiman bolsang – Matai bol.' This proverb as it were establishes the peculiar hierarchy of the Kazakh clans and tribes, while ensuring that Kazakhs from other clans do not take offence at my grandfather!

My ancestors were generously provided for as far as lineage is concerned. From the Matay came the Scythian king Madius (or Matay), after ruling Babylon for 28 years in the 7th century BCE; also from the Matay came Modu Chanyu (Matay), leader of the Huns, who in 209 BCE established an empire in China to which the rulers of the Celestial Kingdom paid tribute. And finally the Bible mentions that one of Noah's grandsons, one of his son Japheth's seven sons, was called Madai (Matay). Curiously, a Finnish-language edition of the Gospel of St Matthew reads as though it were the 'Gospel of Matay'. Another of my ancestors created the Yin-Shang dynasty in China, which ruled that people for 600 years from the 18th century BCE. Later, in Roman-ruled Britain the Sarmatian Iazyge Jasak created the kingdom of the Britons ruled by King Arthur, whose descendants can be found among the Karaul Jasak of the Naiman. Many great individuals were born to the Samara region; its sons include men of the Sumerians (or Samarans) who, in the fourth millennium BCE, founded the most ancient civilisation, the Sumerians in the land between the Tigris and the Euphrates.

And so it was during my third year at university, in 1974-1975, that I first became acquainted with the tribal divisions of the Kazakhs. Sadly, however, my historical investigations were not prolonged, because at that time we were little interested in our past, and least of all in our national and tribal roots and shrines. We were part of the Soviet people and were required to speak in Russian only. I remember my mother reproaching us as children for not knowing our native language; as a diligent pupil I responded to her with the words of my school teacher: 'There will be communism in the USSR by the 1980s. There will no longer be Russians, Kazakhs or Germans but instead there will be one nation, the Soviet nation, that will speak a single language – Russian.'

Had that continued much longer, we would have ended up as just that – Kazakh *mankurts*, lost persons without a sense of our origin or tribe, our culture or our history. The word 'mankurt' stems from Turkic mythology and refers to a captive who has been forcibly deprived of his ability to think in order to become a docile slave. It was used by Chingiz Aitmatov in his novel *The day lasts more than 100 years* for a man who has been brainwashed, deprived of any memory of his people or origin.

Happily, nobody today is startled if a person takes an interest in his ancestral roots. And I do not find anything reprehensible in that desire. Let me make one thing clear: we are not speaking here about tribalism, a bugbear that was exploited by Soviet ideologues to control the national self-consciousness that was arising within the system. My wish to know my roots is governed purely by my interest in my humanity.

Recently I met for the first time some members of the Merkit, a clan that played an immensely important role in the life of Genghis Khan. Genghis' father took the wife of a Merkit warrior and the Almighty alone knows whether at this time she was carrying the future Great Terror of the Universe in her belly. I also experienced an unspeakable joy at meeting a representative of that great (I am not afraid to use such a word) clan the Koralas, from which descended the entire dynasty of Genghis Khan by the maternal line, and of the Baganal, of whom, I am convinced, Genghis Khan himself was a descendant.

Ever since it first started to attract me long ago, this interest in my own history, which can be explained only by the genetic memory of one's family, has been a major preoccupation for me. This interest has focused primarily on the great figures from our ancestral history such as Confucius, Alexander the Great, Genghis Khan, Attila and Tomyris, partly also because I share another of Thomas Carlyle's views, namely that 'The history of the world is but the biography of great men'. One of the outcomes of my enthusiasm was that I began to work on creating a series of paintings, working together with an artist of similar outlook, Zhomart Ibraev. My role in this collaboration was to substantiate the ideas, the concepts – and to provide the financing. Together we have, I hope, been able to revive our history and also to introduce it to our students.

Of course, the history of the great among one's ancestors is far from the whole of that history. Still, as the German thinker Bertolt Brecht said, it is a poor and indigent nation that has not given birth to a genius. I therefore also place great importance on seeking to understand the sources of the greatness of the Kazakh nation, for our blood flowed in the veins of some of the greatest figures in history. Those I have mentioned – Tomyris, Confucius, Alexander the Great, Aristotle, King Arthur, Attila, Genghis Khan and Timur – are without doubt among them, for they have left deep footprints in the history of all humankind, and not only that of the Turkic world. And thus the blood of our great ancestors flows today, in us, the Kazakhs of the 21st century.

Additionally, the person of Genghis Khan is now an immense storehouse of riddles and enigmas, and the search for answers to these is highly complex. And on top of this, the rigid stereotypes about this figure that have formed in the minds of many, including historians, have bolstered the popular notion that he is of Mongol descent.

We may suppose that even just ten years ago, suggesting that Genghis Khan was related to the Kazakhs would have been equivalent to indecent exposure in public, and yet, as the Persian poet Ferdowsi intimated, without pricking yourself on thorns you cannot pick the beautiful rose. So I had to make my choice, and I have done so. Today the picture is changing fast and in our favour.

The number of works devoted to the red-bearded genius is in the thousands. Yet there is almost no material regarding his descent and origin, since it is simply taken as axiomatic that his roots are Mongol. So imagine my astonishment when I first came across a particular original source – an outstanding book by the Persian scholar Rashid ad-Din Hamadani, published in 1305, a fundamental work that gave descriptions of a large number of tribes and clans that live today in what are now Kazakhstan, Mongolia, China, Turkey, Iran and so on ('Collected Chronicles', see *Sbornik letopisey*, USSR Academy of Sciences, 1952).

I have already pointed out that Hamadani approaches the problem of relations between the Turkic and Mongol clans entirely differently. His second chapter, for example, is titled: 'Of the Turkic tribes that are **at present** called Mongols but in ancient times each had its own name and sobriquet, and had both ruling positions and positions of dependency' (my emphasis – K.Z.). The third chapter title is 'Of those Turkic tribes of which each separately had a king and leader, but which were not related to those tribes that have been mentioned in the preceding chapters'. A further chapter is called 'Of the Turkic tribes that were known as Mongol'. In short, whenever he refers to the peoples that inhabited Mongolian territory in the 12th and 13th centuries, he describes them as Turkic tribes. In the course of time some of them began to call themselves Mongol. **And so I naturally found myself asking who, then, are the Mongols of today, if all their ancestors are descended from Turkic peoples?**

It is true that translators working for the USSR Academy of Sciences explained, and indeed cautioned future scholars of the Turkic republics of the USSR who would not be indifferent to the fates of their own peoples, that by the ethnonym 'Turk' Hamadani meant the entire nomadic world. But it is evident that this assertion cannot stand up to any criticism whatsoever.

In the period of the Turkic khaganates (6th-8th centuries) the ethnonym *turk* was understood to mean a strongly circumscribed union of related tribes, a significant part of which later became part of the Kazakh nation. This union did not include, say, modern Turkic groups such as the Kyrgyz, Uigurs, Tatars, Karluks and so on. The ethnonym *turk* spread later to a large number of peoples, but the ancestors of today's Mongols – Mancho-Tungus hunting and fishing tribes – were manifestly not included among the Turks by Hamadani.

Jumping forward a little, let me give my interpretation of the terms 'Turk' and 'Mongol' within Hamadani's works. When he titles one of his chapters 'Of the Turkic tribes that were known as Mongol', he means those Turkic tribes that came from the Ergenekon and from whom Genghis Khan and his 'Mongols' descended. When Hamadani refers to 'the Turkic tribes that are at present called Mongols' he means the following. Genghis Khan, in creating his empire, united all the Turkic peoples living in the eastern region of the Great Steppe into a single body, and therefore all Turkic peoples that were added to Genghis Khan's empire became known over time as Mongol. But the 'Mongols' of Genghis Khan are the people of the Mangi El ('Eternal Land' or 'Eternal People'), the name of which was given by Genghis Khan himself. We will discuss this later.

In seeking an answer to my question about the origin of the modern Mongols I have obtained much assistance from the works of Kalibek Daniyarov, a man whose background is far from historical studies: he is a doctor of science in the engineering disciplines, worked in the Soviet and Communist Party organs and taught at the Kazakh State Polytechnical Institute. Today he enjoys a well-earned retirement, but continues to write books that, in my view, are greatly needed by our people. It was he who first stated, boldly and out loud, that Genghis Khan was unrelated to modern-day Mongols but was in fact Kazakh, or more accurately, he was from one of the clans that later formed the Kazakh ethnos. The official historians naturally ostracised him at once – who after all could these Kazakhs be if the Kazakh nation did not appear until after the fall of the Golden Horde? Or, put another way, what Kazakh ancestry can one speak of for Genghis Khan if in the 13th century the ethnonym Kazakh did not exist?

Such were their arguments. But I decided to act differently and set to examining the primary sources and a considerable volume of research, including Hamadani as described above, and Hamadani's teacher Ata-Malik Juvayni, who in 1260 wrote an account of the Mongol empire titled *History of the World Conqueror* (Rus. ed. *Chingiskhan: Istoria zavoevatelia mira*, Moscow: Magistr-Press, 2004). I read Mahmud Kashgari, Abu al-Ghazi Bahadur and Kadyrgali Zhalairi, Nikolai Aristov, Vasily Bartold, Nikita Bichurin and Vasily Radlov. I also familiarised myself with that most important of all documents concerning Genghis Khan, written in 1240 (and known in Russian as 'The Hidden Legend of the Mongols' ever since it was translated at the order of Stalin in 1940 by the Soviet historian S. Kozin, though it is known everywhere else in the world as *The Secret History of the Mongols*).

From my efforts I realised that 'Mongol' was the name of a people that emerged in the 13th century, and this name is recorded as spoken solely by Genghis Khan himself. When by 1206 he had conquered and united all the clans and tribes of present-day Mongolia and the surrounding lands, he said: This people, the *bide*, who despite all the suffering and danger that I underwent, joined with me with courage, perseverance and devotion, and who, bearing joy and suffering with indifference, multiplied my strengths – I wish that this people, as noble as rock crystal, who showed me the deepest loyalty in all dangers and constancy until I achieved the objectives of my ambition – be given the name *keke*, 'Mongol', and that they be first among all peoples on the earth.' This is described by Erenjen Hara-Davan in his work *Chingishan kak polkovodets i ego nasledie. Kul'turno-istorichesky ocherk mongol'skoy imperii 12-14 vekov* (Almaty: KRAMDS – Ahmet Yassaui, 1992).

There is considerable disagreement about the interpretation and deciphering of this ethnonym. Kalibek Daniyarov maintains, for example, that the appearance of the concept of 'Mongol' is linked to Genghis Khan having created a people in the mode of an army, dividing its entire population into units of tens, hundreds and thousands. His genius lay in the fact that he did not make these military divisions on the basis of tribal groups but rather ensured that in every unit of ten or a hundred was a mixture of different groups. These units, moreover, were inviolable, and an attempt, say, by an individual to move from one unit to another was punishable by death. Genghis realised that this was the only way he could unite these people. Execution awaited any who left his comrade lying on the battlefield, regardless of whether you were Naiman or Dughlat, Alban or Khongirad – for in the ten or hundred you were all of one, and to leave any individual without aid was unthinkable. Thus he cemented his nation and made its members into citizens of the Great Empire.

In essence this consisted in creating a new community, a new nation with the name 'Mongol', where there were no titled or serving clans and where all the groups, living in felt yurts, shared the same rights and obligations. It was not easy to forget one's past heritage, such as Naiman, Kerey, Jalayir, Khongirad, Qatagan or Dughlat, but Genghis Khan literally forced everyone to style themselves with the proud name Mongol. Consider the analogy that the citizens of the USA do not consider themselves Portuguese, Spanish, Belgian or French, though they are so by blood – on the contrary they take pride in considering themselves Americans – and note that this could not be said of the citizens of the former USSR, which fell apart precisely because of a lack of a real feeling of participation in a single nation. All its citizens hurried to forget the term 'the Soviet people' as quickly as they could. Genghis Khan, on the other hand, succeeded in creating a new Mongol nation. Today the ideologists of Kazakhstan have a concealed desire to create a Kazakh nation, but this will not find popular support for one simple reason: for the Americanised Spaniard there still exists a Spain, where his original culture and language are still cultivated, but the Kazakhs do not have a country other than Kazakhstan itself, and likewise with the Kazakh language; there is no alternative motherland, and we Kazakhs alone are responsible for our national future.

Kalibek Daniyarov gives the following etymological derivation of 'Mongol': *myng qol* means 'a thousand warriors', or, literally, 'a thousand hands'. However, the young scholar Tleuberdy Abenay, who published a brilliant piece in the first issue of the periodical *Juldyz* in 2006, has given his version of the origin of the name, which is that the word 'Mongol' comes from the word *mangqul*, which translates from the Turkic as 'person in a condition of movement', that is, a nomad. The Kazakh word *qul* does not only mean a slave, but also a people. Literally – slaves of God.

People who lead settled lives are similar to animals, he suggests, particularly to dogs, who mark their territory with their urine; these people he calls *sartqul*, from the Kazakh *sary*, to urinate. Whereas those who live freely, without ties, are the *mangqul*. This then explains the ethnonyms 'Sart' (a term used in various contexts for settled peoples of Central Asia) and 'Mongol'. He believes that the division between *sartqul* and *manqul* took place in the 7th century. Following the Arab invasions that brought Islam by force of arms to Central Asia and southern Kazakhstan, those that accepted the new religion remained in their lands and began to call themselves *sartqul* (the Sarts), while the mobile nomads, preserving their belief in Tengri, migrated to northern and eastern Kazakhstan, Mongolia, Siberia and northern China and adopted the name *manqul*, which later evolved into 'Mongol'. If we recall that this was the time at which Börte Chino probably brought his fellow tribespeople from Central Asia to the mountain of Burkhan Khaldun, having crossed some kind of inland sea, then it is entirely probable that their great descendant Genghis Khan named his people the *manqul* (Mongols) in the sense of nomads. In this connection we obtain two possible explanations for why the nomads came to Burkhan Khaldun under the leadership of Börte Chino. Either it is true that, as we have suggested, certain tribes that did not accept Islam migrated out of Turkestan, or else it is possible that following the collapse of the First Turkic Khaganate, when its inhabitants dispersed the length and breadth of Eurasia, some of them, including Börte Chino, came to the source of the rivers Onon, Kherlen and Tuul and to Burkhan Khaldun.

In his book *Kipchaki – Oguzy* (Moscow: Tipografia 'Novosti', 2001, p.171) Murad Adji asserts that the word 'Mongol' appeared in the 11th century to name certain eastern Turkic tribes, the Tele. It is known that the Turkic Tele tribal union consisted of Sir and nine Oghuz clans. Once the Seir branched off from the Tele in the 7th century, the remainder became known as the 'Toguz Oghuz'. All in all, however, as far as I know Murad Adji explicitly does not associate Genghis Khan with the ancestors of the modern Mongols. If one looks a little deeper, then at the time of the Biblical Flood, which according to various sources took place more than 20,000 years ago, one learns from the writings of Bahadur Khan of Khiva, living in the 17th century (*Rodoslovnoe drevo tiurok*, TKISO, 'Turkestan', 1996) that the only human creatures to survive the Flood were Noah and three of his sons. Noah sent the eldest, Ham, to Hindustan; the middle son Shem he sent to Iran, and the youngest, Japheth, was charged with the northern lands, the Volga and Ural. Japheth, after living to the age of 250 years, left eight sons, the eldest of whom was known as Turk; the entire Turkic people is said to descend from him. Seven generations after Turk, the twins Tatar and Mongol were born. Nine generations after Tatar, Suyunush Khan was born, and from Mongol was born Ilhan. They were implacable enemies; they fought, and the eventual victor was Suyunush, but Ilhan's surviving children, Qiyad and Nukuz, left for the Ergenekon some 700 years BCE, and roughly 450 years later they set off into the steppe as a populous nation.

And so, the interpretations are various, but one thing is entirely clear: the name 'Mongol' was introduced by Genghis Khan to name the Turkic people (this is recognised by even Mongolian scholars) that was made up of all the tribes and clans that it united. This definition may be regarded at the same level as such collective terms as 'Aryan', 'Hunnic', 'Scythian', 'Saka', 'Alan' and – ultimately – 'Kazakh'. In general terms; one or another 'sobriquet' of a people may sometimes have curious origins, such as the case with *nemets* [the Russian word for 'a German person'], which literally means *nemoy*, 'dumb'. In other words, the Russian ear, unable to make sense of German speech, has transferred its own incomprehension onto the very name it gives to the foreign nation.

It is important then to clearly discriminate between the meanings of the ethnic term 'Mongol' in the 13th century and in the 21st. Today it represents the large ethnos currently living in Mongolia, while **800 years ago we, today's Kazakhs, also proudly called ourselves Mongols.** On the matter of present-day Mongols and their relationship to Genghis Khan, the Russian writer Aleksandr Bushkov states unequivocally that '... Without doubt he was not a Mongol. What we have here was, of course, a Turk' (*Chingiskhan. Neizvestnaia Azia*. Moscow: Olma Media Group, 2007). Asking himself the question: 'So who here in Asia in the 13th century had experience of building a state, creating a professional army or an administrative system, or organising large masses of people into military or large-scale economic projects?' he gives the answer: 'The Turks, of course, who had behind them centuries of experience of the khaganates, of statehood.' For the Turkic Genghis, he continues, 'creating a new state was not some exotic experiment but simply a task, something entirely ordinary, that his ancestors had practiced for long centuries before his time.'

It is unlikely that 'Mongol' was the name of the specific clan or tribe from which Genghis Khan was genetically related, although the Turkologist Lev Gumilev and also certain Mongol scholars, particularly Maydar, assert that there was a small tribe that moved about the Onon-Kherlen basin and whose name was in fact Mongol. Perhaps that is how it was, but the tribe has not left any discernible trace in history, and it is obvious that it could not have defeated million-strong groups such as the Naiman, Kerey and so on. Maybe Genghis Khan knew of the existence of this small people and used its name. On this point let me tell a story I heard from a well-known public figure, the writer Omirzaq Zholymbetov as he talked about the Academician Kuziev of Bashkortostan, who in turn was discussing the epics of Korkyt Ata. In the late 4th and early 5th centuries the leader of the Huns, Chanyu Monshaq, who ruled his people in the west of Mongolia, had six wives, one of whom – Tangut by nationality – he loved particularly. She bore him a son who was named Karakesek, since he had a powerful build. Later she bore a second son, but meanwhile the other wives, jealous because they were unable themselves to bear the leader of the Huns a son, poisoned her. The newborn child was found abandoned in the steppe, and owing to his great thirst he lay there with his tongue thrust out. This is why he was named Attila (in Kazakh, lit. 'horse's tongue').

Chanyu Monshaq, grieving for his wife, built her a mausoleum in black granite at a place on the Orkhon river that became known as Karakorum. Thereafter this place grew into a major settlement and eventually became the capital of the Turkic khaganates. In accordance with Tengriist rite, forty days after the burial of his favourite wife Monshaq had torches lit by a thousand slaves or *mingqul* (*ming* – 'a thousand', *qul* – 'slave') brought in from Manchuria. The descendants of these slaves later created their own clan that was given the name 'Mongol', and which roamed the Onon and Kherlen basin in the 12th century.

This clan of 'Mongols', according to Omirzaq Zholymbetov, was also directly related to Genghis Khan for the following reason. When Alan Gua was roaming with her tribe the Qorilar towards the foot of Burkhan Khaldun, she married Dobun Mergen, and after his death she bore three more sons, the youngest of whom was called Bodonchar – because he was born in the early dawn, when the horizon was only beginning to grow light. In Kazakh this 'colour' is called *bozan*. It is known that Bodonchar grew up and gained a reputation among his brothers for being warlike and aggressive, and that he took captive a group of migrants from an alien tribe who had arrived in the territory in which Dobun Mergen and his people wandered. He married a woman from among these captives, who bore him a son Qabichi, who was the ancestor by eight generations of Genghis Khan. Meanwhile the migrants taken prisoner by Bodonchar were also of the same clan of Mongols whose ancestors had lit the torches over the grave of Chanyu Monshaq's favourite wife, whose sons Karakesek and Attila later became renowned leaders. One became the ancestor of the large Kazakh clan of the Karakesek, within the Argyn, while the other received the Pope on his knees, begging him not to touch Rome. Nor did Attila harm Rome, as is well known, though he ravaged the remainder of Italy that same year.

So we see here yet another possible origin of the term 'Mongol': not a thousand warriors but a thousand slaves.

So much for the various ways of interpreting the ethnic term 'Mongol' that I have so far discovered. They are all plausible and all deserve respect. In my view, however, Genghis Khan knew of the hostage dream of his ancestors – the rulers of the Turkic khaganates, the capital of which lay close to Karakorum in what is now Mongolia – of the great people of the Eternal Land, Mangi (or Mangilik) El, and after five centuries he realised the long-standing aspiration of the Turks, uniting his peoples into his great empire and naming them the Mangilik. Move forward another 800 years and a triumphal arch is erected in Astana, the new capital of the Kazakhstan at the initiative of the first Kazakh president, Nursultan Nazarbayev, to commemorate that great event – and a celebration of the eternal People of the eternal Turkic El.

It should be admitted, of course, that Genghis Khan was not the first and will not be the last ruler to dream of eternal renown for himself and his people. As Lev Gumilev states, both before Genghis Khan and after him, strong nations in the phase of 'passionarity' have striven not only for power and world domination – they have hankered for eternity and to produce superlative leaders.

Here one could recall ancient Greece, where people did not rule, but the gods: Zeus and Hera and the council of Olympic gods. And what of 'eternal Rome'? Its 'divine' leaders were cruel, insidious and bloodthirsty – though also great. Julius Caesar, Alexander the Great – before them and after them – both tragedy and greatness in their wakes.

Later the idea and dream of a third Rome reached Moscow. Ivan 'the Terrible', as lustful as any Roman emperor and **of Turkic blood**, conquered all his neighbours and revived Great Rus – which he then impregnated with force, debauchery and lawlessness.

In the 20th century was Hitler with his idea of a Third Reich that would last a thousand years – in effect forever – and his 'master race' of Aryans, **again Turkic by blood**. So in terms of meaning the Germans also regarded themselves as 'Mongols', but in their own language, and took their swastika symbol from the Kiyat Borjigin. Then, of course, there was Stalin and his idea of people as cogs in the gigantic machine of world happiness. Both these leaders all but achieved the impossible, forcing much of the world to live by their rules for large parts of the 20th century.

So let us return to the time in question. A people of the Mangilik El – this is the dream of all peoples in all times, both east and west. It is not world leadership as we currently understand it but rather a universal harmony that has no equal in nature. How does one achieve this and how does one conform to it? Evidently Genghis Khan could grasp this immense secret. Three hundred years of the so-called Mongol 'yoke' was for Russia an era of unification and conception of the great, singular Russia that has to this day no equal.

Was Genghis Khan able to comprehend, with his genius, this philosophical problem that has no precedent in history? We will never know this either.

We know from various sources that towards the end of his life Genghis Khan called the Daoist monk Qiu Chuji to him in Samarkand to ask him the recipe for eternal life. Hearing that this was unattainable, he repeated what the monk had said: 'Eternal alone will be my people beneath the Eternally Blue Sky'.

More detail can be found on the various possible origins of the name 'Mongol' and also a thorough reasoning for the last explanation above about 'Mongol' deriving from 'Mangi El', can be found in Hasen Kozha-Ahmet's work *Zabluzhdenie, dlivsheesia vekami*, mentioned above.

CHAPTER III
THE GENOME OF GENGHIS KHAN

Is Jochi the son of the Great Terror of the Universe?

For every mortal born by the will of Tengri only that piece of ground is sacred on which the first drop of blood was shed when his umbilical cord was cut.

Genghis Khan
(spoken in 1218 during meeting with the Muslim clergy of Bukhara to counter the canons of Islam, which stated that for all Muslims only the birthplace of the Prophet Muhammad is sacred)

There are occasions in history when the ethnonym of a specific clan became the generic name of an entire people or vice versa. For example, the Kazakh clan Balgaly, consisting of the Jalayir Syr-Manaq, which still roams today in the Caspian and Black Sea steppe, gave its name to the great Volga river. This hypothesis, incidentally, has not been discussed elsewhere and appears in this book for the first time. In turn the name of the river gave the name to the Bulgar people, which formed in the region of the lower Volga at the start of the Common Era. M. Barmankunov proposes, in support of my view, that Dicleas and Nicephorus Gregoras consider that the Bulgars 'are named after the river Volga, having once dwelled in its surroundings; but Miller doubts this, since the Greeks and Romans called it Ra, while the Eastern peoples called it Atel or Etel' (*Khrustal'nye mechty tiurkov o kvadranatsii*. Almaty: Bis, 1999).

Continuing with this idea, Murad Adji believes that during the Migration Period there came to the Baltic steppe from the Altai a Turkic clan called the Balt. I suspect however that this in fact refers to the ancestors of the Kazakh Baltaly, who also gave their name to the Baltic

Sea. Similarly, then, the name of the Kazakh clan Balgaly gave its name to the entire Bulgar people, while the other tribe, the Baltaly, gave its name to the large Balt people, whom Murad Adji calls the Goths. In the Kazakh *Shezhire* (family tree) a number of tribes of the Junior jüz such as the Tortkara, Karasakal, Teleut, Jagabaili, Shekti and Baybakty all have as their *tamga* the symbol of a hammer (*balga*), and so, in my view, are related to the Balgaly that comprise the Jalayir and Naiman.

Today the Balgaly are a part of the large Kazakh tribal union of the Jalayir, while the Baltaly belong to a still larger tribe, the Naiman, and all the evidence suggests that before the Common Era there were numerous warlike tribes of the Balgaly and the Bataly in the Volga and Ural river basins and around the Black and Caspian Seas. It is probable that they were members of the Sarmatian Iazyges, who together with the Roxolani were dominant among the Sarmatian union of tribes. Today the Iazyges (Jasak) include the Naiman and live in the Eastern Kazakhstan region. More will be said later about the Baganal, who belonged to a tribal union with close ties to the unions of Kazakh clans mentioned and played a decisive part in that union.

Now an example of the opposite. In the Middle Ages the entire land from the Irtysh to the Danube was known as the Desht-i Qipchaq (Cumania), named after the Kipchak, a large Turkic tribe that inhabited this vast space. Today the Kipchak is relatively small and is part of the Middle *jüz*. The etymology of this clan name is interesting. Olzhas Suleimenov, for example, considering the *tamga* of the Kipchak – two vertical rods that suggest knives or spears – suggests that the word *kipchak* derives from *eki pshak* (remove the first letter and one obtains *kipchak*), while Kalibek Daniyarov, considering the warlike nature of this tribe, gives a different explanation – *qyp-shaq* amounts to 'pursuit and defeat'.

Rashid ad-Din Hamadani considers the Kipchak to be an ancient tribe that is related to the Naiman, Khereid, Uigurs, Kyrgyz, Karluks and others. However, the origin of the ethnonym 'Kipchak' can be explained as follows. During the time of Oghuz Khan some warriors found a pregnant woman hiding in a hollow tree; her husband turned out to have been killed. Oghuz Khan took the boy as a son when he was born and gave him the name Kipchak, from a Turkic word that meant 'the hollow of a decaying tree', and accordingly, the generation of the Kipchak descended from this boy. Abu al-Ghazi Bahadur adds that Oghuz Khan gave Kipchak many peoples and sent him to rule on the banks of the Don and Volga rivers. He ruled for 300 years and all Kipchaks were descended from him.

For me a bigger impression is made by the viewpoint of many Orientalists as described in S.G. Klyashtorny's *Istoria Tsentral'noy Azii i pamiatniki runicheskogo pis'ma* (St Petersburg, 2003). According to this, firstly, the face-value meaning of the word *kipchak*, which appeared in the second half of the 8th century, in the old Turkic language of runic monuments, means 'ill-fated', 'unfortunate'. Secondly, however, it is important to remember that after the collapse of the First Turkic Khaganate in the early 7th century, the core of Sir or Seir of which it was made up was forced to endure misery at the hands of the Chinese or Uigurs. Thinking about the future, however, and in keeping with their spiritual beliefs about the interrelationship between an object and its name, they selected a new name by which to call themselves, *kipchak*, which served as an amulet or protector.

Traditionally, our ancestors would drive away evil forces from the other world that were pursuing an individual or a clan by giving that person or the whole clan a pejorative name that served as a charm. The ethnonym 'Kipchak' also became such a charm, which **was taken unexpectedly by the Uighurs**, who were the successors to the Turkic Khaganate from 744 to 840. The Sir or Seir were a powerful tribe to whom the Uigurs submitted for many centuries, and thus from their side there was a direct interest in the name Seir being obliterated; thus, **partly aided by them**, the name of the Seir became established as 'Kipchak'. Much later, by the time of Genghis Khan, the majority of Turkic clans, including the Kazakh, were returning to the use of their ancestral names, while a part of them continued forever to use the name Kipchak.

And so, in this instance we have a case of the name of a large tribe becoming established as the name of a small clan.

One way or another, the question of the origin of Genghis Khan remains one of the greatest riddles: if he was Mongol (Mangi El), this is a collective name for an enormous number of clans and tribes and not the name of a single clan. So to which of these did he belong?

The works of Ata-Malik Juvayni, Rashid ad-Din Hamadani and Kalibek Daniyarov assert unambiguously that he is from the 'Qiyad', but Qiyad, according to Hamadani, is also a collective name for a large number of clans and tribes that emerged from the Ergenekon; today these include parts of the Argyn, Naiman, Jalayir, Dughlat, Teleut, Tabyn, Tarakt, Jagabaili, Khongirad, Koralas and other Kazakh groups. It is a fair enough question, but to which of these did Genghis Khan belong?

Of course, if his grave had been discovered, it would not be difficult today to determine his genetic makeup from a DNA analysis. For now, however, the location of his resting place remains one of the secrets of world history.

At any rate, modern methodology allows us to give a reasonably reliable answer to the question of Genghis Khan's tribal affiliation. Unfortunately, only the remains of one son is available to Kazakhstan, and whether this son in fact is one of Genghis Khan's is the source of furious arguments among the Kazakh population. Still, there are many direct descendants of Genghis Khan whose remains lie at rest on Kazakh territory. The historian Tursun Sultanov, for example, considers that the bones of Genghis' grandson, the great khan Güyük, lie at rest by the Emil river in the Tarbagatay district of East Kazakhstan region (*Podniatie na beloy koshme. Khany Kazakhskikh stepey*, Astana, 2006). Here also, according to some data, are the remains of Ögedei's grandson Kaidu, who restored his grandfather's settlement in what is now Eastern Kazakhstan and Sinzyan. We can demonstrate theoretically that fabrications about Jochi being from the Merkit do not have any serious basis, and further will show that despite what has become the conventional view, Genghis Khan's eldest son Jochi Khan was truly his son. We shall require the empirical method of carrying out DNA testing on Jochi's remains and also on members of the Merkit, to whom Jochi is said to have belonged, and there are many of these in Kazakhstan. If they turn out to differ, this will prove that Gengis Khan was indeed the father of Jochi, and by this the idle fabrications of ill-wishers who seek to show that Genghis Khan ran away out of cowardice when the Merkit attacked, leaving his wife Börte, pregnant with Jochi by a Merkit, alone in his camp.

This outcome will also disperse another myth about Genghis Khan himself being descended from the Merkit, since his father, Yesugei, took Hoelun from a Merkit warrior when she was already his wife, although the Merkit origin of Genghis Khan would also indicate that he was of Kazakh origin. Therefore if the results of the DNA tests prove different for Jochi and the Merkits, this will demonstrate Genghis' lawful descent from Yesugei and Jochi's from Genghis. Again, however, the Kazakh people have a sacred place in the Ulytau where the remains lie of a great son of the Alash. Even by way of fulfilling its filial duty, the government of Kazakhstan should carry out a suitable investigation. If however Jochi turns out to be of Merkit descent, then there are two possibilities. The first of these is that Genghis Khan himself was Merkit, in which case it turns out that the father of the Great Terror of the Universe had taken from the Merkit warrior a wife who was already pregnant. In this case we are unable to give a unanimous answer to the question of the ethnicity of Jochi, as either Genghis or the Merkit warrior Chiledu could be his father – but at any rate we obtain Kazakh genes for Genghis, in this case of the Merkit. If however we determine the genes of Genghis Khan through other direct descendants and it turns out that he is not Merkit, then Jochi is patently not his son, since we are considering the variant of a Merkit descent for the latter.

I am however certain that Hamadani is also correct in that, through the intermediary of the Khereid Wang Khan, Börte was returned to her lawful husband honourably and with dignity.

Sooner or later, at any rate, we will obtain the genetic code of the 'Great Terror of the Universe'. After this an entirely routine undertaking to test members of the various Kazakh clans along with the Mongols, Buryat, Kalmyk, Tuvans and other pretenders to kinship with the great military leader should lead to an exhaustive conclusion as to just which people on planet Earth can truly consider itself to be the ancestor of this exceptional individual?

Investigations of this kind are in fact already being carried out. Russian researchers have performed DNA analyses on persons living in Russian regions that border on Mongolia. The researchers report that a genetic correspondence with the DNA of Genghis Khan has been found in 1.7% of the inhabitants of Tuva, Buryatia, Kalmykia and the Altai. But an astonishing result was obtained from tests on Altai Kazakhs: here the percentage is 8.3%.

Western researchers are also examining this problem. Oxford geneticists led by Spenser Wells took 2000 samples from inhabitants of the Asiatic steppes. In a published article they gave a list of the genetic markers that in their view were characteristic of Genghis Khan, from the gaplogroup C3. To their surprise these were distributed less among the Mongols than among the Turkic peoples and, highly unexpectedly, among the North American Indians. As we will demonstrate later, there is not in fact any cause for surprise in this; it merely confirms the likelihood that the North American Indians and the Turkic peoples have a common root. Again, we will discuss this below in a different context.

However, as they freely admit, the Western researchers' conclusions are based on assumptions, since they are not confident of knowing the genetic code of Genghis Khan, and so they have not performed analyses on the remains of the latter's direct descendants.

I remain surprised at the indifference shown towards this problem by the Kazakh authorities and Kazakh scholars – after all, the direct descendants of Genghis Khan live primarily in Kazakhstan. I am certain, however, that proving that Genghis Khan also belonged to the Kazakh nation will open up new opportunities for our young government to make efforts to rise to an economic status equivalent to those of the developed countries of the world.

CHAPTER IV
SECRETS OF BIRTH AND DEATH

Crimes and delusions

From black dust to the celestial bodies
I unravelled the secrets of wise words and deeds
I ran from treachery, untangled all knots,
Only the knot of death could I not unravel.
Avicenna (Ibn Sina)

In the numerous sources I have consulted that investigate this problem there is no shortage of riddles. Let us begin with Yesugei, father of Genghis Khan, and his mother Hoelun, or Oyan, as Kalibek Daniyarov suggests. For Genghis' mother the Kazakh author Ilyas Esenberlin chose the name Ulpan, while others have more poetically named her Oleng. The professor of history M. Orazbai maintains that Hoelun is in fact Ulykun. In this book however we will refer to the mother of Genghis Khan as Hoelun.

It is worth pointing out that marrying lawfully was difficult for the Mongols at that time: a potential husband was required to work literally as a labourer in the bride's house for five or six years to gain the right to take her as his wife. Because of this, I suspect, the Kazakhs adopted the tradition of *kalym*, or payment, whereby this working off of a debt in advance came to be replaced, by mutual agreement between the parents of the groom and those of the bride, by a payment to the latter of a given amount of livestock. It is known that the northern lands of Genghis Khan's father, in the Orkhon and Selenga basins, were roamed by the Merkit, of whom a noble member was Chiledu, the younger brother of the Merkit khan. And while he was riding with his young wife Hoelun (possibly already carrying the child that would become Genghis Khan) across these lands at the foot of the Khentii mountains, close to the sources of the Tuul, he happened to meet Yesugei with his future wife, whose beauty had made an impression on him at first sight.

He hurried away to his brothers and together they caught up with the newlywed couple. Hoelun was clever and, as it is told in *The Secret History of the Mongols,* she said:

'Did you see the look on the faces of those men? They wish to kill you. As long as you remain alive, there will be girls on the front seats of carts and women in the black-covered wooden carts. If you live, you will perhaps find a girl or a woman for yourself. If she has another name, you can call her Höelün. Save yourself. While you live, smell my fragrance.'

And Chiledu left her. Thus she became the wife of Yesugei. Let us also note that he already had a first wife, who had borne him two sons, one of whom, Behter, was killed by Temirshin and his brother Qasar at a young age. Historians regard him as brutal and inhuman because of this deed, but while not acquitting Temirshin in any way, it is inappropriate to judge events of the Middle Ages with 21st-century morals. Had Temirshin not killed his elder stepbrother, then Behter would have had every justification for claiming the leadership of the Borjigin and marrying Temirshin's mother: such were the laws of the 13th century. Among the Kazakhs this law remained in force right up to the 19th century. Here Temirshin had good enough reasons: his jealousy over his beautiful young mother, left a widow at scarcely over 25 years old, but, more significantly, the possible loss of his right to become head of the clan. It is also possible that Gumilev is correct in his hypothesis of Temirshin killing his stepbrother, which also justifies him for his action. According to Gumilev's version, Behter was a spy for the Taichuid leader Targitay-Kyryldak, since Behter's mother was of Taichuid stock, while the Taichuids, after their famous relative kinsman Ambaghai Khan, were also laying claim to the Mongol throne, which now by rights should be given to the sons or grandsons of Khabul Khan, and Temirshin, following the death of his father, was one of the main candidates for the khan of the Mongol nation. And according to Gumilev, Behter should have warned Targitay-Kyryldak of Temirshin's possible actions. With all due respect to the great Turkologist, however, I support a different version, which proposes that the informer of the Taichuids was not in fact Behter but his mother Sochigel. She was not Yesugei's lawful wife, since she was a close relative to him, and such a marriage among Mongols in the 12th century was forbidden. It seems then that Targitay-Kyryldak had promised her a higher status in the event of the elevation of the Taichuids to the khans of all the Mongols.

In any case, the episode of the killing of Behter remains one of the least studied pages of the biography of Genghis Khan to this day. Many sources try to avoid the topic altogether, beginning with Hamadani. But *The Secret History of the Mongols* describes in detail Hoelun's grief when she addresses her sons after the boy has been killed: 'Apart from our shadows we have no friends. Apart from our tails we have no fat.' So why, she is saying, when we are abandoned by our kin to the vagaries of fate and there is nobody on whom we can depend except ourselves, do you treat each other so brutally?

There are good grounds for supposing that Hoelun saw Behter as her potential future husband. This is what everything was moving towards...

To this day, meanwhile, there is a view held among the Merkit that they are of royal blood, that is, they are the direct descendants of Genghis Khan. Today this clan is part of the Kazakh Abaq-Kerey and inhabits a compact region of eastern Kazakhstan. Another small group of the Merkit lives in the Chinese borderlands in the Kara-Irtysh river basin. In essence they are a small part of the modern-day Kazakh people.

In the central region of what is now Mongolia is a low mountain range, the Burkhan Khaldun, with a height of some 2500 metres above sea level, and here three major rivers have their source – the Onon, the Kherlen and the Tuul. It is around this mountain that the chief events linked to Genghis Khan took place. As we mentioned earlier, Alan-Gua (or

Alan Goa, as the chroniclers tended to call her), considered the original mother of all Nirun Mongols, is said in *The Secret History of the Mongols* to have come to the foot of this mountain with her family the Qorilar, famous for its hunters and trappers, from Hori-Tumat (north of the Selenga). According to my data this took place around 850 CE.

The descendants of the Qorilar clan are the Kazakh Koralas.

She then married Dobun-mergen. There were two brothers: Duwa-soqor and Dobun-mergen. And having married Dobun-mergen, she bore him two sons. After he died Alan-Gua gave birth to three further children. The elder sons began to mutter that their mother should, according to their ancestral custom, have married one of her late husband's brothers or other relatives, but this did not happen and it is stated directly in *The Secret History of the Mongols* that there was not a man in her home, apart from a servant boy, Ma'aliq, whom Dobun-mergen had once been given in exchange for a hind leg of deer meat. Ma'aliq was of the clan of Baya'ut (the Bayad), known by the Chinese as the Bayegu. Another member of the Bayad was the mother of Khorezmshah Muhammed, whom Genghis Khan crushed in 1220 as punishment for killing his messengers. The Bayad and the Changshi'ut later made up the guard of Onggyr (Ongur), the son of the elder brother of Genghis Khan's father Yesugei.

After Temirshin was proclaimed Great Khan in 1206 he said to Ongur: '... and you, Önggür, the son of Mönggetü-kiyan, with your Changshi'ut and Baya'ut [men], became one camp for me.' And when Genghis Khan asked him what reward he wanted for his loyal service, Ongur replied: 'If I may choose my favour, [let it be this]: My Baya'ut kinsmen are scattered across the tribes. As your favour, allow me to assemble my Baya'ut kinsmen.' The Baya'ut or Bayad, again, are an ancient clan that emerged from the Ergenekon in the 4th century BCE and later formed the framework of the Mongol Darlekin. Meanwhile, I suspect that Ma'aliq Baya'ut was unlikely to have been a servant in Alan Gua's household, as his status was far higher, and this fact may be pivotal in determining the genealogy of Genghis Khan. **We may thus note that Ongur, Genghis Khan's first cousin, considered the Baya'ut to be his brothers, and so it is possible that Genghis Khan is himself Baya'ut, part of the tribe of the Kiyat.** Nothing is mentioned in the ancient sources, except that Genghis Khan belonged to the Kiyat, with the exception of this extract from *The Secret History of the Mongols.* Unfortunately, the existing sources contradict one another. For example, Hamadani, enumerating the houses of the Mongols (page 87), does not name Ongur, leader of the Baya'ut, as Genghis Khan's cousin and accordingly does not consider him to be the son of Mungetu-Kiyan. Evidently the anonymous author of *The Secret History of the Mongols* had other information – that Bodonchara was the offspring of the servant Ma'aliq – and therefore stated that Ongur was Genghis' cousin.

Tleuberdy Abenay claims that the Bayad are today's large Bayuly, a tribe that lives in western Kazakhstan and consists of twelve clans: the Aday, Jappas, Cherkesh, Bersh and others. The Changshi'ut, he maintains, are today's Kazakh Shanyshkyly, which includes the ancient Kangju. Incidentally the *tamga* of the Aday, which includes the Bayuly, and the *tamga* of the Shanyshkyly coincide; it is an upward-pointing arrow ↑, so one can see that Ongur's Baya'ut were later part of the Kazakh Bayuly, while the other brothers of Ongur, the Changshi'ut, formed part of the Kazakh Kangju. The root of the word Shanyshkyly in Kazakh means a 'fork' or trident, as per the arms of the clan of Genghis Khan. In the current *Shezhire* the *tamga* of the Shanyshkyly is an arrow, but this may be an error. In my understanding the symbol of the Shanyshkyly in Genghis Khan's time was a trident. Let us make a note of this, as it will help us later.

So, Alan-Gua bore three sons. Later, seeing the confusion of the elder children, she gathered them together and explained in her own way the family situation. As narrated by *The Secret History of the Mongols* she said:

'Every night, a shining yellow man came into the yurt through the light of the smoke-hole and over the top of the door. He caressed my

belly and his light sank into it. He [slunk] sheepishly away like a yellow dog by the light of the sun and moon.
Why do you talk unwisely?
Evidently it is a sign
that they are sons of Heaven.
Why do you compare them
to the black-haired commoners?
When they become lords of all,
the common people must understand.'

Incidentally, the same divine light that penetrated Alan Gua's belly translates from the Kazakh as *nur.* The Mongols that consider themselves related to Genghis Khan call themselves the Mongol Nirun, that is, the Mongols born of a divine otherworldly light. An analogy of sorts is possible here with the birth of Jesus Christ by the Virgin Mary through the action of the Holy Spirit. If we abstract ourselves from the myth, however, it becomes necessary to assume that there existed an earthly man by whom the young widow Alan-Gua bore her sons. So who was he? After all, he was also a forebear of Genghis Khan!

Yet if we go along with *The Secret History of the Mongols,* there was, again, only one man present – Ma'aliq of the Bayuly (Bayad). In that case this warlike Kazakh tribe may claim that the world is indebted to it for the appearance of Genghis Khan, whose life became one of the cornerstones of human history.

Which tribes, however, were living beside Burkhan Khaldun at that time? With whom, other than Ma'aliq, could Alan-Gua have had contact, a representative of which clan could have become the common-law husband, so to speak, of this beauty? In summer 2006 I set off for Mongolia again in search of answers to this and many other questions, with the aim of acquainting myself with the Mongol people and its history on its home territory. I wanted to clarify the origins of the Mongols as a nation, both before Genghis Khan and after him – because this was the key to the mystery of his origin. The chief objective, however, of the expedition was to convince myself that Genghis Khan came from a Kazakh (Turkic) descent, having demonstrated that his family had lived solely among Turkic tribes that later became part of the Kazakh nation. This was the only available route to the truth. There simply was no other option.

Already in the mode of a researcher, I decided to begin with the most immediate question – how did the present-day Mongol nation come into being? The correct answer to this would contain within it the solution to our main problem. I spent some 20 days travelling some 5000 kilometres in total. This gave me a rare opportunity to compile a suitable map of our journey through Central, Eastern and Western Mongolia. After visiting Genghis Khan's birthplace I spent a lot of time talking with local inhabitants through an interpreter, my colleague Semey Moldakhan. We also visited the place where in either 1186 or 1182, depending on which source one believes, Genghis Khan was proclaimed khan of his related tribes. Later, once the related Naiman had submitted to him and following the conquests of the Kerey, Merkit and other tribes he was proclaimed in 1206 as Khan of the Mongol Empire.

A meeting with the leading scholars of the Mongolian Academy of Sciences proved of immense interest – and specifically with the leading archaeologist and professor Doldoy Bayar and with the director of the National Centre for the Study of the Secret History of the Mongols, Professor Dalantay Tseren Sodnom. We held many passionate arguments and substantial discussions. For example, the response of Professor Sodnom to my initial question as to the language spoken by Genghis Khan was 'In Ancient Mongolian, of course'. He cited an extract from *The Secret History of the Mongols* to substantiate his point.

Rather than relying on this, however, it is necessary to remember the situation concerning the Khereid Wang Khan, whom Yesugei himself – the father of Genghis Khan – helped to gain the Khereid throne. And of course, when Genghis Khan was left without a father, when he was abandoned by his closest relatives, he sought protection from the strongest of his world, in particular from the powerful Kerey khan Togrul. Togrul Khan was indeed a help; he gathered together his people and helped him consolidate his power as a minor appanage prince. Here, of course, Togrul's gratitude to Yesugei for having helped him attain the Khereid throne played a role, but the young Temirshin in any case demonstrated his natural awareness of the art of diplomacy. When Börte's parents contributed a fine sable jacket as dowry, it was this that Temirshin presented as a gift to the Kerey khan. In *The Secret History of the Mongols* we see Togrul Khan's words thus: 'In return for the black sable jacket I will bring together the people who abandoned you. In return for the sable jacket, I will unite your scattered people.'

Also, rather than continuing to describe my conversation with Professor Sodnom, let me mention again an event during which the Merkit, in revenge for the wife of one of their tribesmen having been taken by Genghis' father, made a night raid on the place where Genghis Khan was stationed. His young wife Börte with whom he had lived for only a few months was taken captive in the raid.

So here yet another riddle arises: he had eight horses, and these were provided for him, his mother, his brothers, his sister and his two closest friends. After this there was still one horse in reserve. Yet he left his wife without a horse; he left hers to the enemy. This is a curious situation; Aleksandr Domanin proposes in *Mongol'skaia imperia chingizidov* that it 'baffles many scholars of Genghis Khan... to the majority of historians (particularly in the West), Genghis Khan's behaviour appears wholly inexplicable...'

Domanin offers various possible explanations for this act of the future khan. He mentions dislike of his wife, which seems unlikely; an assumption by Genghis that the Merkit would not find her or would not touch her, which is absurd; and finally the possibility that Genghis Khan acted in a cowardly manner by running away in panic, leaving even his wife to be violated by the enemy, and so on.

In what follows, this talented scholar tends to be disparaging towards the dignity of the nomads, reducing their life values to a primitive level, suggesting that Genghis Khan had no choice, but his life (as the head of the family) was of the greatest worth, and that preserving this had cost him his spare horse. Moreover he assumes that for a mediaeval nomad, this behavioural stereotype is normal.

I will allow myself not to agree with this view, since I have another perspective on the apparently paradoxical behaviour of Genghis Khan. Firstly, in *The Secret History of the Mongols* the Chinese Qo'aqchin, a maidservant in Temirshin's house, hears with her sensitive hearing the trampling of approaching horses at dawn and calls out: 'Mother! Mother! Rise quickly! The earth is shaking! I can hear the sound of swift horses' hooves. Are the terrifying Tayichi'uts coming? Mother, rise quickly!'

My first reading therefore suggests unintentional disinformation on the part of Qo'aqchin, but this disinformation acquits the action of Genghis Khan in not taking his wife with him when he ran away. Genghis Khan believed that the kindred Taichuid would not touch a woman, including Börte. It is possible that Genghis Khan built his reasoning on the character of the raid, since the Merkit had travelled hundreds of kilometres while the Taichuid were close by. There was one thing, however, that Genghis Khan did not take into account: following the support he received from the powerful khan of the Kerey, his name became familiar on the Steppe, but taking their revenge on such a man, even twenty years later, was a matter of honour for the Merkit. It was one thing to take revenge on a child or a youth, but an entirely different matter to do so on the leader of a clan, albeit not a large one, but one that was well established and whose ancestors had been the khans of Mongol tribes.

Yet even if we suppose that Genghis Khan had suspected that the attackers had been the Merkit, I believe that his actions would nonetheless have been guided by rational principles and cold reasoning, two factors that he applied on an everyday basis and that made him a great commander and statesman. His personal desires never took priority over necessities of state in his actions, his emotions were under control and his decisions were made solely in order to achieve his specific objectives.

So Börte was left without a horse; everybody else galloped off to Burkhan Khaldun to escape and take cover, while she was kidnapped by the Merkit. There is a Kazakh parable, a semantic analogy of which can also be found in Russian folklore, for example in the historic song *Avdotia Ryazanochka* (Eudoxia of Ryazan), which tells of the events of the year 1237 when Mongol warriors seized the city of Ryazan. The heroine of the song addresses the Mongols, asking them to release her husband, her son and her brother from captivity. They reply that her request may be granted for only one of these three. She elects for the release of her brother with the reasoning that one can find another wife or husband, and can give birth to new sons or daughters, but a father, a mother, a brother or a sister can never be replaced. The Kazakh version runs along similar lines. And so the basis of Genghis Khan's action, which by 21st-century standards would be deemed perhaps unmanly, is in fact deeply rooted in Turkic tradition. This was reflected in particular in the practice of the succession of power, in which the throne passed not from father to son but from the father to his brothers, and only after that to his sons. So brothers by blood had a higher status than sons.

That is how it was when, after the death in the 8th century of the founder of the Second Turkic Khaganate, Ilterish Qaghan, his power passed to his brother Qapaghan Qaghan, and only after his death did it pass to Bilge Qaghan, the son of Ilterish. It is worth noting that this law remained firmly in place at all times and for all the Turkic peoples. When Qapaghan Qaghan, who had done more for the Turkic world than others, had thoughts of violating this law of the steppe and passing the power to his children in a sudden raid on Qapaghan Qaghan's headquarters. And so the sons paid for their father's actions. By the 12th century, after the death of Genghis Khan's great-grandfather, power did not pass to one of his seven sons but rather to his father's cousin Ambaghai Khan, founder of the Taichuid clan. So it can be seen that from ancient times the Turkic peoples valued their siblings higher than their children. This is then a plausible reason for Genghis Khan saving his brothers and sisters from the vengeance of the Merkit while abandoning his wife.

In excusing Genghis Khan for this act I may also suppose, indeed I am sure, that he must have known that Börte was pregnant, and the fact that he did not take her with him is explained solely by this; in other situations Temirshin would have acted in more manly fashion and not left his wife to the enemy. He simply did not want to cause physical suffering to a pregnant woman, or, put more simply, was afraid of causing an abortion, for they had a gallop ahead of them of many tens of kilometres. So in this critical situation he chose the lesser of two evils: allowing the Merkit to satisfy their lust for vengeance while leaving him alone. He realised that blood feuds were *sine qua non* among the Turkic peoples. My theory about Börte being pregnant at the time of the Merkit raid is supported by Temirshin's full-scale operation to rescue her from her imprisonment by the Merkit. In point of fact this may have been less an operation to return his favourite wife than a decisive action to secure his future firstborn son and heir. His attitude to his eldest son Jochi (Juchi) when he defended him from accusations of being of Merkit stock and delicately prevented his other sons from attacking him, considering him his successor, speaks in favour of my suggestion.

* * *

During excavations of the tomb of Jochi Khan, Alkei Margulan noted that his right hand was missing, which suggests that he died while hunting when his hand was bitten off by a wild onager, rather than that he died at the hands of his father's agents, who would have broken his spine, without shedding blood, for disobedience towards his father (a version sometimes held by ill-wishers of Genghis Khan). To substantiate this let us turn to a 16th-century source, the *Chingis-name*, the work of Utemish-Hadji, court clerk to the Shaybanid khans (see e.g. *Chingis-name*, Almaty: Gylym, 1992). He writes as follows: 'Jochi Khan was the eldest of his sons. He [Genghis Khan] gave him a large army and sent him to the province of Desht-i Qipchaq [the Danube], saying: 'Let this be grazing for your horses'. He also gave him the province of Khorezm.

When Jochi Khan set off to Desht-i Qipchak, he came to Ulug-Tag, which is well known. One day while he was hunting in the mountains he encountered a herd of maral. Pursuing them and letting fly an arrow, he fell from his horse, broke his neck and died...'

Jochi Khan died three months before the death of Genghis Khan himself. *The Secret History of the Mongols* relates the words of Yesui-khatun, wife of Genghis, before the Mongols' campaign against Khorezmshah Muhammed:

'[But] no creature is born eternal.
When your body, like an old and withered tree,
comes crashing down,
to whom will you bequeath your people,
like tangled hemp?
When your body, like the stone base of a pillar,
comes tumbling down,
to whom will you bequeath your people,
like [a flock of] red-polls?'

It is also believed that it was on this day that Genghis Khan nominated his successor – his middle son Ögedei, since his second son Chagatay was said to have doubted that Jochi was a son of Genghis Khan. However, here is what another source – the *Tong jian gang mu* (see e.g. Nikita Bichurin's translation *Istoria pervykh chetiriekh khanov iz doma Chingisova*) – says on this point: 'In the summer, Genghis Khan travelled to the Porman river to avoid the heat. His **successor** (my emphasis – K.Z.) Juchi, the prince Chagatay, Ögedei and Bala returned with the armies and joined Genghis-Khan...' (Note: the summer referred to was the time when Genghis Khan was already on the Khorezmshah Muhammed campaign. We also understand that, contrary to *The Secret History of the Mongols*, the heir to the throne at this point was Jochi and not Ögedei.)

This early source, deserving of some trust, on the history of China thus speaks of Jochi as the successor to Genghis Khan. Since however *The Secret History of the Mongols* was written during the period of Ögedei's rule, I suspect that a decision was 'put into the mouth' of Genghis Khan in favour of Ögedei as a way of legitimising his position. Evidently it was only his death that prevented Jochi Khan from becoming the Great Khan following his father's death. Today we can only conjecture about this.

Many chilling and ominous secrets concerning births and deaths remain linked to Genghis Khan – those of his own birth and death, those of his eldest son Jochi and his burial and his mound – and it is as though these will forever remain unsolved pages of human history.

I will state that one of my main purposes in writing this book has been an attempt to liberate the name Genghis Khan from lies and slander and to present him not as a cruel conqueror and tyrant but as an ordinary steppe-dweller who was not without common human feelings. More than this, there are two acts and omissions, or crimes and errors, of his that I wish to discuss in particular. When I speak of a crime, I mean something that would be considered as such by the laws that were in force before Genghis Khan and before he was proclaimed khan. In fact, however, by breaking the law described below and thereby committing a crime, he nevertheless committed one of the most fundamental reformative measures, by changing the system of succession of power among the Turkic peoples that had prevailed from the time of the Khaganates.

As mentioned earlier, in his running from the Merkit and the captivity of Börte, he was on the one hand intuitively upholding ancient Turkic conventions – saving the lives of his brothers by giving them horses on which to escape and giving priority in the matter of life or death to those born of the same womb as himself. Yet later he violated another law rigorously upheld over many centuries concerning the succession of power. According to that law he himself should have rallied his native tribes around him and proclaimed Daritai-otchigin, the younger brother of his father, as khan, as once did Kultegin, raising his elder brother Bilge Qaghan to the Turkic throne. Here, incidentally, Kultegin was in fact more deserving of the throne and Bilge Qaghan acknowledged this openly.

In the case of Genghis Khan, his father's cousin Daritai-otchigin, along with many other blood relatives, condemned Temirshin's actions. The Taichuids, the closest tribe to Genghis Khan, became sworn enemies and a schism occurred on the steppe. A prolonged civil war began, the apogee of which was the confrontation of Genghis Khan and Jamukha. Genghis' closest relatives by blood line were on Jamukha's side. And it was certainly not a battle of the aristocrats of the steppe, led, according to Vasily Bartold, by Genghis Khan, against the ordinary people led by Jamukha, as Soviet historians liked to portray this conflict, that could explain a heated civil war. The reason was different: it was the violation by Genghis Khan of centuries-old rules of the Great Steppe and ancient ancestral customs. It should be pointed out that disdain for the laws of the ancestors also persisted after Genghis Khan, when not the latter's brothers but his middle son Ögedei inherited the throne of the empire. Maybe there were none of his brothers still living? But that is not so. Before his Khorezm expedition, when he nominated his successor allegedly at his wife's request, Genghis Khan said: 'Although she is [merely] a lady, Yisüi's words are beyond correction. None of you **younger brothers** (My emphasis – K.Z.) or sons – Bo'orchu, Muqali, and the others – have spoken along such lines.'

We also know for certain that his brothers Temüge and Belgutei were still alive.

And so, with power bypassing Genghis' brothers, henceforth it passed to one of his sons. By the old Turkic custom, the natural lawful successor to the throne on the deaths of Jochi and Ögedei would have been Batu Khan, since at that time neither Chagatay nor Tolui were alive. But Batu Khan did not inherit the throne. This is the only point in which I see a reason for confrontation between Batu Khan and the khan Güyük. On the one hand, in accordance with Genghis Khan's testament, power passed from father to son and Güyük was the lawful khan, but on the other, the old Turkic custom was still in living memory. And this situation repeats later when, in defiance of the will of Genghis Khan, power passes from the house of Ögedei to that of Tolui, Genghis' youngest son, resulting in a missed one-off opportunity to restore the Mongol Empire under Kublai. As is well known, Kaidu, the grandson of Ögedei, appeals against the testament of Genghis Khan, declares himself and his supporters khan over the territory of what is the Zheytsu (Seven Rivers) region of Kazakhstan and thereby brings about the final schism in the great *ulus* of the Mongols and initiates the decline of the empire of Genghis Khan. Nikolai Aristov asserts that the majority of the army of Kaidu Khan (1270-1301) was formed of Naiman and Kerey that lived at that time in the upper reaches of the Irtysh.

Genghis Khan's violation of the old law of succession to the throne had a ruinous effect on the entire moral fabric of the nation as, one might say, he rode roughshod over the centuries-old structure of the Turkic people. And the Chinese did not fail to exploit this situation when, after the death of the khagan Möngke – grandson of Genghis Khan and son of Tolui – Kublai was raised to the throne of the Mongol empire and not Ariq Böke, who was his elder brother and stood up for the preservation of the ancestral customs. Carrying out the will of the Chinese, who helped Kublai Khan to the throne, he first moved the capital from Karakorum (or Ötüken, as the Turks of antiquity called it, and which had been the site of the Turkic capital since the empire of the Huns of Modu Chanyu, the Matay, then the Turks of Bumin Qaghan and Ilterish Qaghan) to Beijing, the northern capital of the Chinese. This step proved fatal for the Mongol empire.

So what high matters of state can have nudged Genghis Khan towards such radical reforms?

On the one hand, in justifying Genghis Khan and not wishing to wrongly accuse him of violating the ancient Turkic customs, I would like to cite an episode from *The Secret History of the Mongols*. When Genghis Khan escapes by a miracle from a trap laid by the Khereid Wang Khan, he sends the following message to his close blood relatives:

'Quchar, when I said that you, as the recognised son of Nekün-taishi, should become Qan, you were not willing. Altan, when I said that you should become Qan and govern as your father, Qutula Qan, governed, you too were unwilling [to do as I proposed]. When I said: 'Sacha and Taichu, because you are [a generation] above us, and the sons of Bartan-ba'atur, you should become Qans,' I was unable to [persuade them]. I said that all of you should become Qans [but] **I was unable to [persuade you]. [Then] you said [to me]: 'You become Qan.' So I did as told, and governed.'** (My emphasis – K.Z.)

Only matters of high national interest prevented Genghis Khan from being able to follow in the footsteps of his predecessors and declare somebody else khan. This was a responsibility he had taken on himself. Having united the scattered Turkic tribes, he came closer than anybody else to realising the age-old dream nursed by the Turkic peoples and their khagans of establishing the people of **Mangilik El** – the 'Eternal Turkic Land' (or 'Eternal Turkic People').

And he did not miss that opportunity.

In fact the individuals mentioned did have higher status by lineage than Temirshin. For example, Nekün-taishi was the elder brother of Yesugei; Altan was the son of Qutula, the younger brother of Bartan-ba'atur and father of Yesugei; and Sacha and Taichu were grandsons of Ökin-barqaq, Bartan's elder brother and the grandfather of Genghis Khan. By birth they were all higher than Genghis.

Let us go on. Having voided the old tradition of the succession of power, Genghis Khan asserted a new order, according to which power was transferred from father to son and not to his brothers. By doing this he centralised the power and prevented many possible instances of separatism. This was the main essence of his reform in the ruling of nations, because in the specific hierarchical system of succession of power the khan's brothers, waiting for their turn on the throne, allotted themselves their own separate principalities with populations and armies. This brought with it the danger of separatism, whereby brothers who disagreed with the khan's policy would simply move to a new place and then use every opportunity to create power for themselves. Such a situation was always fraught with political and military cataclysms and posed a real danger to the central power.

It is worth pointing out at the same time that Genghis Khan showed a certain inconsistency in not completing the reforms in the ruling of his empire. Having created a new system of transferring power from father to son, he should not have invested his sons in independent principalities, an error that ultimately led to the fall of his immense state. Let us recall the situation under Möngke Khan when the latter's younger brother Hulagu, carrying out his grandfather's wishes, set off to conquer Persia and the Islamic world. The khan of the Golden Horde, Batu Khan, did not wish to see his cousin gain strength and so did not permit him to enter Khorezm, which Genghis Khan had left to Batu's father Jochi Khan. Then, worse still, Batu's successor Berke Khan took the side of the Mongols' enemy, the Egyptian sultan Baibars in the battle of Ain Jalut against Hulagu, rather than that of his blood relative.

It is known that in 1259 the Egyptian Mamluks defeated Hulagu's army under the command of a Naiman named Kitbuqa and thus spared the Muslim world from enslavement to the Mongols.

For the sake of fairness it should be said that the bulk of Hulagu's forces – some hundred thousand units, along with the khan himself – had returned east to tackle further unrest in Genghis Khan's native lands, where problems had arisen in connection with Kublai being proclaimed Great Khan. So what remained available to Kitbuqa in the battle with Egypt was only three *tumen* (each of which equalled 10,000 men). The name Kitbuqa is immortalised in the *Shezhire* of the Naiman, in which he is identified as the ancestor of the Teristamgaly tribe.

The historian Mukhtarkan Orazbay maintains that the Mamluks beheaded the captive Mongol commander Kitbuqa and that it was because of this act that the head of the Mamluks, Qutuz, was overthrown by Baibars, who thus gained complete power in Egypt and also sent an official apology to Hulagu for the execution of his commander who was well known and respected within the Turkic world.

Today the Naiman and the Bersh are large Kazakh tribes, but even in the 13th century the two were related, and major representatives included Baibars and Kitbuqa.

* * *

It is now time to discuss Genghis Khan's major omission. His omission, like his victories, was great. As Francois de la Rochefoucauld later wrote, 'Large faults are only found in great people.' Even today many in the West regard the only positive aspect of Genghis Khan's actions as his religious tolerance. As is well known, unlike the Arabs or the Catholics, Genghis Khan did not impose the beliefs of his ancestors, Tengriism, on the lands and peoples he conquered, requiring his subjects to adopt it on pain of death; all that he did impose were economic sanctions, in the form of a 10% tax. This situation in fact established countries and peoples among the conquered, but had an adverse effect on the empire of Genghis Khan himself. His forces stationed in conquered lands, as a rule, gradually adopted the beliefs of the local population. This occurred both with Islam and Christianity in the West and with Buddhism and Confucianism in the East.

Rafael Bezertinov, and indeed a number of other scholars, consider that any civilisation rests on three foundations: language, religion and a body of literature. The loss of any one of these will result in the death of that civilisation. This occurred, for example, among the ancient Uigur civilisation when it abandoned Tengriism in the 9th century, adopting first Manichaeism and later Islam. Today, millions of Uigurs do not have a land of their own or a state, far less a civilisation. Perhaps Tengri punished this people for their disloyalty. A nation loses its face and gradually its being when deprived of its literature and language, and above all its religion. Today the Turkic world is split; it lacks cohesion or the might it had, say, at the time of Genghis Khan. And it may be that if it revives its ancestral religion, Tengriism, its Turkic language and its literary fabric, the Turkic people will once again acquire its previous greatness.

In his work *Nasledie Chingiskhana* (Moscow: EKSIMO, 2007) Nikolay Trubetskoy observed very accurately that the weak point in Genghis

127

Khan's state structure was the fact that Tengriism did not become the domestic religion of the peoples of his empire, as occurred with Orthodox Christianity in Rus' and with Shinto in Japan. The canons and rites of Tengriism thus did not penetrate into the daily life of the nomads and did not become commonplace features for daily use. **I believe that the greatest omission and error of Genghis Khan was that he missed the unique opportunity to make Tengriism the practical religion of the nomads. God and fate offered him the chance, but...**

Genghis Khan created a system of state power that was not based on a particular social estate or a religion, but rather on the specific psychological makeup of the carriers of that power – a makeup that was intrinsic, he was certain, to the nomads, but not to the settled populations. Unfortunately – and this is in the laws of nature – his successors lacked his own talents and abilities and allowed perhaps the greatest empire of all times to fall into decline.

The Mongol empire of the Yuan dynasty with its centre at Beijing fell into ruin after surviving only slightly over a hundred years; its literature became Chinese and its religion became Buddhist. A similar situation occurred with the Golden Horde in the west, where the state religion became Islam. While still far from having exhausted its potential, it broke into numerous small kingdoms and princedoms. In this sorry group the Japanese, a nation related to the Turks, stands out favourably. This nation never deviated from the path of its ancestors, nor did it alter its gods or its customs. In spite of its exceptionally advanced state of development, it remains, as suggested by Nurlan Amrekulov (reference from first book) a highly conservative country. It has been able to retain its royal authority and to preserve its historic belief system, Shinto. This has much in common with Tengriism, and in essence the two religions are each based on the worship of ancestors and of nature. Shinto teaches personal responsibility towards the state and to the common cause, and its product is the Samurai – a way of life that places spiritual values over wealth. The Samurai values honour, duty, nobility and loyalty, and it was this belief and support that enabled Japan to become a world leader despite its paucity of natural resources, overtaking many Western countries.

CHAPTER V
THE TURKIC LANGUAGE OF GENGHIS KHAN'S MONGOLS

To know the disposition of one or another people, seek above all to learn their language.
Attributed to Pythagoras

Languages are a ford across the river of Time
Vladislav Illich-Svitych

Let us return and picture the following: Jamukha, Genghis Khan and the Kerey khan Togrul are on their way to rescue Börte from captivity by the Merkit. I ask Professor Sodnom what language they would be speaking, if Genghis Khan and Jamukha spoke Mongol but Togrul spoke the Kazakh of the time. He replies: 'In ancient Mongol, which was also spoken by the Khereid Wang Khan'. Even a scholar such as Michel Hoang (*Genghis Khan*, Eng. ed. Saqi Books, 1998) freely asserts that the Naiman were a Turkic tribe that had become Mongolised, but nevertheless speaks of the Kerey as 'a precarious union of Turkic clans'. The language of the Kerey in the 12th century was what is now Kazakh. Muhamedzhan Tynyshpaev, in reference to Nikolai Aristov, asserts that the Kerey as a people are recorded in Chinese chronicles from the 9th century and that they descended from the Huns, thus, from Turkic-speaking peoples. So it is unsurprising that the Kerey of Genghis Khan's time spoke in the Turkic Kazakh of the time. It is interesting that in the 12th century the Kerey included, as noted by Rashid ad-Din Hamadani, Turkic-speaking Yakut (Sakha) who, according to some sources, belonged at various times to the Kazakh Argyn. The Kerey also included what are today the Kazakh

Alban and the Tangut (called the Tongoit by Hamadani). The Tangut are known in Kazakhstan as the Dungan.

So why, I continue to ask Professor Sodnom, if you are the descendants of the Mongols of the 13th century, do you not understand their language of that time? And why do you, today's Mongols, not understand the language of *The Secret History of the Mongols*, whereas we, today's Kazakhs, recognise more than 60% of the words from our modern language? This question was examined in depth by Kalibek Daniyarov in his book *Istoria Chingiskhana* (Almaty, 2001). If the Kerey khan Togrul spoke ancient Mongol, then why is it that the Kerey who remained on the territory of Mongolia, together with those Kerey that returned there after defeat by the Xirong in the 17th century and indeed the Kerey who today live in Kazakhstan, all speak the same Kazakh language? Is it, I squeeze from the professor, that ancient Mongol is in fact modern Kazakh, and the language of Genghis Khan's Mongols coincides with the Kazakh of that time? Apart from this, I reminded him that the Mongol translator-editors of another epic work, the *Altan Tobchi*, discovered in Mongolia in 1926, noted that 'the ancient Mongols [i.e. of Genghis Khan's time – K.Z.] spoke differently to modern Mongols...'.

A leading expert in the comparative linguistics of the Mongolian and Kazakh languages, Professor B. Bazylkhan remarks in his major work on the compilation of a Mongol-Kazakh dictionary (*Mongol-Kazakh tol'/ Mongolsha-Kazaksha sozdik*, Ulan-Bator: Olgiy, 1984) that the phonetic system of ancient Mongol is closer to that of modern Kazakh than it is to that of modern Mongolian. For example, the ancient Mongol words *zhadagay, chalma, syltaq, qara* and *taqa* are written in modern Kazakh as *zhadagay, shalma, syltau, qara* and *taqa*, i.e. they coincide almost completely, whereas in modern Mongolian they are written *zadgay, tsalam, shaltag, khar* and *takh*, thus, changed largely beyond recognition.

Another well-known Turkologist, Karzhaubay Sartkozhauly, wrote in a popular article for the weekly *Moskovsky Komsomolets v Kazakhstane* (1-7 May 2013) that while it was possible, with great effort, to find a similarity between the primary words of modern Kazakh and modern

Mongolian dictionaries of some 60-70%, nevertheless 'today these are completely different languages', i.e. the languages of Ulan Bator and Astana in the 21st century are completely different.

To confirm this conclusion we analysed the words in Yuri Kruchkin's Mongol-Russian/Russian-Mongol dictionary (*Mongolsko-russky, russko-mongol'sky slovar'* (Moscow: AST: Vostok-Zapad, 2006). In a study of 240 randomly selected words beginning with the letter *kh* (this is a single character in both languages), only 27 were similar in both sound and meaning in both languages, though one could, at a stretch, consider words such as, say, the Mongolian *khavsrakh*, meaning 'join in with' or 'affiliate with', the Kazakh equivalent of which is *zhapsyru*, or, say, *khadkhalagakh*, 'to keep', 'to store', which in Kazakh is *qadagalau*, as being similar. Thus only 13.5% of words, and that with a great stretch, can be said to coincide in sound and meaning between the two modern languages.

Similarly, in analysing 150 entries from Professor Bazylkhan's dictionary (*Mongol-Kazakh tol'/Mongolsha-Kazaksha sozdik*, Ulan-Bator: Olgiy, 1984) we found only 24 words (16%) with similarity of both sound and meaning in the two languages.

A professor of contemporary Mongolian linguistics admitted that modern-day Mongols have forgotten the Mongol spoken by Genghis Khan and repeated the basic theories that used to be given in Soviet-era history textbooks that the Naiman, Kerey, Khongirad, Jalayir and Merkit were Mongol tribes that spoke Middle Mongol in the 13th century. According to this argument, when they rode with Genghis Khan to what is now Kazakhstan, they became assimilated into the Kazakh tribes living there and consequently began to speak Kazakh. So my assertion that there had been no 'assimilation' came as a surprise to the professor; yet the matter is self-evident, since Genghis Khan's warriors were, as the professor had said, of the Naiman, Kerey, Jalayir, Khongirad, etc., and their route took them through the Seven Rivers region, which was inhabited by those same tribes – Naiman, Kerey, Jalayir, Karluk, Merkit and Argyn and into southern Kazakhstan where lived the Khongirad, Kangju and Wusun, and later reached central and western Kazakhstan, home to the Alshyn and Kipchak. In short, they were passing through their own kind and assimilation was not an issue. They all spoke a similar Kazakh language of the day, since the Naiman, Jalayir, Kerey, Kongirad, Merkit, Ongud, Manghud, Baarin and Shyryn, having arrived with Genghis Khan in Central Asia, formed a single nomadic people with the Kazakh tribes living there, with a common culture and common language. Grasping at a final straw, Professor Sodnom pointed to the episode in *The Secret History of the Mongols* in which the three men meet to go and rescue Börte from the Merkit. He recalled the moment when Jamukha reproaches Wang Khan and Genghis Khan for arriving late for their meeting at the appointed place and is said to have asked, 'Did we not make our agreement in the Mongol tongue?' In response to this I turned to the page in question of *The Secret History of the Mongols* and cited the entry correctly: 'Did we not so agree? [When] we Mongqols say 'yes', are we not bound by oath?' It must surely be agreed that 'the Mongol tongue' and 'we Mongols say 'yes'' are two different things. Moreover the ethnonym 'Mongol' meant an entirely different ethnic group in the 13th century to that of the present-day Mongols. We will discuss this later.

As we parted, the professor congratulated me on the fact that the Kazakhs had preserved their language, unlike today's Mongols. Of course, it would be absurd to claim that Genghis Khan spoke modern-day Kazakh (if only because, according to linguistic statistics, the language renews some 15% of its lexis every hundred years, and the same percentage of the language becomes obsolete). Rather, Genghis would have spoken in the Kazakh of his time, and this is entirely unambiguous.

To support this argument let me mention an eloquent fact from the dynastic chronicles of the house of Ögedei preserved in oral tradition. The great khan, having inherited the empire of Genghis Khan, relied considerably in his daily governing duties on his chancellor, the Naiman-Khitan Yelü Chucai and in general on the wealth of state-building expertise that the Naiman possessed. Of course, this closeness of the Naiman to the khan's court did not please the other tribes and clans of the Mongol empire. The situation particularly irritated the Jurchen, who had ruled the Celestial Empire prior to Genghis Khan (the Jin dynasty).

Let us note – and later we will show – that the modern Mongolian language is also the language of the Jurchen of the 13th century, and is of Tungus origin. And so, according to a scenario planned in advance, a Jurchen shaman approached Ögedei Khan and told him that he had had a dream in which Ögedei's father, the great Genghis Khan, instructed him that it was necessary to beware the Naiman, to whom the successor to the throne had become too close, and that they were planning a conspiracy against him, intended to betray him and so on. 'In which language did my father speak to you?' Ögedei asked the shaman. 'In our language, Jurchen', answered the shaman candidly.

The khan immediately commanded that the shaman's spine be broken, saying to him: 'My father knew only one language in which he spoke with my chancellor Yelü Chucai.' And that language was the Kazakh of the time, which was also spoken by the Naiman.

In Hasen Kozha-Ahmet's previously cited work *Zabluzhdenie, dlivsheesia vekami* the question is raised of whether there was an 'ancient Mongol language'. He analyses 57 words and phrases from the *Compendium of Chronicles* of Rashid ad-Din Hamadani that the author or translators reckoned to be 'ancient Mongol' words, then, comparing them to dictionaries of modern Mongolian and Kazakh, he reaches the unambiguous conclusion that the words are Turkic and many of them Kazakh. For example, the word *yusun* in Hamadani's source is ascribed to ancient Mongol with the meaning 'custom', 'convention'. The modern Kazakh equivalent for this is *zhosun*. Meanwhile the modern Mongolian word with the same meaning is *zanshil*. Or let us take a phrase from the *Compendium* that reads 'Foreigners there were called the Jad'. In modern Kazakh the word *jat* (or *zhat*) means 'foreign', 'alien'. In Mongolian, this sense is carried by the word *har* or *khar*. Next, the term *keshik* or *kezik* in the *Compendium* is considered to be the ancient Mongol phrase 'regular guard'. Meanwhile in Kazakh, *kezek* means 'queue', 'turn', for which the modern Mongolian equivalent is *eelzh* or *daraalal*. In the *Compendium* the word *kushluk* is considered to have the sense in Ancient Mongol of 'strong', while the word for this in modern Mongolian is *huchtey*; the modern Kazakh sense of a 'strong man' is however *kushti*. I will discuss one more word, *buyuruk*, taken to be Ancient Mongol for 'giver of orders'. Now, in modern Mongolian the word 'order' is represented by *tushaaz*, while in today's Kazakh – 800 years after the formation of the Mongol Empire – the equivalent is *buyryk*. Hasen Kozha-Ahmet points out that in all the volumes of the *Compendium of Chronicles* one encounters clarifications such as: 'In Mongol this word means X, but in Turkic it means Y'. The ordinary reader thus comes to see that the Turkic and Mongol languages existed side by side in Genghis Khan's era, but if this was so, then there existed a Mongol people independently of the Turkic. We have sought to explain in simple terms that this reading of Rashid ad-Din Hamadani is erroneous. **We may thus conclude this chapter by asserting that the language that was called 'ancient Mongol', which was spoken by Genghis Khan, was in fact the language of the 13th-century ancestors of the Kazakhs, while the modern Mongolian language has little in common with that of the Mongols of Genghis Khan,** although they both relate to the same Altaic group of languages. We will discuss this in the following chapters.

There are also other, indirect proofs of what has been said. Recently I read in Russian translation the work of the American scholar Jack Weatherford (*Genghis Khan and the making of the modern world*, New York, 2005), who spent a long period in Chinese archives and lived in Mongolia once it was open to foreigners after the fall of the USSR. His work deletes at a stroke the negative representations of Genghis Khan that have been prevalent in the West for centuries. In their place he skilfully develops the notion that the Renaissance in Europe was made possible by the reforms of Genghis Khan.

CHAPTER VI
THE KHITAN AND JURCHEN OF MANCHURIA
ASSIMILATED BY THE KAZAKH NAIMAN
(My amendments to Lev Gumilev)

By Hercules, I prefer to be wrong with Plato...
than be right with these idiots.
Cicero

We will continue our discussion of Jack Weatherford's book and again pose ourselves the question of Genghis Khan's native language. In 1211 he decided to invade northern China, which at that time was ruled by the Jin dynasty of the Jurchen – a series of tribes of Tungus origin that lived in eastern Manchuria. Earlier the Jurchen had forced out the Liao dynasty of Khitans, which had ruled northern China from 947 to 1125 (Genghis Khan was born in 1155). Thus, for thirty years before the birth of Genghis Khan northern China was ruled by the Khitan, who, according to official sources, were of Tungus-Manchurian origin. But was this really the case? Discussing the Khitan in his work *Ocherki istorii Semirech'ia*, Vasily Bartold states that '... they are usually considered to be a people of Tungus origin, with an admixture of certain Mongol features' [i.e. Mongols of Genghis Khan – K.Z.]. However, the editor of the 2005 edition of this work, A. Abishev, published by the Kazakh 'Svobodnoe Obshchestvo' ('Free Society') institute, points out in his commentary that 'The Chinese [i.e. the Khitan – K.Z.] were incorrectly considered to be Tungus tribes...'. In the *Khronika chelovechestva* of Bodo Harenberg (Moscow: Slovo, 2000) it is again merely suggested that the Khitan are probably of Mongol-Tungus origin.

The leading Turkologists Lev Gumilev noted in his book *Chornaia legenda* (Moscow: Airis Press, 2003, p.238) that a small people related to the Khitan referred to itself in the 8th century as 'Tatar'. In another of his works, however (*Ot Rusi k Rossii*, Moscow, 2004, p. 114) he states that 'the Naiman are successors to the Khitan who had forced the Jurchen from their camps'. I am willing to agree with this leading scholar but nevertheless, considering that the Naiman, a large tribe, was formed only in the 8th century, as agreed by Chinese chronicles, I would state my point of view that the Khitan were a Turkic tribe that was assimilated by the ethnically close Naiman, and this will be discussed below. One may also say that the Khitan became dissolved in the new people that began to be known as the Naiman. For now, though, let me recall the fact, noted by Claudius Ptolemy, that north of the Hwang Ho lived Turkic tribes, beginning with the Huns of Modu Chanyu-Matay, and this land had always belonged to the Turks – the ancestors of the Kazakhs. The Khitan, the Ongud Kumo Xi (today these are the Kazakh Waq clan), the Chinese Tuoba (whose descendants are today among the Kazakh Argyn), the Oghuz Toguz (the Uigurs) and the Tatar Otyz – were all inhabitants of northern China and all had Turkic roots. Northern China in fact only became Chinese from the time of the Ming dynasty in the mid-14th century. It is in no way a coincidence that on his first campaign into the Celestial Empire, Genghis Khan captured what is today Beijing and, by way of an ultimatum to the Jin emperor, laid down the condition of giving him all the land north of the Hwang Ho. Further, he made the very ruler of the Jin empire take the inferior tittle of wang, which put him in a position of vassal dependency. If we recall, the title Wang was also granted to the khan of the Kazakh Kerey, Togrul, for aiding the Chinese in their battle with the Tatars.

Thus according to Gumilev, the dynasty that ruled northern China for 200 years from 947 was that of the ancestors of the Naiman, or at least was related to them. Developing Gumilev's position, let me give the fifty-first line of the inscription in honour of Kultegin on the Orkhon-Yenisei monument, which contains a list of the embassies that arrived at the Orkhon headquarters of the eastern Turkic khagans in the year 732 to participate in the funeral of Kultegin: 'As those weeping and groaning [i.e. expressing mourning] there came the Khitan and the Kumo Xi led by Udar-Sengun...'. The Kumo Xi were Ongud living along the Great Wall of China who subsequently formed a significant element of the Kazakh Tatars, while a certain part of them became part of the Kazakh people under the name of the Waq clan.

If the Khitan had not been closely related to the Turkic khagans, is it likely that they would have come to 'weep and groan' at the funeral of a Turkic khagan? In *Istoria naroda khunnu* (Moscow: Ast, 2004) Lev Gumilev discusses the Khitan as a northern group of ancient Donghu who lived in the western areas of northern Manchuria, with similarities of language to the Kumo Xia or the Ongud. In Chinese scholarship the Kumo Xio are often still referred to as the Yuwen.

Let us return to Jack Weatherford, who suggests that during the first battles in northern China, where there were still many Khitan (after all, they ruled there for almost two centuries following their defeat of the Balhae state),

In a masterful propaganda campaign, the Mongols entered Jurched territory announcing themselves as a liberating force intent on restoring the older Khitan royal family that had ruled before the Jurched overthrew them a century earlier . Before the fighting began, many Khitan fled to join the Mongols, **whom they saw as relatives speaking the same language** (my emphasis – K.Z.)

Weatherford, Jack: *Genghis Khan and the making of the modern world.* Kindle location 1967.

According to Gumilev the Khitan spoke the language of the Naiman, but in this case what language was used by Genghis Khan's warriors? Clearly the language of the Mongols was also that of the Naiman.

Another example. Another American scholar, John Man in his work *Genghis Khan* asserts:

So it proved, when Mukhalil and Genghis's brother Kasar swept across all Manchuria in 1214-16. Mukhali – reputed for his powerful build, curly whiskers, superb archery and meticulous planning ability – was, at 45, already one of Genghis's greatest generals, having been with him for fifteen years, and he would become the anchor-man in the long struggle to subdue north China. One major task was to capture the old Liao provincial capital of Pei Ching, which fell into his lap in an extraordinary fashion. A Mongol officer named Yesen, who spoke both the local Turkish language and Chinese, ambushed a new Jin commander arriving to assume control of the city, took over his documents, persuaded the guards that he was actually the incoming general, and then, as the city's new boss, ordered all the guards off the walls.

(John Man: *Genghis Khan*, 2nd ed. London: Bantam, 2005, pp. 164-165)

Thus we see that the 'local Turkish language' is also the language of the Khitan who lived in Manchuria, their historical homeland, at that time. And so Gumilev is correct in asserting that the Naiman are descendants of the Khitan.

Let us add another argument. In 1205 in what is today the Katon-Karagay district of eastern Kazakhstan, by the headwaters of the Bukhtarmy there took place a large battle between the Mongols (with Genghis Khan present in person) and the united forces of the Naiman and Merkit, who suffered a crushing defeat. The commander of the Naiman was the prince Kuchlug, who had taken the place of his father Tayang Khan in 1204. Many of the fighters on the losing side escaped the battle only to drown in the Irtysh; and only a small proportion of them got away with their lives. Kuchlug found refuge with the Gurkhan – the head of the Kara-Khitan khanate, which was established after the Liao were replaced in China by the Jurchen dynasty of the Jin.

The capital of the Kara-Khitan khanate was initially the city of Chuguchak (today's Tacheng, in the Dzungarian Basin on the Chinese side of the border between Xinjiang and Kazakhstan). West of here, on the Chu river near modern Tokmak, in some sources located close to what is now Bishkek, was situated the khanate of the Karakhanids with its centre at Balasagun (955-1130). Other data, as shown by recent research by the Kazakh archaeologist U. Shalekenov, suggests that Balasgun was in fact in Kazakhstan, in today's Zhambyl (Taraz) province. Faced with an attack by the Kangju and the Karluk, the leader of the Karakhanids appealed for help to the Khitan. The Khitan-Naiman, having assisted the Karakhanids, then captured Balasagun and made that city the capital of the Kara-Khitan khaganate. The latter included Naiman, Kangju, Karluk, Uigurs and others. So it was here, to Balasagun, that the prince Kuchlug came after the fight with the Mongols. It is also interesting to note that Genghis Khan referred to the Karluk as the Tajiks (according to Tleuberdy Abenay and *The Secret History of the Mongols*). Gumilev on the other hand regarded them as Uysyn, dispersed among Tajiks. Does it follow from here that, contrary to conventional opinion, the Tajiks were not an Iranian but a Turkic-speaking people? Vasily Bartold believed that the Turkic peoples called all Muslims Tajiks or Taziks, but of all the Turkic peoples, the Karluk were the most influenced by Islam. Among the Kazakhs the word *taz* is used to mean 'bald-headed' and coincides semantically with the definition 'Muslim'. Unlike the Muslims, the Turks did not shave their heads. It is most likely that the Tajiks have Turkic blood but an Iranian language. In any case, in the 2nd century BCE the Turkic-speaking Saka migrated from the Seven Rivers region (Kazakhstan) to the Pamir, and in the 5th century CE the Uysyn made the same journey. The 7th-century Byzantine historian Theophylact Simocatta wrote the following in his *History* (see e.g. *Istoria*, Moscow, 1996, p.20): '... It was the Huns, who lived in the east, alongside the Persians, whom the majority were used to calling the Turks...' In my book *Under the wolf's nest: a Turkic rhapsody* I pointed out that the Persian empire was created by the Kazakh Alban, and therefore, if the Persians themselves were Turkic-speaking, then what can one say about the Tajiks who lived in those days in the back yard of the Persian empire?

Evidently, Genghis Khan knew this information.

So the Naiman prince Kuchlug ran from Genghis Khan and found refuge with the Kara-Khitan Gurkhan, who received him like a family member. In other words the Naiman Kuchlug came to his own kind, the Khitan. The Gurkhan gave him his daughter and in due course the Naiman Kuchlug became 'Gurkhan', that is, khan of the Kara-Khitan state. And could the fugitive, disgraced, prostrated prince of the Naiman have depended on such a reception from non-relatives? The conclusion is straightforward: the Khitan were not strangers to the Naiman.

Aleksandr Domanin stated in his work *Mongol'skaia imperia chingizidov* that 'The Naiman are overall one of the most enigmatic of peoples. We do not know what language they spoke, although this was presumably one of the dialects of the Mongol language. We do know that they had a highly developed culture (probably the most developed of any of the steppe peoples)... The Naiman kingdom was surrounded by nomadic tribes with a clan system based on a much lower level of evolution... Some historians, following Gumilev, consider them as the **northern branch of the Kara-Khitan**' (my emphasis – K.Z.).

By the way, it was the Naiman-Khitan Yelü Chucai, chancellor of the empire of Genghis Khan, who persuaded the emperor not to subject the population of China to total extermination following its conquest. Genghis Khan, as an adherent of the nomadic way of life, saw in wealthy, sedentary China the main threat to the nomadic way of life, for it has been the case all through the history of the Turks that it was the wealth of the Celestial Empire that attracted and ultimately corrupted the nomads with its life of plenty. This was the reason for the destruction of the empires of the Huns and of the Turkic khaganates.

Yelü Chucai demonstrated visually to Genghis Khan how the million-strong Chinese population, by paying taxes in an orderly fashion, could support and provide a financial mechanism to sustain the vast empire.

Going back, let us once again confirm Gumilev's hypothesis that the Naiman and Khitan were related, but nothing more.

I believe that we should draw a line under the question of what language Genghis Khan's Mongols spoke and take it as axiomatic that Genghis spoke the same language as was used by the ancestors of the Kazakhs in the 13th century. It is therefore no coincidence that not one of the sources suggests that, spending the last ten years of his life on the territory of Kazakhstan, Genghis Khan spoke with the local population through interpreters.

If we consider that the name 'China' derives from the ethnonym *qtan* or *khitan*, it becomes evident that the Turkic clan of the Khitan, after their losses to the hegemony in northern China (Liao dynasty) in 1125, losses from Khorezmshah Muhammed in eastern Turkestan (following the formation of the Kara-Khitan khanate) and, finally, after the defeat inflicted by Genghis Khan's forces in which the Khitan were led by the Naiman prince Kuchlug – after all these losses – the Khitan 'dissolved' into the large clan of the Naiman. And so, to 'correct' Gumilev, I propose that the Khitan were not the ancestors of the Naiman but rather were dissolved among the Kazakhs of Naiman origin and became one of their sub-groups.

In *Naiman khandygy* (Almaty, 2002) by Sabetkazy Akatay the clan of the Tolegetay, which comprises one third of all Naiman, derives its lineage from China and consists of old Kazakh clans such as the Matai and Karakerei, that formed the basis of the Seir-Sir and lived in the 6th-8th centuries alongside the Khitan. It may be asserted that the Khitan Liao dynasty that ruled china for two centuries was led by members of the Kazakh Matai, as it was these who created the great Hun state led by Modu Chanyu-Matay. Incidentally, this dynasty replaced the Tang dynasty of the Tuoba, which was governed – as we shall discuss later – by ancestors of the Kazakh clan of the Argyn. It may be said that China, settled and with a developed artisanal culture, was always a wealthy trophy for the nomadic tribes that, one after another in turn, ruled this hardworking people. After 1125 a group of the Naiman that largely comprised Matay and Karakerey moved to the lands of the Seven Rivers (south-eastern Kazakhstan) and established the Kara-Khitan khanate, and, a short time afterwards, joined the empire of Genghis Khan. Evidently it was this event that prompted Gumilev to assume that the Khitan were ancestors of the Naiman. As regards the Jurchen of Manchuria who ruled northern China in 1125, after the Mongols took control of the country they became part of the Naiman. Today the major Naiman union of tribes includes the Shurshit clan, known as the Teristamgaly, and these are the descendants of the Jurchen.

Another important piece of information is as follows. Grigory Grumm-Grzhimaylo (*Zapadnaia Mongolia i Uriankhaysky kray*, Leningrad, 1926, v.2) discusses the 'Kete' clan as a tribe related to the Khitan. This is evident with the 'naked eye', since the etymology of the words *kete* and *ktan – khitan* is the same. Today the Kete form a significant part of the Alimuly tribal union within the Kazakh Junior *jüz*. It follows that the descendants of the Khitan live today not only among the Naiman but also among other Kazakh tribes.

In *Under the wolf's nest: a Turkic rhapsody* I mentioned that after the fall of the Hittite state in the 12th century BCE in Asia Minor, the Hittites migrated to western China, where they ousted the Shang (Yin) nomads and created the Zhou empire. Thus among the descendants of these Hittites are today's Khitan-Ktan-Kete. The descendants of the Hittites are the Ket of Siberia, the Kazakh Kete and the Germanic Goths of the early first millennium CE. There are also descendants of the Khitan among the Kipchak. Along with the Kara-Kipchak, Sary-Kipchak, Tory-Kipchak and Khulan-Kipchak, this important clan of the Middle *jüz* also includes the Kitay-Kipchak. The 19th-century Russian ethnologist Aleksey Kharuzin (see Alash journal, no. 3, 2007) wrote in his work 'K voprosu o proiskhozhdenii kirgizskogo naroda' that according to a claim by Abu al-Ghazi Bahadur, from the time of Oghuz Khan to that of Genghis Khan there had been no other peoples on the banks of the Don, the Itil (Volga) and the Yaik (Ural) rivers there had been no other peoples than the Kipchak.

It is appropriate to add the following episode at this point – the approach by Genghis Khan to the frontier city of Otrar, which was defended by the Kipchak and situated in the domain of Khorezmshah Muhammed. Genghis said to the defenders, 'Why, my brothers in blood and language, should we fight one another?' And the Kipchak changed over to Genghis Khan's side.

There was no heroic defence of Otrar in the early 13th century by the ancestors of the Kazakhs. The gates of the city were open to Genghis Khan. The only resistance to be shown was by the guard of the residence of the frontier governor Qadir Khan, who killed the messengers of Genghis Khan in violation of all accepted diplomatic norms. In response to this, Qadir Khan's residence was razed to the ground and the man executed by brutal means.

Genghis Khan's warriors spoke with the Kipchaks in the same language, and that language could only have been Kazakh. So what sort of Mongols were they? And another example: when Khorezm was fully captured, Genghis Khan decided to carry out a reconnaissance by means of a battle – through the 'Iron Gates' at Derbent. Subutai and Jebe, taking only a force of 20,000, moved onto the southern Russian steppe – where the famous battle of the Kalka also took place. En route they conquered the Georgians, and their queen Rusudan, successor to the great queen Tamar, wrote to the Pope that her country had been invaded by 'hordes of Tatar savages' (John Men, *Genghis Khan*). Note that she said not Mongols but Tatars – this is a crucial distinction.

CHAPTER VII
THE TURKIC UNION OF THE OIRAT
Why did they become enemies of the Kazakhs?

Truth is born as a heresy and dies as a superstition.
Hegel

To further clarify the circumstances connected with the **ancestry of the Mongols of Genghis Khan** we must also clarify the ethnic origin of the Oirat people. The orientalist I. Zlatkin states in his major work *Istoria Dzhungarskogo khanstva* (Moscow: Nauka, 1983) that the history of the Oirat contains many other unresolved problems. He gives an analysis of the views of various leading scholars on this question – among them Bichurin, Uspensky, Dorzhi Banzarov, Grigory Grumm-Grzhimaylo, Pallas and others, paying particular attention to both the origins of the Oirat known as the Western Mongols and the reasons for their tough confrontational attitude towards the so-called Eastern Mongols. Zlatkin acknowledges that all the scholars are unanimous with regard to the formation of the Oirat union of the Dorben Oirat – such a union was necessary for them in order to fight the Eastern Mongols.

It should be remembered that after Genghis Khan departed west, there remained in Mongolia only 6 *tumens* (units of 10,000 men); in this case these were mostly Kazakh clans from the heartlands of Genghis Khan whom he had left in Mongolia to take Beijing. On the topic of the Dorben Oirat, none of the scholars named by Zlatkin, in my view, noted the main point about the origin of the Oirat, which was that, according to *The Secret History of the Mongols*, they came from the four sons of Duwa-soqor, the elder brother of Dobun-mergen, and according to Hamadani these were both of the Qiyad clan.

145

The *Secret History of the Mongols* thus mentions that the four sons of Duwa-soqora originated the 'Four Oirats' or Dorben Oirat. This union of four (*dorben*) Oirat has included at various times such tribes as the Choros, Hoshout, Torghud, Khoid, Oeld etc. For example, the 18th-century scholar Peter Simon Pallas (*Sobranie istoricheskikh isvestiy o Mongol'skikh narodakh, sochinennoe gospodinom P.S. Pallasom*. St Petersburg, 1766) maintained that the Mongols of the time of Genghis Khan were divided into two main branches – the Mongols proper (understood as the Nirun Mongols descended from Alan Gua, her husband Dobun Mergen and the divine light – K.Z.) and the Dorben Oirat (the descendants of Duwa-soqor – K.Z.). And so it was, except perhaps that one could add the Darlekin Mongols, originating in the Ergenekon, to the 'proper' category. Grigory Grumm-Grzhimaylo (*Zapadnaia Mongolia i Uriankhaysky kray*, Leningrad, 1926, v.2) also believed that the Dorben union of Oirat was formed in Genghis Khan's day. We should note here that Pallas understands the Dorben as a single people, while Grumm-Grzhimaylo considers them to be different but related peoples. And naturally we should pay attention to the view of the great orientalist Dorzhi Banzarov (*Ob Oiratakh i Uigursakh*, Kazan, 1849, v.1), who believed that the term 'Dorben-Oirat' appeared in Genghis Khan's time, when the entire population was divided into *tumens*, units of ten thousand; the Dorben-Oirat consisted of four such *tumens* (i.e. the number of Duwa-soqor's sons – K.Z.). The ethnonym Dorben Oirat may therefore be considered to mean a union of four Oirat tribes. **Incidentally, the ethnic term *dorben* is easy to decipher using Turkic syntax. The root of the word *dor* in Kazakh is the same as that of *tort* or *dort*, meaning the number 4 (as per Dowa-soqor's four sons). The suffix *ben* or *men* is a suffix of attraction, so that *dorben* can be read as 'union of four tribes'.**

On the basis of the scholars mentioned here, then, we will take the Oirat or Dorben Oirat to mean the descendants of the four sons of Dobun-mergen's elder brother Duwa-soqor.

In the work of the Khivan Abu al-Ghazi Bahadur we note that the Oirat, Torghud, Khori-Tumat and so on are Turkic tribes (*Rodoslovnoe slovo tiurkov*, 'Turkestan', TKISO, 1996, p. 34). This information will be helpful in what follows, as we examine the process by which the Dzungar entered Kazakhstan in the early 15th century.

After Genghis Khan set off for Khorezm the fertile lands that he and his people left behind were occupied by the Oirat, who had hitherto lived in the forests and mountains of northern Mongolia. And from this point onward they came into conflicts with the eastern Mongols, who consisted, as mentioned above, of six Turkic *tumens*. Zlatkin suggests that the cause of this conflict is unknown and has tried to resolve the question himself, suggestion various possible explanations.

In my view, however, the reason for the confrontation between the Oirat and the so-called Eastern Mongols – or **Darlekin Mongols** – is as follows. The Oirat, as representatives of the clan of the Qiyad, wanted to predominate in Mongolia after Genghis Khan's departure, and they believed that their ancestry gave the right to do so. The Eastern Mongols could not agree to this, however, as they also regarded themselves as successors to Genghis Khan. Mongolian researchers differ in their opinions; Manchurian tribes arrived, willingly or otherwise, to help the Eastern Mongols fight the Oirat. When I discussed this with members of the Mongolian Academy of Sciences they expressed diverse views. Some said that the Eastern Mongols called the Manchurian tribes to their aid, while others thought that the latter came as conquerors by themselves. Either way, the fact remains: large numbers of Manchurian tribes poured onto the fertile lands of Mongolia. After all, this land was almost empty – only six tumens occupying this vast territory. **And here is an explanation of the origin of the modern Mongols!**

As concerns the Oirat, meanwhile, they were subsequently forced out of Mongolia by a new people, the Khalkha, of Manchurian descent. After this the Oirat first settled in Xinjiang, then later migrated into eastern Kazakhstan; by 1420 they were living in what is now the Lepinsk district of Alma-Ata province (Muhamedzhan Tynyshpaev: *Istoria Kazakhskogo naroda*, Almaty: Sanat, 2002). Yet oral records do not mention any salient factors that would indicate a bitter confrontation here between the arriving Oirat and the local Kazakhs. So why not?

I believe – as stated earlier – that the tribes that constituted the Oirat union were ethnically close to the Kazakhs that had gone west with Genghis Khan and also with those already living in Kazakhstan (the Argyn, Wusun, Kipchak, Kangju, Alshyn and others) at the time that Genghis Khan arrived in the land.

Nevertheless, the arrival of the Oirat on Kazakh lands was not entirely straightforward. Nikolai Aristov mentions that in 1400, during the rise of the Dzungar, the latter arrived on Kazakh territory, while Uwais Khan of Moghulistan fought the Dzungar a total of sixty-one times between 1400 and 1428, being the victor only once. Muhamedzhan Tynyshpaev also describes a crushing defeat of the Kerey in 1400-1410, as a result of which only six brothers remained alive of the original twelve. The Kerey of today descend from these six surviving brothers. On top of all this, there were always more conflicts between related Turkic tribes over grazing land, as discussed in Part 1 above, which were a constant throughout the history of the Turkic nomads. They had no peers other than one another, so fought one another. It should be noted that the ancestors of the Dzungar Oirat reached China from Central Asia back at the end of the third millennium BCE; a Turkic nomadic tribe, it created the first Xia dynasty there under the leadership of the Shang tribe. After this came the Zhou dynasty under the Kete-Khitan, and so it continued up to 1910, when China was ruled by the Turkic **Qing dynasty** of Manchurian origin 1911, (clans of the Naiman Shurshit tribal union of modern-day Kazakhs).

The Turkic tribes that migrated to China naturally returned in the course of time to their homelands in the Eurasian steppe, but meanwhile other groups had settled here – related Turkic tribes, but still distant. The result was a frequent, wholly explicable state of war over grazing land and the means of subsistence, including that between the Dzungar and the Kazakhs in the 18th century CE.

The situation changed dramatically in 1644 when the Manchurian Qing dynasty took power in China. The Oirat tribes in what are now southern and eastern Kazakhstan became swollen by numerous Manchurian tribes whose purpose was colonisation on behalf of the Qing, who already ruled the millions in China. These colonising tribes included, for example, the Mohe, Mukri, Ugi and others, who were not linked to the Kazakh Uz related by blood. A bloody war ensued that reached its climax in 1723 and was known by the Kazakhs as *ak tabandy shuburyndy*. It is recalled in the Kazakh folk lamentation-song 'Elim-ay'.

There is plenty of evidence and explanation for the increased aggression by the Dzungar (i.e. the symbiosis of the Oirat with the arrivals from Manchuria) in 1723. The conspiracy of the Russian imperial dynasty of the Romanovs that was consolidating at the time with the court of the Qing may be compared to the Molotov-Ribbentrop Pact of 1939, as a result of which a number of European nations disappeared from the map. In exactly the same way, as a result of 18th-century Russo-Chinese accord the border between Rus' and China extended over the territory of the Kazakh khanate. In *Skhvatka shesti imperiy* (Moscow: Veche, 2007) Vadim Obukhov states: 'The Oyrot (or Dzungar) embassy came to Moscow...' (p.7) and '...In 1722 (a year before the Dzungar entered Kazakhstan, - K.Z.) the artillery commander Ivan Unkovsky set off with a diplomatic mission to the Dzungar *khong tayiji* (crown prince) Tsevan Rabdan. At that time the Oirat khan maintained a hostile policy towards China. However, the eight-year war with the Qing empire had significantly weakened the Dzungar, and rumours began to circulate that the *khong tayiji* was ready to accept Russian citizenship. The objective of the expedition was to persuade the Oirat to come under Russian rule. The dispatch received by Unkovsky from the headquarters of the *khong taiji* convinced the Russian autocrat that 'the Kyrgyz-Kaysak horde to all Asiatic lands and nations... key and gates... irrespective of the great outlay of which that horde claims it is needful to be under Russian patronage, in order to have communication with all Asiatic nations only through them and to undertake useful and capable measures in respect of the Russian nation...'

Does this not seem like an ideological basis for the future colonisation of the Kazakh khanate by Russia under the plausible pretext of 'voluntary accession'?

What happened after the completion of Ivan Unkovsky's diplomatic mission has already been discussed. On a visit to Kazan in 2007 I was struck by a manifesto by the Russian emperor Peter I on display in the National Museum of the Republic of Tatarstan. It turns out that a year before the Dzungar entered the lands of the Kazakh khanate, Peter paid a visit to Kazan. At that time Kazan lay on the outer limit of the Russian empire, beyond which was the Kazakh steppe. It seems hardly a coincidence that these events – Unkovsky's mission, the Tsar's visit to Kazan and the Dzungar invasion of the Kazakhs – all happened at the same time. That was the time of Peter's manifesto, the wording of which was telling – to the effect of '…and the infidel [should be treated] exceedingly softly, so that he does not realise how much can be taken away…'.

The toponomy of Kazakhstan still includes a number of Dzungar place names – examples include Narynkol, Bayankol, Qapshagay, Burunday, Kegen, Charyn, Mukry, Kaskelen, Zaysan, Urankhay and others.

It should be noted that the interpretation of the Dzungar invasion into Kazakh lands is ambiguous in Kazakh historiography. I have given my own view above. The historian Irina Yerofeeva believes that there was no scheme between the Russian empire and the Qing for stirring up the Dzungar on Kazakh lands and supplying them with firearms ('Sobytia i liudi Kazakhskoy stepi (epokha posdnego Srednevekov'ia i novogo vremeni) kak ob"ekt istoricheskoy remistifikatsii', published in *Nauchnoe znanie i mifotvorchestvo*... previously cited). Examining in detail material from the *Shezhire Shapyrashty Kazybek-beka* and *Otryvki iz dastana Elim-ay*, the work of the popular Kazakh author Mukhtar Magauin, *Azbuka Kazakhskoy istorii. Dokumental'noe povestvovanie*, Almaty, 1997, Kalibek Daniyarov's *Al'ternativnaia istoria Kazakhstana* and the four-volume *Illiustrirovannaia istoria Kazakhstana* (a project led by B. Ayagan and compiled and written by the poet Orynbay Zhanaydarov), Yerofeeva gives scholarly arguments against Russian or Chinese involvement in the

Kazakh-Dzungar conflicts of 1723. I am naturally in agreement with her where the authors of the *Illiustrirovannaia istoria Kazakhstana* give their version of the appearance of the Swedish sergeant Johan Gustav Renat among the Kalmyk forces. Some of their arguments strike me as weak, however, such as the idea of the Russian general staff, keen to realise the doctrine of Lomonosov and Peter that 'Russia will take Siberia', sending the captive Renat, an expert in artillery matters, onto the Kalmyk steppe to weaken the powerful Kazakhs and Oirat who were hindering Russia's eastward progress. Similar arguments could and should of course have been made differently and with different reasoning, without the need to start again from scratch. Still, as they say, 'you don't wave your fists after the fight'. Irina Yerofeeva further claims that a primary source for the views held among the Kazakhs about the character of the Dzungar invasion is Muhamedzhan Tynyshpaev, who suffered repression by the Soviets in 1937; as a result of this, '… all the factual information and opinions contained in his printed works on the history of Kazakhstan in the early 18th century came to be seen as truths that had long been concealed from the people, that were worthy of blind faith and did not demand any kind of documentary substantiation…'.

In my view Yerofeeva greatly underestimates our compatriot when she says that '… he never worked in any archive, and in particular not with primary documentary sources on the history of Russian-Kazakh and Russian-Dzungar relations, and therefore did not have reliable historical information at his disposal, either on the specific circumstances of the captivity of the Swede Gustav Renat by the Dzungar or, more importantly, of the exact date of the appearance among the Oirat of types of firearms that were new at the time'.

So is our honourable scholar aware that Muhamedzhan Tynyshpaev was not only well acquainted with 'Kazakh folk traditions and the literature of oriental studies of his time concerning the Kazakhs…', but had an encyclopaedic level of education? As a member of the Russian State Duma Muhamedzhan Tynyshpaev had access to many secret archived materials of the Russian state, while as the president of the government of the Kokand Khanate, unrecognised by Soviet authority, he also had unparalleled access to Eastern archives.

Also unconvincing in my view are her arguments that 'the archival documents of the 1730s and 1740s indicate that the Tsarist government not only did not send its staff to stir up war among the Oirat but, on the contrary, one of the special instructions with which it charged the envoy L.D. Ugrimov was to demand insistently of the Dzungar khan Galdantseren (r. 1727-1745) that Renat be returned, along with various Russian captives, from Urga [Ulan Bator] to Russia, which had serious fears that the Oirat might use its artillery against the Altaic peoples that were now naturalised Russians...'.

History knows any number of diplomatic receptions in which the official message was one thing but the 'inside-track' information was entirely different.

CHAPTER VIII
THE UNREAD STONE OF KULTEGIN

The Mongols of today and the Mongols of Genghis Khan

When a thing ceases to be a subject of controversy,
it ceases to be a subject of interest.
William Hazlitt
(English essayist and populariser of Shakespeare)

On arriving in Mongolia I asked myself the question: who exactly are the people that lives in this land today? To my great delight I have been able to obtain a work by the Mongolian scholars Taijiud Ochir and Besud Serzhee, *Mongol chuudyn ovgiyn lavlakh*, published in Ulan-Bator in 1998. The two authors have carried out an immense amount of work in 20 of Mongolia's *aimags* (administrative subdivisions). This was a major expedition, during which they carried out their own form of population census, asking local people, 'Who are you? Where are you from? What are your roots?' From their results it appears that there are representatives living in modern-day Mongolia of 769 clans, yet when I recounted carefully the clans mentioned in *The Secret History of the Mongols* and the other sources that list all the clans living on the territory of Mongolia in Genghis Khan's time (regardless of whether they were allies or enemies), I could find only 67 in all! Among the 769 modern clans were representatives of 35 modern Kazakh clans that live in Mongolia up to the present. Admittedly, their names have changed slightly, at least in pronunciation – the Dughlat pronounce their name like *dolood*, the Alshyn like *altchin*, the Wusun like *uysyn*, the Qatagan like *hatagan*, the Qiyad like *hiyad*, the Khereid like *hereed*, the Merkit like *merged* and the Koralas like *gorlos*, etc.

Naturally, I was left with a perfectly reasonable question – where had the extra 700-plus new clans come from since Genghis Khan set off for the West? From here I also began to examine the question of the ethnicity the modern Mongol people. Here another interesting find should be mentioned. I visited Avarga, some 25 km from the Kherlen river, a place with excellent mineral springs and that Genghis Khan used as his summer residence. In point of fact the Japanese have been excavating extensively in this attractive location because according to one account, Genghis was buried here.

In 1990, on the occasion of the 750th anniversary of the publication of *The Secret History of the Mongols* (which took place in 1240), a large monument was erected to Genghis Khan in Avarga. I examined the monument closely and was struck by the fact that it was covered on all four sides with decorative symbols, many of which were identical to Kazakh *tamgas* or clan symbols. I photographed them meticulously and enlarged each of them to the maximum, and saw that the monument bore the symbols of the following Kazakh clans: Argyn, Baganal, Baltaly, Balgaly, Bersh, Oshakty, Jalayir, Tarakt, Tama, Tabyn, Kangju, Teleut, Kerey, Alash, Taz, Jappas, Ysty, Shanyshkyly, Aday, Shekti, Saryuysun, Dughlat, Waq, Khongirad, Ramadan, Altyn, Kete, Tortkara, Karasakal, Zhagalbayly, Cherkesh, Siqym, Alban, Botbay, Shaprashty, Shymyr, Matai – a total of 40 clans (and note that the Kazakhs today are only some 75 clans altogether)!

Surprised at what I had seen, I asked Professor Bayar: 'Do you know what these engraved signs are?' He replied, 'This monument was made by my friend, and he went round collecting all the petroglyphs in Mongolia and copied them onto this stone'. I told him to thank his friend heartily, for he had confirmed for me that many Kazakh clans had lived on the territory of modern-day Mongolia, their historical homeland, and had left their family symbols here. And there was little more that I could say to him.

Now I may begin to answer the question about what constitutes the modern Mongol nation, if in Genghis Khan's era there were recorded some 60 clans and today there are over 700. Let us begin by turning to the book of the well-known Mongolian historian Baabar, *History of Mongolia*, which was published on the occasion of the 800th anniversary of the Mongol Empire. To our shame, Kazakhstan did not mark this date at all, although – and this is a fundamental objective of my research – the great empire was founded in 1206 that created the ancestors of the present-day Kazakhs. Even Murad Adji, who spoke negatively of certain modern Kazakhs in one of his latest books, *Dykhanie Armageddona* (Moscow: Khranitel', 2006), nevertheless asserted in another work, *Tiurki i mir: Sokrovennaia istoria* (Moscow: Khranitel', 2004, p. 367) that 'in the 13th century the greatest Turk of all times and all peoples was born – Genghis Khan'. At the same time, in telephone conversations with me he reproached me for trying to 'appropriate' Genghis Khan for the Kazakhs. To that I can only say that each of the Turkic peoples has the right to search for and find evidence of its relationship to its famous ancestor. And my right as a scholar and a citizen of Kazakhstan is to insist on the point of view held by Kalibek Daniyarov, Mukhtar Magauin, Tleuberdy Abenay, A. Tarazi, Omirbek Baygeldi and many, many other citizens of our country. There is no desire here to reduce the role of another people, and far less any pretension to foreign territory, such as China has asserted, having proclaimed that all lands on which the hoofs of Genghis Khan's horses ever trod are the age-old lands of the Celestial Empire and are even shown as such on their geographical maps. (On top of this, several years ago Genghis Khan was officially added with great pomp to the list of the great Chinese emperors.)

So what then does constitute the modern Mongol people in ethnic terms? Baabar acts against his conscience by saying that in 924 (the point at which government in Mongolia and northern China changed hands from a dynasty of Yenisei Kyrgyz to the Liao dynasty of Khitan Naiman – K.Z.) the territory of Mongolia was abandoned by the Turkic tribes and the Mongols themselves began to rule there. At that time Mongolia was mostly populated by Naiman, Kerey, Jalayir, Khongirad,

Dughlat, Merkit and other Kazakh clans and tribes that still exist today, plus Tatar, Ongud, Manghud, Baarin, Shyryn and other tribes that were ethnically close to Kazakh groups. In general the Turkic tribes did not leave Mongolia in 924, as Baabar suggests, but rather after 1218, when they left with Genghis Khan to participate in his Khorezm campaign. Genghis Khan left his trusty general Muqali with some 40,000 Jalayir, Ongud, Manghud and Khongirad, while the remainder of the Kazakh tribes were left to his younger son Tolui, to whose lot fell Genghis Khan's native lands of Burkhan Khaldun and Karakorum.

Muqali, of the Jalayir, had been charged with conquering northern China; however, he died in 1223 and northern China was not taken until 1234, by Ögedei, who by then was khan and successor to Genghis Khan since the latter's death in 1227. Baabar states that during Genghis Khan's time there were forty princedoms or *tumans* on the territory of Mongolia, plus the four Oirat tribes. After Genghis Khan set off for the west there remained only six Mongol *tumans* and the four Oirat. Nevertheless, Mongolia continued to be known as 'the forty plus four'.

Following the death of Ögedei's son Güyük in 1248, the throne was occupied by sons of Tolui. This, it should be added, would not have occurred without the help of their wise and experienced mother Sorghaghtani of the Kazakh Kerey. In 1259, however, after the death of the khan Möngke, a struggle for power began between Ariq Böke (*buqa* translates from Kazakh as 'bull' or 'ox', while *aryq* means 'thin'), who was left in Genghis Khan's native country, and Kublai, who had elected to live in northern China. The winner was Kublai, who founded the Yuan dynasty in China in 1260 and made its capital Beijing, which remains the Chinese capital to this day. From that point, even Mongol scholars admit, the decline of the Mongol Empire was rapid.

In moving the capital to Beijing Kublai made a fateful mistake, going against a warning that had long ago been given by Bilge Qaghan, one of the founders of the Second Turkic Khaganate. There is a prophetic message engraved on the stone dedicated to Kultegin that stands near Karakorum, which I visited in 2006, which reads: 'The Tuoba (Turkic clans that were **ruled by** northern China) who give without limit so much gold, silver, intoxicating drinks and silk, usually speak sweetly and their gifts are luxurious. By enticing with sweet talk and luxurious gifts, they always brought close to themselves peoples who lived far away. Those peoples (Turkic – K.Z.), once they settled close at hand, acquired evil knowledge... By letting yourselves be tempted by their sweet talk and luxurious gifts, O Turkic people, you will be killed in great numbers! ... O Turkic people, if you settle in that land (the land of the Tuoba – K.Z.), you may be killed. But if you settle in Ötüken (Karakorum – Bilge Qaghan's headquarters on the Tuul river – K.Z.) and send from there caravans (for gifts, i.e. for tribute), you will suffer no grief. If you dwell on the soil of Ötüken, you may live and create (support) your great state...'

At the initiative of the current mayor of Astana and former prime minister of Kazakhstan, Imangali Tasmagambetov, **a copy of this stone is on display in the lobby of the L.N.** Gumilev Eurasian National University in Astana, Kazakhstan's capital, as a testament and moral from the Turkic ancestors to the new generations. Regrettably, the new generations have not fully read and understood it. Meanwhile the minister of education for Kazakhstan, Krimbek Kusherbaev, has also initiated the publication of the 9-volume encyclopaedia *Qazaqtar* (edited by Yerlan Aryn). These initiatives are aimed at initiating and cultivating a national self-awareness for the successors to the great khaganates.

It may be recalled that the Tuoba were a Turkic-speaking tribe of the Xianbei state that grew in strength at the end of the 4th century when its leader Toba Wei founded the Northern Wei dynasty (386-532), which united all of northern China under its protectorate. We have already mentioned that all down the millennia it was Turkic tribes, one after another, that established the ruling Turkic dynasties in the Celestial Empire. It is very interesting to observe the relations that arose here between the indigenous ethnic Chinese and these ruling Turkic elites on the one hand, and the Turkic tribes and states that existed outside the Great Wall of China on the other. Considering the interests of the indigenous, conquered ethnos, the Turkic rulers of the Celestial Empire were forced to maintain policies that went against the interests of their own relatives living inside the Great Wall. This is what happened with relations between the Shang and Zhou rulers of China and their **fellow countrymen**, and the same was true for the rulers of the Tuoba.

It is well known that after its defeat by the Huns of Modu Chanyu-Matay, the Tatar tribe of the Donghu divided into three parts: the Wuhuan, Xianbei and Toba. The Tuoba are also the Toba, while the Wuhuan were the ancestors of the Khitan Naiman; meanwhile the Xianbei were the ancestors of today's Siberian Tatars. By the end of the 5th century, however, the Tuoba tribe had already fully assimilated into the Chinese ethnic milieu, and the runic monuments of the Orkhon already meant by this name the ethnic Chinese population under the emperors of the Tang dynasty. Evidence of this is given in part by S.G. Klyashtorny. Mirzabek Kargabaev, listing the Kazakh clans by *jüz*, states that the Middle *jüz* included the strong Toq branch within the Argyn, which had historically been known as the Toba, Tuoba and later the Tocharians (*Atlantida kochevnikov*, Karaganda, 2007, p. 52). I fully admit that one of the branches of the Argyn was assimilated into the Chinese in the 5th century, but the ancestors of the modern-day Argyn were the leaders of the powerful Tuoba dynasty of the Tang from the 7th to the 10th century, which was then supplanted by the Naiman Khitan Liao dynasty. In the literature, however, the Tocharians are more usually called a **tribe** of the Yuezhi, the ancestors of the Kazakh clan of the Kangju, which in its turn established the great Kushan empire. Mirzabek Kargabaev also maintains that the large Turkic clan of the Karluk were once part of the Argyn tribal union. This is also mentioned by Muhamedzhan Tynyshpaev, who asserted that at a certain point in history, the ethnonyms *argyn* and *qarlyk* indicated the same people. Earlier we argued that northern China and Mongolia were always ruled by Turkic clans – starting with the Shang, then the Hittites or Khitan and the Huns of Modu Chanyu-Matay – right up to the middle of the 14th century (when the Chinese Ming dynasty took power).

Bilge Qaghan believed that the Turks, having conquered the Chinese, should not live among them, where they would be in constant danger of assimilation, but rather, having collected the tribute due to them, should continue to live in their habitual, austere situation, always maintaining a military configuration. And who knows how many centuries the empire of Genghis Khan would have survived if his grandson Kublai had not broken the commandment of his illustrious grandfather, who knew and respected his predecessors – Bumin Qaghan, Ilterish Qaghan, Qapaghan Qaghan, Bilge Qaghan and other outstanding leaders of the Turkic state. Incidentally, the Turkic khaganates themselves also collapsed – I will dare to suggest – at the fault of certain short-sighted khagans. S.G. Klyashtorny writes that in his proclamation to the (Chinese) throne in 629 the Chinese ruler gives various reasons for the inevitable end of the Turkic khagan; among them, 'Kheli separated himself from his Turks and put his trust in the Khu (the Sogdians); but these Sogdians are unreliable. When we send a large army, they will give him up...'.

In another chronicle of the period we read: 'Kheli always acted in ways that were beneficial to the Khu (Sogdians) while neglecting the people of his own tribe. The Khu were self-interested, arrogant and unreliable...'. Meanwhile the original home of the Sogdians was northern China (before the Common Era); later they moved to Central Asia, settling between Bukhara and Samarkand. According to Olzhas Suleimenov the Sogdians were in fact Asiatic Persians. Laypanov and Meziev meanwhile consider them to be related to the Kanly. Later the Sogdians moved back to eastern Turkestan, to what is today Mongolia (during the time of the Turkic khaganates). Some sources suggest that today's Uigurs are the descendants of the Sogdians of Central Asia.

This is what happens to a ruler who neglects his own people!

The Second Turkic Khaganate also fell, lamentable as it is to say so, through the fault of Bilge Qaghan for changing the strategy of his predecessor Qapaghan Qaghan, whose impetuous raids had kept the Tuoba in a state of permanent fear. Bilge Qaghan instead made friends with the Chinese, continually accepting generous gifts and noble brides from them. This life of plenty, however, corrupted and weakened the Turks, ultimately leaving them amid their own ruins. To be complete, one should also give an account for the fall of the Hunnic empire Modu Chanyu-Matay. The Huns' domain reached its apotheosis under Mode's grandson Gunshen Chanyu. By an agreement of 152 BCE, at the Turks' request a series of border markets were opened for exchanging goods. This was unprofitable for the Chinese, but the steppe was now amply provided with exotic and attractive Chinese goods, and moreover they could now be had without fighting. A pro-China party formed among the Huns that split the Hunnic empire into northern and southern Xiongnu in 48 CE. The rest, as they say, was technical.

Bilge Qaghan's admonition is particulary relevant in the 21st century, as the Chinese yuan actively encroaches on the economy of Kazakhstan. It does no harm to recall this harsh lesson learned by our rulers.

Generally speaking, a carrot-and-stick policy of, say, initially tempting one's neighbour and then bleeding him, was always part of the Chinese rulers' policy towards the nomads. The principle of 'divide and rule' was most current among the political heavyweights of that time. Here is how Michel Hoang describes this phenomenon in his book *Genghis Khan*: 'To gain a favourable disposition among these peoples (the Turkic nomads – K.Z.), it was sometimes enough for the Jin emperors to send their khans gifts that were rare on the steppe – various objects made in Chinese workshops (how similar this is to the present! – K.Z.). Sometimes they sent concubines with whom they were bored or princesses who had ceased to please at the court. On other occasions they handed out titles to members of the barbarian nobility (for example, the khan of the Khereid was granted the title Wang Khan, and Genghis Khan was given the insignificant title of *jautuhri* – K.Z.). This subtle politics inevitably brought compromise with it, even discrediting. It could sow implacable animosity between unconnected tribes that were then defenceless against the intrigues of Chinese diplomacy. In about 1150 the Tatar thus gave the Beijing authorities the Khereid ruler

Margus Buyrak, and then the Mongol prince Oekin-barkak, the son of the first 'unifier of the Mongols, Kublai Khan... They also handed over their powerful neighbour Ambagay Khan, the leader of the Tayichuid...'

The process of assimilation and absorption of the Turkic clans occurred on a still larger scale after the collapse of the Yuan dynasty and the accession to the throne of the Ming in 1368. For a short time the six Turkic *tumens* **together with a small number of Genghis Khan's warriors who returned after his death** were assimilated by Manchurian tribes, while **the Mongolian people itself** began to assume the name of the Khalkha Mongols from the 15th century. I have already considered the reason for the arrival of the Manchurians in Mongolia following Genghis Khan's departure with his 34 *tumens*. This is why more than 700 tribes are present in contemporary Mongolia of Tungus origin, who re-coloured the ethnic map of Genghis Khan's Mongolia from the Turkic to the Tungus-Manchurian.

Today practically any inhabitant of Mongolia will say, when asked about his ancestry, that he or she is of the Khalkha. A few minor Turkisms remain in their language, and this makes sense. **And these are the present-day Mongols whom I met in Mongolia in 2006, who do not have anything in common with Genghis Khan or the Kazakh tribes that followed him west to Central Asia and present-day Kazakhstan.**

When I shared this conclusion with Professor Bayar, he disagreed, arguing that the Manchurians had now degenerated as a people, while their pitiful remnants could be seen in the character of Dersu Uzala in the novel of the same name by the Russian author Vladimir Arsenyev. Yet how could this populous race vanish from the face of the earth if it had formed the framework of the Manchurian Qing dynasty from 1644 to 1911 in China? **The Mongols and Manchurians of the 14th-17th centuries are in principle one and the same people, who in the 21st century are known as the Khalkha Mongols. Similarly almost identical are the Kazakhs of the 21st century and the Mongols of Genghis Khan who lived on the lands of present-day Mongolia in the 12th-13th centuries.**

My conclusion is also upheld by scholars of the Institute of

Mongolian Studies, Buddhology and Tibetology of the Siberian branch of the Russian Academy of Sciences and the Institute of History, Archaeology and Ethnography of the Far Eastern branch of the Russian Academy of Sciences, (N.N. Kradin and T.D. Skrynnikova: *Imperia Chingishana*, Moscow: Vostochnaya literatura, Russian Academy of Sciences, 2006), who identify the present-day Mongolian language as Tungus-Manchurian.

Let us return on this point to Olzhas Suleimenov, who said that 'Languages are a fount of historical information that has not survived in fragmentary manuscripts. Languages are an archive that cannot burn or be lost, does not moulder and is not subject to ideological influences'. Moreover, no less than archaeological excavations, languages give immensely valuable information about civilisations that have long vanished. Continuing the poet Suleimenov's line of thought, let us also recall the famous phrase of the Soviet Russian linguist Vladislav Illich-Svitych, 'Language is a ford through the river of Time'. Indeed, when millennia separate us from the civilisation of an unfamiliar people, it is above all the language of our ancestors, and then archaeological findings, that give us the tools for understanding the past.

In further support of this idea, let me add the practical results of a genuinely outstanding discovery by the American linguist Morris Swadesh cited in the work of three Russian authors, V. Demin, Ye. Lazarev and N. Slatin, *Drevnee drevnosti: Rossiyskaia prototsivilizatsia* (Moscow: AiF Print, 2004). The essence of his revelation is that the core lexical base of a given language (as represented in his method by a 'Swadesh list' of vocabulary) changes at a roughly uniform speed: so if two languages have evolved from a common root, then after 1000 years each of them will contain 81% of the original core lexis. The rate of correspondence of the core lexis between the two descendent languages will be 66%. Developed in the 1940s, Morris Swadesh's method is still recognised by scholarship worldwide with some modifications and corrections.

Let us now consider how to apply this discovery to the matter in hand – the question of the language and ancestry of Genghis Khan.

As we established above, Mongolian scholars accept that the present-day Mongols have lost the language of the Mongols of Genghis Khan's day, though they do not like to admit that the Mongols of that time and those of the present are two entirely different ethnic groups. Why this occurred has also been discussed at some length, but I will briefly recall that the six *tumens* left behind when Genghis Khan took his other 34 units on campaign to Central Asia and Kazakhstan simply became assimilated into the large number of Tungus-Manchurian tribes that then migrated into the region from Manchuria and that now form the backbone of today's Mongols. Because of this assimilation, the modern Mongols have lost the language spoken by Genghis Khan. Now if today's Mongols were really the descendants of the Mongols of the 13th century, then, recalling Morris Swadesh's 66%, we could conclude that they would be able to understand a significant amount of the language of *The Secret History of the Mongols*, which was written in the Naiman language of 1240, in which case they would have been the actors in those epic events of history. But, sadly for the Mongols and happily for the Kazakhs, today's Mongols do not understand the language in which the monumental *Secret History of the Mongols* was written, though they would have been able to recognise at least 66% of the words in it, had they been the real descendants...

Thus we have confirmed yet again that the Mongols of the 21st century have no relation to Genghis Khan and the Mongols of the 13th century.

Let us continue to draw on Swadesh's discovery. Many leading Turkologists and orientalists, including the patriarch of the field, Rashid ad-Din Hamadani, maintain that the 13th-century Mongols and the Turkic tribes of Naiman, Kerey, Khongirad and others, who lived as neighbours, spoke the same language. I have even proposed equating the 13th-century Kazakhs with the 13th-century Mongols and equating the 13th-century Tungus Manchurian tribes with today's Mongols.

So, once again keeping in mind Swadesh's formula, let us take for example the Kazakh Kerey, today's descendants of Togrul Khan in the 13th century, and today's Mongols, who consider themselves the descendants of the Mongols of Genghis Khan's era. In accordance with the theory of Swadesh, 800 years after the moment at which the modern Mongols were separated from the so-called 'ancient Mongol' ethnos, the language of the Kazakh Kerey, whose ancestors, in the view of Mongolian scholars, were related to the ancient Mongols and the language of today's Mongols should each contain no less than 85% of known words from the original core lexis. As was pointed out before, after 1000 years a language will contain some 81% of basic vocabulary from its predecessor, while two languages evolving in parallel will share between them 66% of the basic vocabulary of the parent language. Adjusted for 800 years, these figures would then be 85% and 73%. And yet, as pointed out earlier, even vehement opponents of the view that Genghis Khan was related to the ancestors of the Kazakhs such as Karzhaubay Sartkozhauly can find a rate of only 70% – not even of direct equivalence but merely of similarity – of core words between contemporary Mongol and 13th-century Kazakh, particularly Kerey, and even that only with difficulty.

It must surely be agreed that similarity and equivalence are very different concepts. Moreover, arithmetic is an exact science, and 70% does not equal 85%.

As for correspondence **between the two modern languages**, as we have seen, according to the Swadesh formula there should be no less than 73% of common vocabulary, yet, as Sartkozhauly concludes, the two languages are completely different – the rate of correspondence is almost zero.

The crushing argument brought by arithmetic thus draws a line under the question of the language spoken by Genghis Khan's Mongols. That language was Kazakh, the same as that spoken by the ancestors of the Kazakhs in the 13th century, while the Mongols of modern Mongolia have no direct relation to the Mongols of Genghis Khan.

Many exponents of the official historical view that, say, *The Secret History of the Mongols* provides irrefutable evidence that Genghis Khan was related to the Mongols, fail to mention the most important thing – to which Mongols they are referring. Do they mean today's Mongols or those of Genghis' time? I can cite several references from *The Secret History of the Mongols* that supporters of the view that Genghis Khan was related to today's Mongols use to substantiate their argument. Thus when, for example, messengers are sent to the khan of the Kerey proclaiming that Genghis has been elected khan of his related tribes, he replies: 'It was right to make my son Temujin the qan. How can **you Mongols** live without a leader?' And another episode. When the tribes gathered at the Kurultay (council) to elect the new khan, Genghis Khan said: '[According to] **Mongqol practice**, a lord may become a beki. You are descended from the Elder Brother Ba'arin.' Or again, as cited previously, the episode in which Jamukha, Togrul and Temirshin gather to rescue Börte from the Merkit. I mean when Jamukha says: 'Even if a snowstorm stands in the way of the appointment, even if rain hinders the meeting, we [should] not be late. Did we not so agree? [When] we **Mongqols** say 'yes', are we not bound by oath?' (my emphasis in each case – K.Z.).

Let me draw our attention again to the fact that in all these instances what is meant are the Mongols of Genghis Khan's time, whom the great khan so named himself. Thus the Kazakh, Turkic tribes of the Khongirad, Dughlat, Merkit, Naiman, Jalayir, Kerey, Qiyad, Waq, Ongud, Manghud etc. **were also 'Mongols' in the 13th century,** and prior to that time had been the Celts, Cimmerians, Scythians, Saka, Aryan, Alan, Huns, Goths, Tatars and so on, and only later began to be called the Nogai and the nomad Uzbeks of the Golden Horde, and later still the Kazakhs of the Kazakh khanate. Meanwhile the Orat tribes that emerged from the forest and the arrivals from Manchuria and occupied the lands of today's Mongolia gained the happy destiny of being called the Mongols, and accordingly of being treated considerately and enjoying the glory of Genghis Khan while not having any ethnic basis for this.

It should be noted that Genghis Khan called the Turkic tribes and clans eternal (*mangi*) that he himself united under his own banner, and he affirmed this ethnonym at the *kurultay* of 1206. This name did not immediately become well known outside Mongolia and so the chronicles described here that date from that time always refer to the Mongol conquerors as Turks or Tatars.

CHAPTER IX

TURKIC MONGOLIA

The Altaic Ergenekon and the Migration Period

The sleep of reason produces monsters.
Francisco Goya

Let us now turn to another question: into what ethnic milieu was Genghis Khan born? Native Mongols generally believe that his origin was the Ergenekon – the place where, according to Rashid ad-Din Hamadani, after the Mongols had split away from certain other Turkic tribes (i.e. Hamadani regarded the Mongols as a Turkic tribe) some 700 years BCE, two Mongol men and their wives escaped to a high mountain, inaccessible to others but with favourable living conditions. One of the men was called Qiyad (or Kiyad) and the other was called Nukuz. The entire Mongol race is said to have descended from them, and it became known as the Darlekin. The Pirun Mongols were the branch of Genghis Khan and originated from Alan Gua of the Kazakh clan of the Koralas and a mythical divine light. I may suggest my idea of where the split occurred (Hamadani is silent on this point). In the 8th century BCE it is known that the Zhou dynasty that ruled China, made up of Hittites from Asia Minor of Turkic descent, collapsed under the onslaught of other Turkic nomadic groups arriving from the Eurasian steppe. The Hittites later became known as the Khitan or Ktan, the successors of whom formed a part of the Naiman union of Kazakh tribes, while another group of them took the name Kete and became part of the Kazakh Middle *jüz*; a further part of them became the Goths of Europe and the Ket or Ostyak in Siberia.

Evidently having in mind this particular page in the history of the invasions of China by Turkic tribes, Hamadani also tells the legend of the origin of the Mongols, the Darlekin of the Ergenekon.

There is currently no single opinion among scholars about the physical location of the Ergenekon. Some Mongol scholars, including Professor Bayar, believe that it was situated at the sources of the Argun river in eastern Mongolia, while others point to the very north of the country, the Hubsugul *aimag* (region); the majority, however, situate it in the high Altai, a place rich in iron ore. In my view, following losses incurred from other nomadic tribes in the 8th century BC, the Hittites/Khitan often left China and settled in the Altai mountains. In exactly the same way, and following the same route, Turks of the Ashina clan migrated to the Altai in the 5th century BC following conflicts with other Turkic tribes. In the Altai they could recover from their wounds, while also being able to manufacture iron weapons that they could later sell in order to improve their precarious economic situation. In iron production they were unsurpassed. The toponym *ergenekon* is a Turkic word that is used to mean 'stopping place', 'overnight stay'. Having regained their strength and begun to multiply in the fertile lands of the Altai mountains, the Turks began to take over other territories – precipitating the beginning of the so-called Great Migration or Migration Period.

We also know, however, that back in the 8th century BCE two cities were founded on the banks of the Amu-Darya in what is today Uzbekistan, Qiyad and Nukus. In the Soviet period Qiyad was renamed Biruni, but Nukus was unchanged; it remains today the capital of the Autonomous Republic of Karakalpakstan within Uzbekistan. It would appear that those descendants from the Ergenekon who settled in the interfluve between the Amu-Darya and the Syr-Darya named the two cities in honour of their ancestors. It would be helpful to add that the Karakalpaks, together with the three Kazakh *jüz*, the Kyrgyz and the Kurama tribal union that consists mainly of the Qiyad and Qatagan who lived primarily on the territory of Uzbekistan, together make up the major Turkic subdivision of the Alash. Today, Alash is effectively a synonym for 'Kazakh'. It should be noted that different authors have different understandings of which tribes make up both the Alash and the Kurama. For example, in the *Alash* journal in 2005 A. Kalysh made reference to A. Maksheev (1867), considering the Kurama to be made up of the Dughlat, Jalayir, Argyn, Tama, Kerderi, Jagabaili, Khereid and Teleut, all of which are part of modern-day Kazakh clans. Vasily Radlov meanwhile believes that the Kurama consist of the Tama, Jagabaili, Teleut, Jalayir and Tarakt. As for the six tribes of the Alash, in some cases the Tatar are included and elsewhere they are not.

As we have seen, Hamadani considers that the peoples who left the Ergenekon were the Qiyad and Nukuz, and today a significant question arises: from where did those tribes come to Burkhan Khaldun? I have already given my own view on this.

Muslim chroniclers such as Abu al-Ghazi Bahadur, Kadyrgali Zhalairi, Bahadur Khan and others suggest that the tribes from the Ergenekon were taken later to Burkhan Khaldun by Borte Chino of the Kazakh Koralas, Genghis Khan's ancestor by 22 generations. A purely mathematical calculation shows that over a period of 450 years the population of the Ergenekon could have reached several million; the question then arises of how a mountain valley could support so many people. The key may be in the fact that the area was rich in iron ore. According to the legend proposed by Hamadani, the people there lit a gigantic fire that caused the ore to melt and run, leaving a colossal hole, through which the people departed. This was said to be around the 4th century BCE. Here the following situation is unavoidable. If one adopts the view of the Muslim chroniclers, Genghis Khan's ancestor of 22 generations, Borte Chino, brought the people of the Ergenekon to Burkhan Khaldun in the early 7th century CE. There is thus a discrepancy in time from Hamadani's version of nearly a thousand years. This incongruity can be avoided if, as I suggest, we assume that the people Borte Chino brought with him were distant descendants of those who originally left the Ergenekon.

It was at that particular time – and this is historical fact – that the

Migration Period began, starting with populations from the Altai that migrated west, south and east. Ultimately this exodus brought them to what are now Western Asia, Asia Minor, Kazakhstan, India, the Caucasus and Europe – not to mention China, Thailand and Korea.

Mongolian scholars maintain that in roughly the 7th century, during the time of the Turkic khaganate, Burkhan Khaldun, which was the centre of the formation of the Mongol nation, was settled by the arrivals from the Ergenekon led by Borte Chino. These Mongols were called the Darlekin Mongols. Hamadani gives a table listing all the clans that came from the Ergenekon: Nukuz, Uriankhai, Khongirad, Ikiras, Olkhunut, Koralas, Eljigin, Kunkulayut, Ortaut, Konkotan, Arulat, Kilingut, Uysyn, Baya'ut, Kunjin, Suldus, Ildurkin and Kinchit (transcriptions as per Hamadani's translations – K.Z.).

Let us consider an analysis of the ethnic origin of these tribes. The Nukuz, according to Abu al-Ghazi Bahadur and Kadyrgali Zhalairi, consisted of the ancestors of the modern-day **Kazakh** Naiman, Kerey and Jalayir. The Turkic tribe of the Uriankhai, according to Hamadani and Muhamedzhan Tynyshpaev, became at some time a part of the Kazakh Kerey. Two major battle commanders descended from this tribe: Subutai and Jelme, two of Genghis Khan's closest advisors. As for the Khongirad, Ikires, Olkhunut, Koralas and Eljigin, again according to Hamadani, they all descended from three brothers: Jurluq Mergen, founder of the Khongirad, the ancestry of Genghis Khan's wife Börte; Quba Shira, the founder of the Ikires and the Olkhunut, from whom Genghis' mother Hoelun originated; and Tusbu Da'u, the father of Kunkulaidy, who married his father's widow and himself became the father of a son named Koralas, who was father to Alan-Gua. Tusbu Da'u also had another wife, Chinese in origin, who gave birth to Eljigin.

Going on, the Ortaut, Konkotan, Arulat and Kilingut descended, according to Hamadani, from the same branch and are related to Turkic tribes. For example. Tleuberdy Abenay notes that the Arulat are the remnants of the Argyn who left Mongolia before Genghis Khan, and it is from this clan that one of Genghis Khan's closest advisors came: Bo'orchu, who while still very young helped Genghis retrieve eight geldings that had been stolen from his family, and went on to become his first true companion, providing active support to the future leader on his ascent to power. Another member of this clan was Tonyukuk, the advisor to the khans of the Second Turkic Khaganate. The Ushin are without doubt today's Wusun. The Suldus and Ildurkin tribes were also related and belong, according to Hamadani, to the Baya'ut or the Bayegu, who in turn are none other than today's Bayuly, according to Abenay and other Kazakh scholars. The relatively small tribe of the Kinchit, according to Hamadani, was passed by Genghis Khan to his eldest son Jochi when the empire was divided, and its name is also Turkic.

Thus we see that all the tribes that left the Ergenekon and came to Burkhan Khaldun with Borte Chino were Turkic and many of them subsequently became part of the Kazakh people. **So Alan-Gua, travelling with her family to Burkhan Khaldun, was in the company of Turkic, Kazakh tribes, and whoever was the father of her three sons after the death of Dobun Mergen, it was almost certainly a Turk. And most likely a Kazakh.** This analysis entitles me to assert that Genghis Khan, 'the greatest Turk of all time and all peoples', as Murad Adji put it, came from a Kazakh clan.

CHAPTER X
GENGHIS KHAN IN THE CONSCIOUSNESS OF MODERN KAZAKHS

The greatest gratification for a man is to defeat his enemies,
drive them before him, take from them all that they have,
to see the tears on the faces of their loved ones, to saddle their horses
and to hold their daughters and wives in his embrace.
Genghis Khan

We will try to answer the question to which of the Kazakh clans Genghis Khan belonged a little later, and I have my views on this matter. This is necessary in order to answer another question: is Genghis Khan the ancestor of today's Mongols? In popular memory there are no doubts that he had a Kazakh ancestry – the traditions are handed down from generation to generation that he belonged to one or another of the Kazakh clans. I have written about this in previous publications. For example, in a conversation with Erkin Uanbayev, a senior professor at the East Kazakhstan State University and himself a descendant of the Merkit, he told me that the Merkit have insisted for centuries that Genghis Khan shared their ancestry.

We have examined this question above. On the other hand, the prominent writer and poet Aron Atabek gave me serious proof that Genghis Khan was from the Bersh clan, which is part of the tribal union of the Bayuly (Junior *jüz*). By way of substantiation he gave the following piece of information, which was published in the journal *Amanat* (edited by the writer Rollan Seysenbaev). Genghis Khan's banner famously displayed a gyrfalcon, which in Kazakh is *lashyn* – and the Bersh is one of 12 clans that make up the large Bayuly union, which in turn belongs within another union, the Alshyn. As an ethnonym, these two words are equivalent. A second argument consists in the fact that Genghis Khan was related to the Qiyad and also to the Borjigin; the root of the latter can also be derived from the word *bersh*. Accordingly, the Kazakhs of the Junior *jüz* obstinately believe that Genghis Khan was related to the Bersh. If we recall the sole male labourer, Ma'aliq of the Baya'ut (Bayad), who was present with Alan Gua after the death of her husband, we see that the aspirations of the Junior *jüz* to the right to Genghis Khan are eminently well-founded. Another member of the Bersh, incidentally, was the great Egyptian ruler Baibars. The Arab scholar Badr ad-Din al-Ayni (1360-1453) testified that the Mamluk Egyptian sultans Baibars (1260-1279) and Qalawun (1279-1290) 'were Kipchaks from the Brzh-ogly clan' (V.G. Tiesenhausen, *Sbornik materialov, otnosyashchikhsia k istorii Zolotoy Ordy* (vol. 1: Izvlechenia iz sochineniy arabskykh. St Petersburg, 1840).

If we consider the description of the outward appearance of the Wusun given by Chinese chroniclers – blue-eyed, tall, fair-haired, with red beards – and if we recall that Alan-Gua confessed that a strange light used to pour through the smoke-hole of her yurt at night and change into a man who matched that description, and if we take account of the fact that Alan-Gua descended from the Kazakh Koralas, related to the Dughlat (a sub-group of the Botbay), who today form part of the Wusun, then it turns out that some of the Kazakh Senior *jüz* also have no less a claim to kinship with Genghis Khan.

Nor do members of the Middle (or 'Central') *jüz* of the Kazakhs miss out on a claim to such kinship. It is known that the Qiyad, who came to Kazakhstan together with Genghis Khan, settled all over its territory and assumed various names. For example, the 19th-century Kazakh poet Abai Qunanbaiuly also mentioned the relationship of the Tobykty, to which he himself was related, to Genghis Khan's descendants. I found an explanation in the sources for why Abay thought this. It is known that during one of the raids by the Argyn led by Esim Khan in 1629 on Tashkent, where the Qatagan of Tursun Khan lived, they captured 40 girls, of whom the most beautiful, Konyrbike, was taken as a wife for Sary – a member of the Tobykty and a direct ancestor of Abai. But the Qatagan were a kindred tribe to Genghis Khan. Alan-Gua's three youngest sons were called Bukha Khatagi, Bukhatu Salji and Bodonchar. Genghis Khan's family descended from Bodonchar; from Bukha Khatagi came the Qatagan, who today live in southern Kazakhstan and Uzbekistan, and Bukhatu Salji was the ancestor of the renowned Seljuk Turks who conquered Anatolia in the 11th century. If the descendants of the Seljuks are today's Turks of Turkey, and the Qatagan are today among the Kazakhs, then who, ethnically, are the descendants of the third son Bodonchar? And which Mongols could be involved here?

As it happens, one of Abai's direct ancestors married a girl from the Qatagan clan, and she had direct kinship with Genghis Khan, and Abai thus also considered himself to belong to this clan. Today the Tobykty generally belong to the Argyn and live in the Abay district of eastern Kazakhstan, but to tell a member of the Tobykty that he is Argyn would be to make him a mortal enemy. After all, they consider themselves the direct descendants of Genghis Khan. I consider the very fact that so many Kazakh clans regard themselves, on an everyday level, to be closely related to Genghis Khan to be symbolic. And no longer can we ignore the Matai clan of the Naiman union of the Middle *jüz*. This is the only Kazakh clan whose *tamga* is a wolf, in Kazakh, *böri*. If we recall that Genghis Khan was of the Borjigin, the ethnic term of which can be interpreted as a part (*jik*) of the people of the wolf (*böri*), then the argument of this people is also highly convincing.

CHAPTER XI

MONGOLIA FROM MODU CHANYU TO GENGHIS KHAN

The Turkic state in the lands of Karakorum

He who is not predestinced to shatter rocks must kiss and fondle them.
Ancient Turkic saying

Before finally addressing the question to which modern Kazakh clan Genghis Khan is related, let us examine still a further problem: which clans were living on the territory of Mongolia from the 3rd century BC up to the time of Genghis Khan? From Baabar's *History of Mongolia* it appears that a state structure was formed in those lands for the first time in 209 BCE with the name Xiongnu. We are aware that this kingdom was created by a Turk, Modu Chanyu. The professors of history and linguistics Laypanov and Meziev, from the Caucasus, propose his other name – Matai.

Yet Baabar puts the origin of the Xiongnu in doubt – were they Turkic or Mongol? He does however recognise that the direct descendants of the Xiongnu were the Seljuk Turks who now occupy Turkey, plus the western and eastern Huns, the Turkic peoples, the Khitan, Avar, the Mongol Empire of Genghis Khan, the Golden Horde, the Ottoman Empire, Tamerlane's empire – and the modern states of Kazakhstan, Kyrgyzstan, Turkey, Azerbaijan, Turkmenistan and Mongolia.

Paradoxically, Baabar answers his question himself: the state founded by the Xiongnu was Turkic. Today this fact does not arouse the slightest doubt among scholars. So, the Xiongnu ruled for 400 years in Mongolia after Modu Chanyu (Matay). It is worth noting that after the defeats inflicted on them by the Tatar and Chinese tribe of the Donghu in the middle of the 2nd century the eastern part of the kingdom continued to call itself the Xiongnu, while those who had moved west began to call themselves Huns. And after the Xiongnu, Mongolia was ruled by the Donghu. Translated from the Chinese, *donghu* means 'eastern barbarians'. According to the investigations of Qoyshigar Salgarin, the Donghu are the Tatar (*Egemen Qazaqstan* newspaper, nos. 29, 24, 27, 2006). Muhamedzhan Tynyshpaev meanwhile divides the Tatar into three groups: the Ongud, which includes the present-day Kazakh clans the Waq, Sirgeli and Kalkaman-Karakoz within the Jappas clan, plus the Kazan Tatars; the Manghud (95% of which is the Nogai Horde, which later became completely integrated into the Kazakh khanate) and the Shurshit, also known as the Jurchen, who are today's Siberian Tatars. Incidentally, the Naiman clan of the Teristamgaly also includes a subgroup of the Shurshit.

Thus we see that the Donghu were also Turks.

In 156 CE, Baabar continues, the nomads, having united against the Xiongnu, created the state of Xianbei. According to Lev Gumilev, after its defeat the Xiongnu (whom many equate with the Huns) split into four groups; some went west and subsequently conquered Europe under the leadership of Attila, while others settled in the Seven Rivers region (Kazakhstan); a third group formed a union with the Xianbei and the fourth settled along the Great Wall of China.

It remains to be established whether the Xianbei kingdom was Turkic or Mongol. Gumilev mentions one Ashina of the Xianbei who served the Huns of Khessi (a part of western China south of the Gobi Desert and west of Ordos) (*Tysiachiletia vokrug Kaspia*, Moscow: Ayris-Press, 2003, p.166). After their country was conquered by the Tuoba, Ashina took his unit of 500 families to the Altai and began production of iron for the Rouran khaganate. So according to Gumilev, Ashina was the founder of the Turkic ethnos. Gumilev tells the legend of the she-wolf who rescues the Hun prince Ashina, who has been thrown into a lake with his hands and feet cut off. She becomes pregnant and, now in the Altai, bears the prince ten sons who become known as the 'Sons of Ashina'. These go on to be the ancestors of the entire Turkic people.

It is believed that the ethnonym *turk* derived from the Chinese *tukyu*, and reference here can be made to a chronicle of the Sui dynasty of the 7th century in which, describing the place to which the 500 families ran with Ashina, mentions that they '... settled in the mountains of the Altyn (Altai) that had the shape of helmets. Their usual word for a helmet was *tuzhie*, and so Tuzhie became the name of this people...'. In another version, however, the Turks were so called by the Arabs, meaning that they were adherents of Tengriism. Nevertheless I agree with Yuri Drozdov, who proposed a meaning from a deep historical root of a variant of the ethnonym *turk*. This was *aturgy*, meaning 'those who strike from horseback'.

As for the ethnonym *xanbei*, Gumilev states that '... in ancient times the name of this tribe was pronounced Sarbi, Sirbi, Sirvi...', but in the Chinese manner it ended up as 'Xianbei'. The conclusion then naturally arises that even the vast territory of Siberia was named in honour of the Sirbi. The root of this word is *sir*, so it may be stated unequivocally that the nomads of the Xanbei were the descendants of the Turkic Sir or Seir, who lived in western Asia in the 15th century BCE, and then in the 4th century BCE Ptolemy encountered them to the north of the Hwang Ho river.

Shakarim Kudayberdy-uly describes the Hun tribes of the Toba, Xianbei and Rouran being called Eastern Tatars (*Rodoslovnaia tiurkov, kirgizov, kazakhov i khanskikh dinastiy*, Almaty: Zhazushy, 1999, p.23). Now it is known that the Tatar Donghu tribe split into the Xianbei, Wuhuan and Toba. Thus one can say clearly that the Xianbei nation that came to replace the Xiongnu was also of Turkic descent. They were supplanted in turn in the period 345-545 by the Rouran (the latter descended from the Donghu mentioned above), to whom Gumilev refers as 'the fragments of the Xanbei Huns' (*Tysiachiletia vokrug Kaspia*, pp. 161-163). I also consider them to be tribes of Turkic origin and can give the following fact in support of this.

After their defeat by the Turks (or the Turkut, as Gumilev calls them in the plural), the Rouran moved westward and, according to the Great Soviet Encyclopaedia, created the powerful khaganate of the Eurasian Avars in the 6th century. Incidentally, Chinese sources mention the word *khan*, with its meaning of 'great leader' or 'head of a nation' as first being used by the Rouran (and this word has been Turkic from time immemorial). The descendants today of these Avars (not to be confused with the Avar of Daghestan in the Caucasus) are Germans living mainly in Bavaria and other European peoples of Turkic origin. Murad Adji, referring to the work of Orazak Ismagulov, asserts that the genotype of the people of the Altay, the Kazakhs, the Catalans, the Bavarians and the English is the same, as is also the case among many Eurasian peoples. This leads one to suggest that the ethnonym 'Albion' is linked to the Kazakh clan Alban.

Among the Argyn in the Semipalatinsk district of Kazakhstan there lives a strong-willed and historically interesting clan called the Abraly that are, in my view, indirectly related to the Avar. In old Russian chronicles the Avar are often called the Obry, and it is entirely possible that some of the Rouran, as they moved westward, settled in eastern Kazakhstan with the name Abraly and then created the Avar khaganate in Europe.

Attila's forces returned in the 540s to Mongolia having conquered all of Europe. There is a widely-held tradition that when Attila and his forces approached Rome, Pope Leo I came out to meet him together with his cardinals and the ruling emperor Valentininan. Thus the 'representative of God on earth' appealed to the conqueror to spare Rome. The Hun leader, evidently remembering the honours that had been conferred upon him in Rome and thinking of the Pope's religious feelings with respect, did not touch the Eternal City – though he did not fail to conquer the rest of Italy.

After Attila's death part of the Huns settled in western Europe and became integrated into the German, Spanish and English nations, while another group returned eastward to Mongolia. These returning Huns of Attila, who included what are today the Kazakh clans of the Argyn, Matay,

Kara-Kerey, Baganal, Baltaly, Balgaly, Koralas, Siyrshy, etc., together with the Eastern Huns who had remained there, the Xianbei, created the First Turkic Khaganate – having first expelled their relations the Rouran, who, according to Gumilev, were 'true steppe bandits' whom the local population could no longer tolerate. By the formation of this first Turkic khaganate the ethnonym 'Turk' gained official status. As for the Rouran, however, Gumilev's 'steppe bandits' whom the other tribes supposedly could not endure, there is another argument, which is that the formerly Tengriist Rouran had converted to Buddhism, and this was the reason for their being rejected from the Turkic khaganate. The ethnonym *avar*, nevertheless, which was given to the Rouran while in Europe, translates from the Turkic as 'vagabond'. **They called their former compatriots homeless vagabonds – those believers in Tengriism that had remained on the Steppe.** Whether the Avar in fact adopted Buddhism or remained worshippers of Tengri is difficult to establish today. There is however indirect evidence that they adopted the new belief system. It was the Rouran or Avar, for example, who built the city of Buda (perhaps implying 'Buddha'?) on the west bank of the Danube, while the Tengriist Turks counterbalanced this with the city of Pest on the opposite bank, which name translates (*pest* or *peysh*) from the Turkic as 'paradise'. This is the view held by Mirzabek Kargabaev and some others. Today of course the two cities are united into the Hungarian capital Budapest.

Finally, in the mid-7th century the exiles – Turkic Kazakh tribes – from the Ergenekon arrived with Borte Chino at Burkhan Khaldun, a favourable region on the plains beside the Khentii mountains. Then in the mid-9th century came Alan-Gua and her Khori-Tumata, also of Turkic descent, to the same place, and eleven generations on from this, Genghis Khan was born there. After the defeat of the Second Turkic Khaganate in 742 the territory of what is now Mongolia was ruled by the Uigur empire (until 840); after this came the empire of the Yenisei Kyrgyz, and then in the early 10th century the Naiman dynasty of the Khitan known as the Liao took power, as I earlier mentioned with reference to Gumilev. In 1125 the Liao submitted power to the Jurchen Jin dynasty; this also was not destined to last, and half a century later it was merged with the Kazakh Naiman. But not without the 'help' of Genghis Khan.

Summing up all that has been said in this chapter, we may state that throughout the 1500 years from the 3rd century BCE through to 1218, when Genghis Khan set out for Central Asia and Kazakhstan with 34 *tumens* of 'native Mongols', the lands of what is now Mongolia were inhabited by Turkic, Kazakh tribes.

So, what was the ethnic environment into which Genghis Khan was born?

CHAPTER XII
TURKIC HERALDRY AND HISTORICAL MEMORY

Let him who seeks bliss in this world occupy himself with business,
and he who seeks bliss in the next world, let him pursue moderation.
But he who wants bliss in both worlds – let him see it
through study and knowledge.
Prophet Muhammad

In this chapter I shall rely on the historical postulate that each Kazakh clan today has its own ancestral symbol, or *tamga*. The Russian Turkologist Nikolai Aristov made a study of the Turkic ancestral symbols and in his view they are symbols of ancestral ownership, that is to say, a given *tamga* is inherent to members of only one particular clan. It is by means of these symbols that an **individual** could be identified with a particular tribe or clan. As time passed, of course, certain tribes migrated and became integrated into other tribes. There is no shortage of such examples: the large modern Kazakh tribe of the Kerey comprises two clans, the Abaq-Kerey and the Ashamayly-Kerey. In ancient times, however, it consisted of six clans, including two Naiman, the Baganal and the Baltaly, one Argyn clan, the Tarakt, and the independent Middle *jüz* clan of the Waq: all these were related to the Kerey. Meanwhile still earlier, tribes related to the Kerey included the Kazakh Alban, the Yakut, the Tuvans and the Tangut..

The same may be said for the Karakesek, Taz and Khereid, which are found in both the Middle and the Junior *jüz*. So a *tamga* could gain additional symbols over time – for example there are many based on a circle, but to which various additions such as a cross, a line or other modifications have been added. These alterations can be used to trace the migration of a clan; the *tamga* of the Kerey, for example, is a cross of regular limb length, ╬, while that of the Kazakh Alban is ♀, i.e. the cross has been added to a circle, which is the symbol of the Sun and of Tengri. Murad Adji believes with good reason that the Alban were a supporting, fundamental clan that spread Tengriism among the Kazakh ancestors, just as the Khoja clan worked to spread Islam among the Kazakh tribes. Rashid ad-Din Hamadani has already noted the migration of the Alban from within the Kerey; they kept their *tamga* of a regular cross, ╬ , but added a circle to it, the symbol of Tengri. Few people are aware that the helmet of a Saka warrior found during excavations of a burial *kurgan* in Kazakhstan, also had such a regular cross marked all over it. Yet many depictions of the 'Golden Man' do not include the cross. Why? Seemingly because of a lack of knowledge among our scholars or the politicians who, sadly, still control the scholars. They usually associate the cross with Christianity, although we know, for example, that Attila's warriors approached Rome in the 5th century with banners bearing a regular cross. While Rome is now the stronghold of the Roman Catholic faith, it was pagan in those days. Its inhabitants worshiped Jupiter, Mars and other gods, but not the Christian figure of Jesus Christ. The belief in a single deity was brought to the Europeans by our ancestors, the 'wild' nomads of the Steppe.

At any rate, the ancestral sign, the *tamga*, is an unvarying constant that has not changed over time; it belongs *a priori* to only one specific clan. On the basis of this fact, Murad Adji concludes in *Tiurki i mir: Sokrovennaia istoria* that the ancestors of today's Alban, who lived in the Chu Valley long before the Common Era, travelled west on the crest of the Migration Period to create the first Turkic state in the West, Caucasian Albania, and afterwards established Ravenna in Italy and Barcelona in Spain; they participated in Anglo-Saxon campaigns and watered their horses in the Nile. Adji continues,

...And this is supported by the form of the *tamgas* of the Alban, Botbay, Siqym and other clans of the Senior *jüz*, which appear on various buildings and monuments in Caucasian Albania, Europe and the Near

East. Their symbols can also be found in North Africa, where the *tamga* of the Botbay is particularly evident. This is a cult phenomenon and wholly sacred: the sign of the ancestors! It is no coincidence that Eastern symbols appear in Western heraldry. The *tamgas* have survived like the secret of the ancient Turks, like a sign of their epoch. And no Jesuit order and no Pope is capable of erasing what has been inscribed by the Almighty. This is particularly so if one considers that the *tamga* of the Kirey [more correctly, Kerey – K.Z.], as though by irony, has become the symbol of the Order of Malta, one of the Turks' major enemies... Regrettably, nobody has so far given serious study to the history and geography of the *tamgas*. Is then the fact that nobody has paid such attention because the *tamgas* no longer belong anywhere? Yet once appeared on coins and on the signet rings of aristocrats in both East and West, identical in each. Even in signatures that were remodelled in the European manner. **This is History writ large – and unread...** (my emphasis – K.Z.).

The Turkologist Altai Amanzholov mentions that the Russian orientalist Nikolai Aristov disagreed with [the Danish Turkologist] Vilhelm Thomsen, instead supporting Franz Anton Schiefner's hypothesis that Turkic runes derived from the *tamgas*, having discovered a correspondence with Turkic *tamgas* for 29 of the 38 symbols of the Orkhon alphabet. Olzhas Suleimenov, who said that languages are an archive, a fount of historical information, asserts that the *tamgas* of many Kazakh clans were drawn from Sumerian cuneiform texts (Suleimenov, O.: *Iazyk pis'ma*, Almaty and Rome, 1998). I would add that not only the characters of the Sumerian and Orkhon alphabets but also those of the Latin and Greek share an outward similarity with the *tamgas* of Kazakh clans. Compare Σ with the *tamga* of the Alimuly, Δ with that of the Bersh and the Oshakty, and consider all the following comparisons: X – Kerey, Waq, Teleut, Y – Shaprashty, Alasha, Z – Jappas, V – Naiman, T – Balgaly, Kara Kerey, Tortkara, Shekti, Teleut, Jagabaili, П – Kara Kete, Altyn, Khongirad, P – Khoja, Baltaly, L – Siqym, O – Dughlat, Ω – Shomekey, M – Tore, etc, etc..

The oldest depiction of a *tamga* is attributed to the Huns or the Xiongnu. The Huns, who lived in what is now Mongolia, were known for 1300 years BCE. Their *tamga* was a double helix in the form of two infinity signs ‿. This is mentioned in the work of B. Kulikov, *Arabskie i persidskie istochniki po istorii kypchakov XII-XIV vv*, Alma-Ata, 1987. It is possible that the *tamgas* of the Argyn and the Wusun, including the Alban, Suan, Dughlat, Siqym, Botbay and Koralas, plus some clans of the Junior *jüz* such as the Kerderi, Tabyn and Ramadan all derived from this.

No less ancient than the Huns are the Kazakh clan known today as the Kangju, which moved to Turkestan before the Common Era from Mongolia. The *tamga* of the Kangju consists of a vertical line |, from which derived, I believe, the *tamgas* of the Kipchak | |, Khongirad П, Naiman V, Kara Sakal Λ, Jalayir m, Bersh, and Oshakty Δ, Kerey +, Shapyrashty Y, Jappas Z and others.

Many more Kazakh clans could be listed that might be identified by tracing their ancestral symbols. In that case the differentiation of the clans by region of habitation and kinship could have been done not on the basis of *jüz*, but rather on that of *tamga*. This would also be the better approach from a scholarly perspective. For today the Argyn, say, who believe themselves to belong to the Middle (*orta*) *jüz* (though note that in Kazakh, *orta* means 'central' rather than 'middle'; the word *orda* or *orta* meant the headquarters of the khans), are in fact closer – in terms of tracing their *tamga* – to their ancestors the Huns and, accordingly, to the Senior *jüz*, than they are to their supposedly related tribes of the Middle *jüz*. Interestingly, some sources refer to the Argyn as 'white Huns'. Incidentally the Jalayir, as we will demonstrate, once formed a large tribe, the Seir, together with the Naiman, but today belong to the Senior *jüz*, although its *tamga* is a downward comb of teeth, like a combination of lines, close to the *tamgas* of the Middle *jüz* clans.

Another example are the Kipchak, with which Arab, Persian and European scholars associated all Turkic populations between the Irtysh and the Danube (the Desht-i Kipchak). In his work *Kratkaia istoria Kazakhskoy tsivilizatsii* (Almaty: Arda, 2005) E. Omarov proposes (and this is worthy of attention, as also are the views put forward by Nikolai Aristov, S.G. Klyashtorny, Olzhas Suleimenov and Kalibek Daniyarov) that the Kipchak were the direct descendants of the Scythians and Saka (*skifak* = Kipchak). Interesting – if perhaps a little far-fetched. The same people, the Scythians and Saka, though it is not mentioned in the sources even in the Common Era, effectively created, for their two tribes, the *tamga* of the Kipchak – | | . Although the sources do not mention the presence of ancestral symbols among the Scythians and Saka, it seems to me that the Kangju, who migrated before the Common Era to the lands where the Saka lived, gave them their *tamga* or, on the other hand, themselves adopted the *tamga* of the Saka. I prefer the former version, since relations between the Huns and the Kangju were hostile and this hostility could be explained by the fact that their origins were different; this can be seen from the *tamga* of the Huns, based on a circle and spirals, as distinct from that of the Kangju, which features vertical lines.

As we have seen, a *tamga* can aid in establishing possible kinships, for example between the Argyn and Dughlat, whose *tamgas* are OO and O, even where the clans concerned may belong to different *jüz*. There is an analogous situation for the Kangju and the Kipchak, whose *tamgas* are respectively | and | | , but who belong to the Senior and Middle *jüz* respectively.

In this connection it is necessary to devise new principles for classifying the Kazakh clans by the degree of their closeness in terms of their ancestral signs (*tamgas*). Yet the fact that the existing *jüz* system has arbitrarily divided the Kazakh clans on an absolute basis by hierarchy does not give rise to doubts. For example, the clans of the Kara Kesek, Aday, Bersh, Jappas, Kerderi, Taz and Shekty do not agree in any way with the status of being the 'younger brothers' of all Kazakhs that is conferred on them by their belonging to the Junior *jüz*. They justifiably say that many of their clans are older and more representative than certain clans that have 'managed' to be classified in the Senior (sometimes they even use the epithet 'Great') or the Middle *jüz*. As I mentioned earlier, historically the 'orta' (so-called Middle) *jüz* meant the 'central' or main group rather than merely the in-betweeners.

An attempt at re-classifying the Kazakh clans, admittedly not on the basis of the *tamgas*, has been made by the young scholar Timur Jumaqan, who proposes the following principle for dividing them into groups. To the first group, named 'Zhogargy dala' (lit. 'Upper Steppe') he assigns the Dughlat (Dughlata), Jalayir, Sirgeli, Sary Kangju (Sary Wusun), Kara Kangju (Kara Wusun) and Qatagan. A second group, which he calls 'Orta dala' or 'Central Steppe', would include the Kerey, Kipchak, Khongirad (Khongirada), Argyn, Tarakt and Waq (Waq Kerey). The third group, 'Tomengi dala' or 'Lower Steppe' would contain the Bayuly (Aday, Altyn, Jappas, Alash (Altybas), Baybakty, Masqar, Berish, Taz, Esentemir, Ysyk, Tanga and Sherkesh (Kyzyl kurt)), Alimuly (Karasakal, Karakesek, Kete, Tortqara, Shomekey, Shekti) and Zhetiru (Kerderi, Kereyit, Tama, Zhagabayly, Tabyn, Teleut and Ramadan).

Tribes that do not belong to the above groups are related by Jumaqan to the Tore, which consists of the Elata, Kara Kerey, Karatai, Sadyr-Matai and Khoja clans.

In carefully analysing the *tamgas* of the modern-day Kazakh clans, I reached the conclusion that the overwhelming majority of them are based either on a circle in one or another form or on a vertical line – a spear or dagger – or on a combination of the two. Only an insignificant proportion (not in terms of the size or population of the clan but in terms of the number of such clans in relation to all the Kazakh clans) have different, uncharacteristic symbols. Examples include the Matai and Sadyr, whose symbol is a wolf, or the Kara Kerey, whose are the antlers of a deer or ram, and the crescent moon of the Saryzhomart. Perhaps the list of clans whose tamgas are not combinations of lines and circles is exhausted by these Naiman clans, although a crescent moon can also be associated with a circle (though admittedly only its half). As we will demonstrate below, these clans, who are assumed to have come from Western Asia and have a rich history, made up a significant proportion of the Turkic khaganates in the 6th-8th centuries in what today is Mongolia.

For example, the khans of the First Turkic Khaganate made their mark on the Orkhon-Yenisei monuments – a *tamga* in the form of a wolf – while those of the Second khaganate left their *tamga* of a wild ram (*arkhar*). According to findings by Muhamedzhan Tynyshpaev, 'Arkhar' was the *uran* (battle-cry) of the descendants of Genghis Khan (apart from the Tore within the Argyn, whose *uran* was 'Ablay' and the Tore among the Naiman, whose *uran* was 'Sankhay'). But the cry 'Arkhar', according to some sources, belonged to the Baganal clan, from whom, **in all probability**, Genghis Khan descended, with the **trident** as its tamga, Ψ. Nevertheless, the possibility of the khagans of the Second Turkic Khaganate having descended from the Kara Kerey, with the tamga of a ram's horns, cannot be ruled out. Thus it may be supposed that the leadership of the First Turkic Khaganate consisted of Kazakh Matay and Sadyr, who later combined with other related peoples to form the large tribal union known as the Naiman, while the Second Turkic Khaganate was led by either the Kara Kerey or the Baganly, which also belonged to the Naiman. Incidentally, the advisor and general to the Turkic khaganates mentioned earlier, Tonyukuk, is said by the Chinese chronicler Ma Mang Shu to have come from the Senduk clan, which later became known as the Suyunduk and became part of the Argyn. In my view the Eastern Turkic khaganates consisted primarily of what are now the Naiman, Argyn, Khongirad, Jalayir, Kerey, Kipchak and Waq. The majority of the clans of the Wusun and Kangju tribes left Mongolia and northern China before the Common Era.

As regards the tribal unions of the Alimuly and Bayuly, who lived before the Common Era in eastern Eurasia and left many toponyms there of their families (e.g. the Bersh, a tributary of the Chulym river, the Cherkish, a tributary of the Katun and Greater and Lesser Ket, near to the town of Achinsk) (compare with the names of the clans of the Alshyn tribe?), they later moved west, before Genghis Khan, excepting a few clans of the Bayuly, and joined the peoples of the ten arrows of the Western Turkic Khaganate – so runs the version related by the Orkhon-

Yenisei monuments.

According to the traditions, Genghis Khan assigned personal *tamgas* to the *beks* (commanders) closest to him. He gave, for example a *bek* from his native Qiyad–Borjigin a *tamga* in the form of a swastika, 卍 which we can see, say, on the Registan and other Timurid monuments of Samarkand; he gave Sengel of the Khongirad a (half-moon *tamga*, and others to the ≪≪≪ Wusun Mayqy bek, Kipchak bek, ﻭﻭ Tamian Bek ↻ and so on. I would not be surprised if Adolf Hitler had wanted to follow in Genghis Khan's footsteps and become a Great Terror of the Universe in his own right, to which end he appropriated the swastika of the Qiyad Borjigin in imitation of the Mongol leader. The swastika was also the ancient symbol of the Aryans, whose purity as a race was one of the Nazi dictator's obsessions. We should also note that the fact that the Qiyad Borjigin had a swastika for its *tamga* is evidence that the Mongols of Genghis Khan were related to the ancient Turanian race of Aryans of the Great Steppe.

Mongol clans, by contrast, do not have differentiating symbols or *tamgas*. Mongolian scholars say that they were thought to once have had them, but that they were subsequently forgotten. In my view, however, which I stated earlier, if they did have them, then these clans were Turkic, Kazakh clans. But after Genghis Khan departed with his 34 *tumens*, leaving behind only six, the latter were assimilated into the many Manchurian tribes and all but vanished, losing their language and culture, including their ancestral symbols.

CHAPTER XIII
UNDER THE SIGN OF THE TRIDENT

Follow your own road, and let the people talk.
Dante Alighieri

As pointed out earlier, the *tamga* of the clan of Genghis Khan was a trident, in which the prongs pointed downwards. It was shown on his banner and his personal standard, as is illustrated elsewhere in this book.

An article by Talas Omarbekov and Kh. Kabzhalilov, 'O rodovykh znakakh drevnikh tiurkov i kazakhov' (*Alash* journal, 2005, no. 1) includes an appended table of Kazakh ancestral symbols compiled by Amanzholov, Tynyshpaev, Dobromyslov, Kharuzin, Kazantsev, Levshin and other scholars of Turkic and Kazakh peoples. After carefully studying these symbols and comparing them to the *tamga* of Genghis Khan, I came to the conclusion that Genghis Khan might have belonged to one of the following Kazakh clans. First among these would be the Baganal, which is today a part of the Saryzhomart, in turn a component of the Naiman union.

A second possibility is that he could have belonged to one of the clans that are today in the Junior *jüz* and collectively known as the Zhetyru. These are the Tama and the Tabyn. In his most recent work, *Istoria Alash* (Almaty, 2006), Kalibek Daniyarov showed that *zhetyru* is a tribal union that consists of 7 clans, all of whom belonged to the Qiyad and thus were descended from Genghis Khan.

When the sons and descendants of Genghis Khan moved and settled across the vast distances of the Eurasian steppe, his closest relatives naturally always tried to stay close to the khan, and so they spread across the huge spaces in small groups. This led to the danger of assimilation by large clans such as the Naiman, Argyn, Dughlat and so on. To avoid this, in the early 18th century the wise Tauke Khan, remembering his filial duty, gathered the seven small clans closely related to Genghis together into a union, which he called the Zhetyru. So the Tama and the Tabyn belong to this tribal union and have a similar *tamga* to that of Genghis Khan; in my view they may also have a relationship of kinship with him.

The Senior *jüz* clan of the Sirgeli, which once belonged to the Ongud and later to the Waq, at some point became part of the union of the Kerey along with the Baganal. Here also was the Middle *jüz* clan of the Tarakt, which now is part of the Argyn. The Sirgeli and Tarakt have similar *tamgas* to that of the Baganal. This can partly be explained, since they were all once part of the same union, the Kerey. And finally, as has been much discussed and many volumes written in recent times, Genghis Khan could have belonged to the Jalayir with its *tamga* of a downward comb of teeth. **The Kazakhs have a belief that a festive** ***dastarkhan*** **(feast) for a special occasion should begin only a blessing has been given by an elder of the Jalayir clan. Note that the members of the Tore – Genghis Khan's own clan – remain to one side.**

While I was in Mongolia I familiarised myself with the standard of Genghis Khan. From the moment of his being proclaimed khan, his standard – his *sulde* (the Mongolians believed that the leader's spirit and ability to act were embodied in his standard) – could be found erected outside his yurt. The design featured a trident, beneath which hung nine bundles of yaks'-tail hair. During times of war a black *sulde* stood outside Genghis' yurt, while during peacetime a white standard was used. Analogously to a modern-day president's standard, the *sulde* was a symbol of power. The upward-pointing trident was also Genghis Khan's ancestral symbol, and this symbol crowns the stele that has been built over Genghis Khan's birthplace. And the same symbol is used today in the coat of arms of Ukraine.

For now, however, let us return to the symbol that allowed the scope of the search to be narrowed, eliminating clans that did not have a similar sign in their *tamgas*. Clans with symbols that have correspondence with Genghis Khan's *tamga*, as noted above, are the Baganal, Jalayir, Sirgeli, Shanyshkyly, Tama, Tabyn and the Tarakt. The *tamga* of the Tarakt (*taraq* translates from Kazakh as 'comb' – K.Z.) is a bold comb arranged with its teeth downwards; the Tabyn and Tama also have a comb, but together with this *tamga* they also have several others, which indicates that they have been linked to different, larger tribal unions at different times. The ancestral symbol of the Sirgeli has similarities to the *tamga* of Genghis Khan but, as was pointed out above, at one point the Sirgeli and the Baganal formed part of a Khereid union of tribes, and in addition, the Sirgeli have a further eight ancestral symbols. It is therefore unlikely, though not impossible, that the Tarakt, Tabyn, Tama and Sirgeli are kindred to the tribe of Genghis Khan. We will discuss the Shanyshkyly separately; but for now we will discuss the Jalayir.

Let us return to Tleuberdy Abenay's article in the journal *Zhuldyz*, 2006 no. 1, which at that time was edited by the prominent Kazakh writer Mukhtar Magauin (who incidentally occupies a firm principial position with regard to the clan allegiances of Genghis Khan, certain of his Kazakh roots and logically therefore an opponent to the well-known writer and poet Mukhtar Shakhanov.) So, the author of the article, Tleuberdy Abenay (himself a Kazakh of Chinese origin, a highly erudite man who draws on knowledge gained from working with sources in Chinese libraries) proposes the scenario of Genghis Khan being descended from the Jalayir. In this connection he considers the Jalayir *tamga* – the comb pointing down – to be identical with Genghis Khan's *tamga* of a trident Ψ with its teeth pointing upward. But it is not the same thing. For example, the *tamga* of the Naiman is **V**, but the sign inverted, Λ, now looks like the *tamga* of the Junior *jüz* clan of the Kara Sakal. Abenay considers the fact that Genghis Khan's *anda* (boyhood friend) Jamukha was related to the Jalayir as further proof of his hypothesis; and consequently, since he was related by blood (in his opinion – K.Z.) to Genghis Khan, it follows that Genghis was also descended from the

Jalayir. However, it is known that Jamukha descended from an ancestor who was born of a woman whom Bodonchar had captured and taken as a concubine while already pregnant, while Genghis Khan was born of a different ancestor – also born of one of Bodonchar's women, but in this case a lawful wife. It follows that the fathers and mothers of Genghis and Jamukha came from different clans.

In more detail: when a foreign camp appeared by Burkhan Khaldun, where the Dobun Mergen clan roamed near the source of the Onon river, Bodonchar and two of his elder brothers committed an act of *barymta* (a raid, common among the Kazakh ancestors, the purpose of which was to seize property and cattle from the strangers) and took the incomers prisoner. The pregnant woman whom Bodonchar took as a concubine appeared to be Uriankhai but said she was of the Jatjurt or Jajiradai, which translates from the Kazakh as 'foreign tribe'. She gave birth to a boy and called him the same name, Jajiradai. She also bore Bodonchar another son whom they called Baaridai, meaning 'born as a result of an act of *barymta*'. Bodonchar meanwhile had also taken a lawful wife and fathered his firstborn, his successor, Qabichi, from whom stemmed the clan of Genghis Khan. From Jajiradai came the clan of Jamukha, and from Baaridai descended the large clan of the Baarin.

I am thus prepared to accept that Jajiradai's father could be a member of the Jalayir, but there is no way that Jamukha and Genghis Khan could be from the same clan because, to repeat, a strange people arrived in the lands of the Dobun Mergen; as 'trespassers' it was permitted to local tribes to plunder these strangers and take their people by force. This is mentioned in both *The Secret History of the Mongols* and in Rashid ad-Din Hamadani's writings.

Thirdly, according to Tleuberdy Abenay, is a detail described by Marco Polo, who lived for 17 years in the camp of Kublai Khan: from the milk of ten thousand snow-white mares was prepared a miracle-working drink, *kumys*, which was permitted only to the direct descendants of Genghis Khan and members of the Jalayir to drink. If one reads Marco Polo's *Livres des merveilles du monde* carefully, however, we see that '... On the twenty second of August, always this day, the great khan [Kublai] rides out from that city and that palace, and this is the reason: he has a stock of white horses and white mares, white as snow, without any blemish, and a great number of them, more than ten thousand mares. Nobody is permitted to drink the milk of these mares except members of the royal clan, that is, of the clan of the great khan; also allowed to drink this milk are the Goriat [i.e. Oirat – K.Z.]; they had such respect from Genghis Khan for having once helped him to victory' (*Kniga o raznoobrazii mira*, Almaty: Kochevnik, 2005, p. 101). **While not fully in agreement with Marco Polo, specifically with his interpretation of particular reverence by Genghis Khan towards the Oirat for having supposedly helped him secure a victory at some point**, I would add that as we established earlier in this book, the Oirat descended from the sons of Duwa-soqor, the brother of Dobun Mergen, by whom Alan Gua bore two sons (but not the sons from whom descended the Nirun Mongols, including the generation of Genghis Khan himself). As Hamadani states, Dobun Mergen and Duwa-soqor were of the Qiyad, but from Khabul Khan onwards all descendants of the Nirun Mongols were considered to belong to the Qiyad. It was because of these circumstances that Genghis Khan showed special respect for the Oirat as very closely related, and created the special exception for them that allowed them to drink the *kumys* of the snow-white mares.

In a word, the Jalayir, contrary to Abenay's assertions, did not have access to the royal *kumys* on equal terms with the imperial household. The reasons for this will be explained below. But such are Abenay's arguments for the Jalayir.

Let us now turn to the leading exponent of Mongol studies, Boris Vladimirtsev:

In the 12th and 13th centuries what was called an *obokh* or clan represented a complex unity. The *obokh* consisted in the first instance of persons with blood ties; then came the *unagan bogol* or feudal vassals, and after these the 'ordinary' servants, *ötöle bogol* and *jalau*. Consequently the clan contained multiple social groups; one might even speak of two social classes, the upper of which consisted of the blood relatives (holders of kinship or *urux*) plus the more prominent and better-off of the vassals, while lesser vassals and servants belonged to the lower class. Some were *noyad*, 'lords', others were *xaracu*, 'black' or 'common people', while others again were *bogol cud*, 'slaves'. (*Obshchestvenniy stroy mongolov. Mongol'skiy kochevoy feodalizm*, Leningrad, 1934)

Concerning the Jalayir, let me provide some information from Hamadani's *Compendium of Chronicles*, where he mentions that when Genghis Khan wanted to make the two Jalayir, Ukha Qalja and Qarasha, into senior emirs, they said that Yesugei, Genghis' father, had commanded them to watch over the sheep, and Genghis Khan abandoned his intention (*Sbornik letopisey* vol. 1, book 1, p. 97). Hamadani states (*ibid*, p. 92 and in vol. 2, p. 150) that the Jalayir had been *ungun bogol* to Genghis Khan's clan, that is, 'trusted slaves', ever since Kaidu Khan, seven generations before Genghis Khan himself. Going on these facts, it can be established that at that time the Jalayir were still in hereditary service to the Qiyad Borjigin. In this sense it is simply not possible to suggest that Genghis Khan descended from this clan, although he **might** have a close relationship to it, for the Balgaly, who today are part of the Jalayir, are closely related to members of the Baganal, from whom Genghis Khan himself **may** have descended. The Baganal are part of the tribe of the Naiman, while the Jalayir and Naiman belonged until the mid-7th century to the large tribal union of the Seir-Sir.

In part 137 of *The Secret History of the Mongols*, the Jalayir Gü'ün brings two of his sons, Muqali and Buqa, to Genghis Khan as servants and says to him:

Let them be the slaves
at your threshold.
Should they escape your threshold,
slice [the sinews of] their heels.
Let them be the slaves
of your felt-door.
Should they depart

from your felt-door,
cut out their livers and cast them out.
Spot on, so to speak. So everything is in its rightful place. **Genghis Khan could not have been of the Jalayir, and what I mentioned about the Jalayir having a special place at the festive table came about at a later time.**

***

What we have said about the trident being an ancestral symbol among the ancient Turks would be incomplete if we did not also mention its use in the modern-day heraldic symbol of Ukraine, and which was inherited from the old state of Kievan Rus'.

According to the Norseman theory that arose in the early 18th century, the Slavs of Novgorod, together with the Krivich, the Merya, the Ves' and the Chud called upon the brothers of Rurik, Sineus and Truvor of the Swedish Varangian tribe, to rule over the Slavic lands. They came from the Swedish tribe called Rus and, consequently, the united state over which Rurik ruled was called Rus. Despite Mikhail Lomonosov's opposition, the 'Norsemen theory' was adopted by the Russian Academy of Sciences and to this day has not been rejected. Another Norse theory appeared later, in which Rurik was written Rorekh and he was Danish by origin, but in the Annals of St Bertin he is unflatteringly described as a pirate and a bandit.

I tend towards to the second version as well as the first, whereby Rurik was Danish – a nation that according to Murad Adji was called the Cumans and the Kipchaks in the Middle Ages. That is, the Danish had a Turkic origin and they came as it were to Kievan Rus' with Rorekh and ruled it. As to whether the local population was in favour of their rule or against it, this is no longer of relevance for our purposes.

Here we might recall lines of the poet Sergei Markov, one of the founders of the *Sibirskaia brigada* ('Siberian Brigade') literary movement in Moscow in the 1930s, which was joined by the talented self-styled 'Russian Asiatic' Pavel Vasiliev and his Kazakh friends, here mentioning the early Russian epic *Slovo o polku Igoreve* ('The Tale of Igor's Campaign'):

In the immortal *Slovo o polku*
Like lush greenery,
Grew up among the Slavic strophes
Words of the Kipchak.

An organic outlook on the world, an inherent poetic awareness and a fine feel for language have in no way deceived this poet who absorbed the culture of steppe civilisations along with his mother's milk.

Bagitzhan Adilov has expressed a familiar point of view in his work *Dolgaia pesn' argunov ili gunni zagovorili* (Almaty: Olke, 2006) – that the Varangians were of Turkic Kipchak origin, and gives convincing evidence of his view with data from a catalogue of Russian surnames of noble descent (N. Baskakov, *Russkie familii dvorianskogo proiskhozhdenia*, Moscow, 1979). The list of such names that have Turkic and Varangian roots is long: Saburov, Mansurov, Godunov, Glinsky, Kurakin, Yermolov, Cherkassky, Ushakov, Suvorov, Apraksin, Yusupov, Arakcheev, Urusov, Aksakov, Musin-Pushkin, Golenishchev-Kutuzov, Akhmatov, Berdiaev, Turgenev, Kornilov, Sheremetiev and so on. Lev Gumilev adds more surnames that are no less famous: Aliabiev, Arseniev, Babichev, Balashov, Baranov, Basmanov, Baturin, Beketov, Bibikov, Bilbasov, Bichurin, Boborykin, Bulgakov, Bunin, Burtsev, Buturlin, Bukharin, Beliaminov, Gogol', Gorchakov, Gorshkov, Derzhavin, Yepanchin, Yermolaev, Izmaylov, Kantemirov, Karamazov, Karamzin, Kireevsky, Korsakov, Kochubei, Kropotkin, Kurbatov, Miliukov, Michurin, Rakhmaninov, Saltykov, Stroganov, Tagantsev, Talyzin, Taneev, Tatishchev, Timashev, Timiriazev, Tretiakov, Turchaninov, Tiutchev, Uvarov, Khanykov, Chaadaev, Shakhovsky, Shishkov.

The preface to Adilov's book was written by Olzhas Suleimenov. I would like to mention a curious incident connected with the launch of this book and Bagitzhan Adilov's work. I gave him access to a sculpture workshop located within one of the accommodation buildings of our institute, and here he created a magnificent composition dedicated to Attila. One day he telephoned me anxiously, saying that Olzhas

Suleimenov would be visiting him at the studio in a few minutes. Aware that, to put it kindly, our student lodgings are not up to the European standards to which this master of Soviet, then Kazakh and if you like, world poetry had grown accustomed, I asked Adilov to explain that the building belonged to a certain vocational college. This incident was subsequently immortalised by our great poet in his preface to Adilov's book: 'I went into his workshop, along the basement corridors of some college on the outskirts of town. The kindly director (me – the rector – K.Z.) had allocated him (temporarily) a small space (10 square metres). Unrendered, raw concrete walls and a low ceiling. On the floor was the sculptural ensemble in green plasticine. Human figures and horses: 'Attila and his sons'. He plans to erect these – as bronze statues – opposite the presidential palace in Astana...'

Adilov has shot to stardom, as they say – admittedly by having the rector turn himself voluntarily into the director of a humble vocational college – but I am certain that his statues, not only of Attila but also of Genghis Khan, will appear in bronze in our capital, our 'Northern Palmyra'.

But let us return to Kievan Rus. The history of the surnames listed above is truly old; their roots go back to the time of the Kievan princes, and so I doubt that it will be unduly surprising to propose that, admittedly a little later, the Kievan throne was taken by the ancestors of today's Kazakh clans – who may have been those very Scandinavian Varangians who had migrated there during the early Middle Ages from the Azov and Black Sea steppes.

We know from the *Primary Chronicle* (*Povest' veremennykh let*) – a history of Kievan Rus compiled in the early 12th century – that Rurik initially made Novgorod the capital of his kingdom, but later his successor Oleg moved the capital to Kiev and established the state of Kievan Rus. In a work on Rurik and his successors V. Kogan and V. Dombrovsky-Shalagin provide the arms of ancient Novgorod – a throne, surrounded by bears, on which can clearly be seen a trident – the *tamga* of the clan of the rulers of Kievan Rus (*Kniaz' Riurik i yego potomki. Istoriko-genealogichesky svod*. St Petersburg: Paritet, 2004, p. 94). Incidentally, while I was in Egypt in January 2007 I visited an Orthodox church dedicated to St Catherine on the Sinai Peninsula, where Moses was said to have received the Ten Commandments. On the iconostasis in the church was clearly shown a trident, executed to a high artistic standard and accompanied by a serpent, dragons and the Christian cross. Until it was settled by Jews and Arabs the Sinai Peninsula had been inhabited by Turkic tribes – as discussed in Part 1 of this book.

Alexei Bychkov mentions a sarcophagus containing sacred relics of the Kievan prince Vladimir Monomakh, discovered during excavations of the ruins of the Church of the Tithes in Kiev in 1635 (*Kievskaia Rus'. Strana, kotoroy nikogda ne bylo?* Moscow: Astrel, 2005, pp. 236–237). The inscriptions on the sarcophagus testify that the bones of the holy Vladimir were laid in it together with those of his wife, the Greek princess Anna. Yet this relic with its inscriptions not in the Slavonic language has since vanished without trace. Who would have taken it? And what was the language in which the inscriptions were written? Presumably a Turkic language – which the later rulers of Russia fervently disowned, beginning with Peter the Great.

Bychkov's book also includes texts from Russian chronicles and Scandinavian sagas from which it can be seen that the rulers of the Huns, the Swedes and the Russians were all known by the same title – *konung*. **Yuri Drozdov has deciphered this title from the Turkic as *kong ong* (lit. 'become the right', i.e. 'assume the head of the structure or the people'.** Citing the orientalist Vasily Bartold, Shamkhurat Kuanganov writes: 'We know from the Russian chronicles that some Slavic peoples paid tribute to the Khazar khan in the later 9th century. How far his influence extended can be seem from the fact that the Russian prince, living far to the north near Novgorod, **when the Russians were still Norse and still spoke Swedish, used the title of khagan...**' (*Ariy-gunn skvoz' veka i prostranstvo: svidetel'stva, toponimy*, Astana: Foliant, 2001, p. 169; my emphasis – K.Z.). Vasily Bartold surely realised that at that time the Russians and Turks were ethnically **related** and spoke the same Turkic language, which was also used by the Swedes of the time, though this was evidently too bold an idea for his time. In his 'Sermon on Law and Grace' that appeared in the 11th century, Metropolitan Hilarion of Kiev wrote of 'the great and wondrous doings of our teacher and mentor, the great **khagan** of our land, Vladimir...' (my emphasis – K.Z.). Alexei Bychkov meanwhile cites (*op. cit.*, p. 313) a description by Abu Hamid ar-Rahim al-Garnati al-Andalusi when he stayed in Kiev from 1131 to 1153: 'And I came to the city of the land of the Slavs that is called Kiev. And in it are thousands of people of the *maghrib* [west], Turkic in appearance, who speak a Turkic language.' On page 319 of the same work is a drawing of the helmet of Alexander Nevsky, on which the renowned armourer Nikita Davydov had inscribed Arabic text from the 13th *ayat* of the 61st *sura* of the Qur'an. And I would point out at this stage that the title of the Turkic khans, 'khagan', means 'heavenly khan' (*kok han*)._

I believe that I have given sufficient examples of the presence of the Turks and Turkisms in the domestic and cultural life of not only Rus but of many European countries as well. But where are the contemporary Mongols? If Genghis Khan really was the ancestor of the modern Mongols and, accordingly, his son Jochi and grandson Batu (who subdued Rus to his will) were also Mongols, then considering that something over two hundred years of Russian history, from the 13th to the 15th centuries, cannot be separated from the Golden Horde, then this should surely have left residual Mongol words and surnames in use in the Russian language. But there are none; however much you search in dictionaries of Russian, such terms are simply not to be found. New vocabulary associated with this period did enter the language, but it was all Turkic. So, judge for yourself from these examples: *ataman, karakul, kolchan, yesaul, bunchuk, oblava, bulat, nagayka, bazar, magazin, tovar, altyn, bezmen, ambar, arshin, kirpich, fitil', telega, kovyor, tiufiak, utiug, karandash, kolbasa, kaftan, khalat, shuba, tulul, sarafan, armiak, bashlyk* and many more. A total of over 250 borrowings by Russian from the Turkic language are included in Mark Fasmer's etymological dictionary. Konstantin Penzev states in his work *Russky Tsar' Baty* (Moscow: Algoritm, 2006) that even if such Mongol words as *dokha* or *malakhay* were used in Russian today, then this would not be thanks to the Mongols but rather to the Kalmyk who lived from the late 16th century on the Volga. It should be clarified that the Kalmyk comprise the Torghut clan of the large Oirat tribe, which, as we demonstrated earlier, has no relationship to **today's** Mongols.

In one of Olzhas Suleimenov's last works, the well-reasoned *Tiurki v doistorii* (Almaty: Atamura, 2002), which makes a logical continuation to his brilliant *AZiYA* (1975), gives a list of 200 words of modern Russian that are borrowed from the Turkic and Kazakh language – and this only confirms what he writes, that is, 'the inescapable conclusion is that to accumulate so many loan words for 'three centuries under the yoke' would have been impossible. A thousand years would have been needed...'.

As regards AZiYA, this is recognised by many politologists as being one of the few phenomena that blew the USSR apart from within and ultimately overturned that once powerful state.

Here are a few of the words from Suleimenov's list: *utro, iarko, osen', tayga, tuman, ovrag, sobaka, sled, volk, shakal, sarancha, pauk, tvar', oriol, berkut, chayka, sevriuga, sazan, iasen', cheremukha, orekh, soloma, seno, pshenitsa, loshad', tabun, bulany, bury, kariy, aly, savrasy, bagrovy, tavro, iarmo, ruzh'io, sablia, kinzhal, molot, chugun, latun, svinets, zhest', kuzov, tabor, balagan, shalash, izba, ochag, skovoroda, shkvarki, bogatyr', boiarin, tovarishch, shayka, orda, bulava, kuter'ma, oblava, ura, shal', kolpak, kaftan, rubakha, shtany, sharovary, karman, kiset, igla, tamga, khoziain, bakaleia, poltina, den'ga, ser'ga, zhemchug, almaz, iakhont, iashma, bolvan, balbes, durak, upyr', stakan, chasha, chay, baraban, ulika, vor, griaz', bumaga, bukva, pis'mo, kniga, iazyk.*

And there are plenty more such words, and they are commonly used in everyday situations.

Let us return to Vasily Bartoldy, who said that in the 9th century the Rus people lived in Scandinavia and their ruler had the title of khagan. In the chapter 'Scythian Rus: who came first?' in *Under the wolf's nest: a Turkic rhapsody* I wrote that in about 120 BCE the ancestors of the

Rus migrated from Gansu province in China to the Seven Rivers region of what is now Kazakhstan, before later moving on to the Caspian and Black Sea steppes – and a part of them went further, to Scandinavia. Referring to various sources, I said that the Rus were a Turkic-speaking tribe. I would now add that according to the Khivan Bahadur Khan, the sons of Japheth, that is, the grandsons of Noah, were Turk, Rus, Khazar and others. In the third volume of his work, oft-cited in this book, *Turan: Vzglyad na istoriu chelovecheskogo obshchestva*, Zhumazhan Bayzhumin mentions that the Byzantine historians Constantine VII, Anna Komnene, Leo the Deacon and John Kinnamos wrote of the Rus as of the Scythians and the steppe nomads; that the Arab scholar Abd ar-Rashid al-Bakuwi referred to the steppe Turks as Rus; that the Syrian chronicler Zacharias Rhetor (of Mytilene) mentioned that the 'Ros' people could be found in the northern Caucasus and Azov and Black Sea steppe regions; that August Ludwig von Schlözer concluded that the Rus of the 9th century were Turanian nomads, and so on (see the chapter 'Tiurkskie kochevniki i Kievskaia Rus', pp. 96-138).

It can thus be stated that at the start of the first millennium CE the Turkic-speaking Rus people were living in the Azov and Black Sea steppe regions, which at the time were part of Old Great Bulgaria and later the kingdom of Khazaria.

After the collapse of Old Great Bulgaria in 640 with its capital at Phanagoria (modern-day Taman), one of the sons of Khan Kubrat – the last khan of Old Great Bulgaria – named Asparukh moved to the Danube and founded what is modern Bulgaria, while another son, Kotrak, migrated first to the Kama river area in the Ural and later to Scandinavia. A third son, Botbay, remained in Khazaria and his descendants became the ancestors of the large Kazakh tribe of the Botbay. We can thus note that some of the Rus derived from Kotrak's people from Scandinavia, but then, as Zhumazhan Bayzhumin puts it, '... a centralised royal power began to form in the Scandinavian lands, accompanied by an active conversion to Christianity of the northern Germanic peoples... for most of the members of the Norse-Germanic nobility, who traced their ancestry to the Turkic nomads... the meek and submissive life of a Christian landowner was wholly unacceptable...'. Thus there arose the Varangian Rus, who, according to the Norseman theory, were present at the formation of Kievan Rus. If this is so, then, as will be shown in the next chapter, the Kazakh clan of the Baganal with its trident *tamga*, who lived in the Baltic regions, was able to become the ruling power in the first Russian state.

Additionally, Bayzhumin gives credible arguments that the first great Russian princes were not the Turkic Rus of Scandinavia but of their relations, the Turkic Rus of the Azov steppe, who had remained with Botbay when he took power in Khazaria.

His principal arguments are the following. At the end of the 7th century the early Eastern Slavic princedoms of Right-bank Ukraine were fully submitted to the Khazars. The 'Patriarch of Russian History' Nikolai Karamzin stated unambiguously that 'Kiev belonged at that time to the Kozars' (*Istoria gosudarstva Rossiyskogo*, Moscow and St Petersburg, 2003, vol. 1). Here he quotes the 11th-century Nestor the Chronicler on how the Khazars levied tax from Kiev. Describing a later time, when the Varangian Rus arrived at Kiev, Karamzin points out that 'It is unlikely that the Khazars, having taken tribute from Kiev, would willingly have ceded this to the Varangians, though the Chronicler is silent on the military activities of Askold and Dir in the Dniepr country...'. On this point Bayzhumin notes that '...it was neither a voluntary surrendering of Kiev to the Varangians nor war between the Khazars and the Varangians. Had there been even a single battle, in which the Varangians gained the upper hand over the Khazars, it would certainly have been recorded in all the old Russian chronicles.'

So what actually happened? Bayzhumin maintains, and I agree with him, that the Khazars in Kiev appointed their *tudun* (local governor) from the Rus clan, and at the time under consideration this was Oleg, or Ulug in Turkic, but certainly not the Scandinavian Helg as supporters of the Norsemen theory assume. As the Turkic language evolved, there was a tendency to discard the velar syllable 'g', and so Ulug shifted towards what is now Uly – meaning 'great'. The Varangian Rus of Scandinavia, related to the Khazarian Rus as discussed above, were drawn towards the government of the Kievan state, but primarily at a middle-management level – collecting taxes, and serving as warriors in private armies. After Khazaria weakened and collapsed it was taken by the Pechenegs, this tradition continues, and after Oleg came his son Igor, to whom, as tradition has it, the daughter of the leader of the Pechenegs was given in marriage. The name Igor, incidentally, Bayzhumin suggests is not the Scandinavian Ingvar but rather a modified Turkic word *igeru*, which has the senses 'to reach', 'to achieve', 'to possess'. Thus the rulers of Kiev, and later of Moscow, were true Rus but of Turkic origin.

In the first edition of this book I wrote that the Taman Peninsula in the Azov region was so called because of the presence of Kazakh ancestors by the name of Tama, whose *tamga* was a comb (not a trident!). Bayzhumin supposes that at that time this clan was part of the tribal union of the Rus, and Oleg, Igor and others were members of it. It may well have been so, but all the same, the trident of Kievan Rus and the comb of the Tama are not the same thing. The version I prefer is that some of the Baganal, who had been part of the Scandinavian Rus, remained in Khazaria and the khagans of the Itil delegated members of these Baganal Rus, with the trident *tamga*, to govern Kiev.

CHAPTER XIV
GENGHIS KHAN AND THE KAZAKH BORJIGIN

Even the gods cannot strive against necessity.
Pittacus of Mytilene

Much of the specialist literature is of the view that Genghis Khan fought a bitter war with the Kazakh Naiman, this being one of the largest Kazakh tribes, with its own nationhood, its own khan, and thereby represented one of the main enemies or competitors to Genghis' striving for power. It is most likely, some claim, that in the 12th century the Naiman destroyed the greater part of the Qiyad Borjigin. If this was the case, though it is unlikely, then such an annihilation would have been carried out by the **future** Khitan wing of the Naiman that ruled in northern China from 926 to 1125, created the Liao dynasty and united with the Naiman in the second half of the 12th century.

Let us try to substantiate a somewhat different perspective on the relationship between Genghis Khan and the Naiman. I have already mentioned Aleksandr Domanin's view that the Naiman was the most enigmatic of the nomadic tribes in the 12th century, with its own highly-developed culture, while all other tribes with a clan structure were at a much lower stage of development. Also in this book I have substantiated the thesis that the Naiman gradually absorbed into itself the powerful Khitan and Jurchen that had always dominated Eastern Asia. There is a popular phrase in the Turkic world: *Qalyn naiman – qytayga qanat zhaygan*, which translates literally as 'the multitudinous Naiman spread their wings over great China'.

Because of this, there may at first sight appear to be a contradiction in my reasoning and conclusion about Genghis Khan being descended from the clan of the **modern** Naiman tribal union. On the one hand, Genghis Khan could be from the Kazakh Baganal or Matai, both of which are today part of the Naiman, but on the other hand, the Naiman were supposedly in a state of implacable opposition to Genghis Khan.

So what really happened?

Load-bearing and supporting... the Kazakh Baltaly-Baganly
The Baltic Vikings... the Kazakh Qoralasy-Kurshi

Qara Balta naymanym – qayran elim
Kazakh saying

I believe that in the 5th to 4th centuries BCE the Baganal, to whom according to one version Genghis Khan might have belonged, and which at that time was part of the large tribal union of the Qiyad and Nukuz, had joined the Naiman at Burkhan Khaldun, exercising its rights as *unagan bogol* ('slaves in attendance'), in Boris Vladimirtsev's terminology, but Genghis Khan, for all the exceptional possibilities open to him, could not become khan of all Naiman by descent. Only by circumstances such as this can Genghis' irreconcilable position towards the dynasty of the Naiman khans be explained. The first task he set his general Jebe after being proclaimed khan in 1206, after all, was to ensure the physical liquidation of Kuchlug, successor to the Naiman throne, since Genghis' power would have no legitimacy if a prince of the khan's blood line were present, yet the majority of the clans he had subjugated consisted of families that belonged to the Naiman tribal union.

A parallel situation may be seen in considering the underlying reason for the reprisals by the victorious Bolsheviks under Vladimir Ulyanov (Lenin) against the deposed Tsar Nicholas II and his family in the 1917 Russian Revolution. The Russian people would never have recognised the legitimacy of Lenin if members of the imperial family, deemed by many to be divinely appointed, had still been alive. The rule of the Tsar was regarded as God-given, whereas that seized by the Bolsheviks was always regarded by the Russians as an unlawful usurpation.

Let us return to the Baganal, which I mentioned as having joined the tribal union of the Kiyat and Nukuz in the 5th-4th centuries BCE after leaving the Ergenekon in the 4th century BCE – and then in the 12th century CE (a millennium and a half later) Genghis Khan was born among them. So on what facts can I base this claim?

The archaeologist and ethnographer Marija Gimbutas mentions in her book on the ancient peoples of the Baltic regions (*Balty. Liudi Iantarnogo moria.* Moscow: Tsentrpoligraf, 2004) that certain peoples who lived in the lands of what are now Lithuania and Latvia were called the Kori or Khori: 'In about 945 an Arab merchant from Andalusia called Ibrahim ibn Yaqub arrived on the shores of the Baltic and noted that the Prussians had their own language and were distinguished for their courageous actions in their wars with the Vikings (Rus). **The Kurshi [Curonians], a tribe that had settled on the Baltic coast in the lands of modern-day Lithuania and Latvia, are known in the Scandinavian sagas as the Kori or Khori**' (my emphasis – K.Z.). I do not mean to state definitively that these are the congeners of the Khori-Tumat forest peoples who lived in northern Mongolia and in the places from which the ancestors of Alan Gua came to Burkhan Khaldun in the mid-9th century – but there is much that suggests this.

Continuing with Gimbutas' passage: '...In about the years 880-890 the traveller Wulfstan of Hedeby sailed along the Baltic coast of Schleswig towards the lower reaches of the Vistula, the river Elbe and the Frisches Haff and described the enormous land of Estland, in which there were many settlements, each of which was controlled by a leader, and they often fought one another. **The leaders and the wealthy members of the group drank kumys (mare's milk) while the poor and the slaves drank mead...**' (my emphasis – K.Z.). As we pointed out in part 1 of this book, one of the ethnic markers of a Turkic-speaking people was frequent warfare with neighbouring Turkic tribes over pasture land in order to increase the number of head of cattle, resulting in the 'exules Scytharum' situation. So who was it that settled in this curious Estland, whose tribes, governed by wise leaders, 'occupied a leading position in extensive trade activities between Eastern Europe, Scandinavia, Kievan Rus and Byzantium'? First, Yuri Drozdov says that 'the information provided testifies to the fact that there were Scythian peoples living on the Baltic Sea cost from ancient times...' (*Tiurkoiazychny period yevropeiskoi istorii*, p. 175). I would add that before this, the Baltic was known as the Scythian Sea, and later the Sarmatian. Next, the Roman historian Tacitus (1st century BCE) supports this notion in his *Germania*: 'Upon the right of the Suevian Sea the Aestyan nations reside, who use the same customs and attire with the Suevians; ... they, being barbarians...' The descendants of these 'barbarians' are today members of the Ysty clan of the Kazakh Wusun tribe. Marija Gimbutas continues to say that 'the absence of concrete data about this prehistoric period could be seen in the widespread idea of the Baltic countries being German and Slavic...' But in that case, whose were they if not Turkic? Gimbutas continues that at this time (after the 7th century – K.Z.) the Kurshi (i.e. the Kori or Khori – K.Z.) turned themselves into Baltic 'Vikings' and became the most active and wealthy of all the Baltic tribes. A special prayer would be read out in Danish churches: 'O Lord Almighty, spare us from the Kurshi'. I think and am almost certain that as Gimbutas suggests, after the 7th century some of the Scandinavian Balts turned into these 'Baltic Vikings' and moved to eastern Europe – to Kievan Rus – where they founded the Rurik dynasty. Meanwhile another group of Balts went to the region of the Selenga river in Siberia, and it was from there that the ancestors of Alan Gua of the Khori or Khorilar clan travelled to Mongolia in the mid-9th century, to Burkhan Khaldun, so preparing the way for the later Genghis Khan. Marija Gimbutas is a well-known and authoritative archaeologist, an ethnic Lithuanian of American descent. In chapter I, incidentally, we mentioned that the Lithuanians and the Old Prussians were descendants of the Turkic Cimmerians, an ethnonym that derives from the Kazakh word *qymbattas* ('precious stone'). The 12th-century Saxon historian Helmold of Bosau mentioned in his *Chronica Slavorum*: 'The Prussians did not yet know the light of belief... For food they used the meat of horses, milk and blood of the same they used as a drink, and, it is said, they drank it until they were intoxicated...' No comment necessary.

Let us consider another important factor. Tleuberdy Abenay indicates that one of Alan Gua's roots lie in the Alan union of Turkic clans. The sixth-century historian Procopius of Caesarea wrote (see *Slaviane i Rus'*, Moscow, 2001, p.246) that 'The Vandals that lived by Lake Maeotis were forced by hunger to move to the Rhine, to the Germanic peoples that are now called the Franks and have been brought into the union of the **Gothic people of the Alan'** (my emphasis – K.Z.). A chronicler from the 11th century, Adam of Bremen, wrote on a similar theme: 'In those places dwelled the Alan or Alban who in their own language were called the Vizz...' The 'places' were regions in ancient times of the Eastern Baltic, but Vizz (?) is a distortion of Uz, as in *guz*, *oghuz*. Today, descendants of these Alban can be found among the Kazakhs under the name Alban. And finally, Murad Adji mentioned that 'in the year 435 the shores of the Northern Sea were washed by waves of the Great Migration of Peoples; the Turkic horde of the Balt had come to northern Europe' (*Dykhanie Armageddona*, p. 234). Adji claims that the Balts became known in Europe by the name of the Goths.

The fact that the Alan, Goths and Balts are related – even identical – is thus clear to be seen. This is a confirmation of the Scandinavian descent of the Khori-Tumat of Alan Gua and their being related to the Balts. A corollary of this is that the Kazakh Koralas and Baltaly must be related. As far as the Koralas can be said to have come from the Ergenekon, the same applies to the Baltaly. Aleksandr Bushkov writes in his astonishingly frank account *Rossia, kotoroy ne bylo. Mirazhi i prizraky* (Moscow: Olma-press, 2004, p.48):

So, let us say, scribes of the Middle Ages insist with improbable obstinacy that the Goths (who according to official history had 'disappeared' seven centuries after Christ), continued to live a quiet life in Europe at a later time. The sixth-century historian Jordanes is echoed by the Polish Wincenty Kadlulbek and the author of the *Wielkopolska Chronicle*, who believed that the Goths were the Prussians and that they never disappeared anywhere but lived peacefully on the coast of the Baltic. Other scribes added: The Goths are not only the Prussians but also the Swedes. A historian of the Petrine period, Andrey Lyzov, gave more detail: some of the Goths migrated from Scandinavia to the Black Sea; the Polovtsians are also Goths. Tens of books labour the same point: 'The Goths never disappeared; they are alive, there are Goths, there really are!

Let me add that Goths or Balts continue to live quiet lives in Kazakhstan in the 21st century in the piedmont of the Ulytau mountains in the Karaganda region, and are known as the clan of the Baltaly. Another group of Goths, known as the Kazakh clan of the Kete, live in western Kazakhstan, while a third group, the Alban, live around Almaty. Meanwhile Aleksandr Buskov gives convincing arguments in his other book, *Chingiskhan. Neizvestnaia Azia* to debunk the myth that the nomads were backward and the Europeans were culturally superior. On the contrary, he asserts, it was the Huns/Goths that brought monotheism to Europe together with new technologies, and if they also destroyed anything, this was the pagan shrines of Greece and Rome. In exchange they brought the 'Gothic style' of architecture, which was much admired by 'enlightened' Europe, which, by way of thanks for numerous architectural treasures being created in the European states, unable to find in themselves the strength to acknowledge their relative cultural backwardness, introduced in every possible way into the mass consciousness a myth that humiliated the nomads, portraying them as innumerable hordes of savages that poured across Europe to destroy the achievements of European civilisation, 'who grilled horsemeat on bonfires of burning manuscripts and stabled their horses in Christian cathedrals', etc, etc, etc.

So we have seen that the coast of the Baltic Sea has been inhabited by Turkic tribes since ancient times. The Russian ethnographer V.I. Anuchin proposed that the Scandinavians were descendants of the Dingling, who were also the ancestors of the Siberian Kyrgyz; and that they all lived in the Baikal region of Siberia (*Ocherk shamanstva u ieniseyskikh ostiakov*, 2nd ed., St Petersburg, 1914). It follows that if there was a migration from earliest times from Eastern Asia to Scandinavia then it is entirely possible that a return migration may have occurred in the early Middle Ages with nomadic tribes leaving the Baltic regions for Mongolia and northern China. Such was observed by scholars after the death of Attila, for example.

Summarising, we have established that the Baltaly – Baganal clans, who lived in the Baltic in the 8th century together with the Koralas or Kori, were related. If the Koralas left the Ergenekon in the 4th century BCE together with the Baya'ut, Nukuz and other tribes, it is logical to assume that the Koralas would have been accompanied by their relatives the Baganal – Baltaly. Later, moreover, having reached Scandinavia and become, as Marija Gimbutas called them, Baltic Vikings, they would have found themselves ultimately both ruling Kievan Rus and present with Alan Gua preparing the ground for the future Mongol Empire at Burkhan Khaldun. It is also entirely plausible that the Baganal, which in the 4th century BCE was part of the Nukuz, later migrated in the 9th century and became part of the Baya'ut, since these had the common origin of the Ergenekon. In this case, Ma'aliq of the Baya'ut (Alan Gua's servant) could have been a member of the clan of the Baganal.

Let us return now to the matter of Genghis Khan's relationship to the Naiman. In my view, let me repeat, Genghis Khan wanted only to remove the current Naiman khan in order to gain his throne, and had no desire for a confrontation with the Naiman people. As will be shown below, Genghis' desire coincided with the aspirations of the ruling elite of the Naiman tribal union, who wished to see the Naiman throne occupied not by the weak incumbents of the current dynasty of khans but by a man of outstanding talent – whether or not he belonged to the ruling hierarchy of Naiman khans.

A similar story occurred a century and a half later when the Chagatay elite of Samarkand preferred Timur (Tamerlane), though he was not of royal blood, since they believed that he could restore the former glory of the successors of Genghis Khan. Timur was not a descendant of Genghis so could not be a khan but instead was given the title of emir, though he gained no less glory than Genghis Khan had done.

So let us substantiate this theory. We may recall the situation when Genghis Khan and the Khereid defeated the army of Buyuruk Khan in western Mongolia and the Altai, but on his return he ran into an ambush set up by another Naiman commander, Koksu Sabrak. The next morning, when the Khereid suddenly abandoned him and Genghis Khan was compelled to escape without accepting battle, Koksu Sabrak started out in pursuit not of him but of the Khereid Wang Khan. And it was not for nothing that Jamukha, who was with the Khereid at that moment, said to Wang Khan: 'Some time ago, my sworn brother Temüjin had emissaries among the Naimans. Now, he has not come with us' (*The Secret History of the Mongols*, part 160). Evidently Genghis Khan had certain connections with the Naiman that were unknown to others.

In my view, and it is probably authentic, it was only among the Naiman that Genghis Khan saw his closest kinsmen and strategic partners for the forthcoming war with Jin China. And so it turned out. In the war with the Jurchen dynasty of the Jin the most responsible and decisive part was played by the Naiman. As it happened, a significant proportion of the population of northern China at the time of Genghis' invasion in 1211 were Khitan, tribes related to the Naiman, who had ruled in China before the Jurchen. And only through the aid of these allied Naiman and Khitan was it possible for Genghis Khan, by becoming the ruler of their territories in northern China and Mongolia, to realise his desire to conquer the million-strong Celestial Empire.

It is interesting to trace the relations of the Naiman with the Jurchen, who had set up the Jin dynasty in China in 1125 that Genghis Khan sought to conquer. Northern Manchuria was inhabited by ancient Tungus tribes who lived in the proximity of the Amur and Ussuri rivers and were known in the 5th century as the Ugi and Mohe. These hereditary hunters and fishers, which by the 12th century had become known as the Jurchen, conquered the Naiman-Khitan dynasty of the Liao in China. The Khitan lived alongside the Jurchen in western areas of northern Manchuria. By the 17th century the Jurchen were already being called the Manchurians, and in 1644 they once again established a dynasty in China, now called the Qing, which remained until 1911. From the literature it can be seen that it was during the period of Qing rule in China that relations between the Naiman and the Chinese were at their most productive, and as a consequence, the greater part of the Jurchen joined the Naiman tribal union. But not only the Naiman were on good terms with Qing China; this was true of all the Kazakhs who fought the Dzungar. The latter in turn fought with the Chinese, who ultimately destroyed the Dzungar state in the mid-18th century.

An example of this is the Shurshit. Today the large Naiman subdivision of the Teristamgaly includes the large clan of the Shurshit, also known today as the Jurchen or the Siberian Tatar, but in Genghis Khan's day the Shurshit, along with the Ongud, were the core of the Tatar nation. In the Pavlodar region of Kazakhstan is a place named Shurshit Kyrylgan where the *batyr* Olzhabay of the Argyn defeated a Dzungar army. Today there are Shurshit Jurchens among the Siberian Tatar.

We noted earlier that the Khitan, which the chronicles cease to mention as early as the 14th century, were simply absorbed into the Naiman. The same occurred with much of the Jurchen, which was partly assimilated into numerous Chinese clans, but another part of which became part of the Kazakh Naiman; and from the 18th century onwards their name does not appear in the chronicles.

The history of relations between the Kazakhs, particularly the Naiman, with the Jurchen remains full of mysteries that await investigation.

Finally there is the major question of the so-called defeat of the large, experienced and well-equipped Naiman army by Genghis Khan, described in *The Secret History of the Mongols*. Let us begin with the words of Koksu Sabrak at the point that they are debating the death of Wang Khan: '... You are weak, my stupid Qan Tayang. You have no skills or desires other than falconry and hunting' (*SHM*, 189). At another point, when the Mongols, far fewer in number, seek to confuse the Naiman by lighting a large number of fires at their headquarters and thereby apply psychological pressure to them, one of Genghis Khan's *noyan* (unit commanders) says: 'They [the Naiman] are said to be many, but their Qan is said to be weak and not to leave [his] yurt. Our fires will distract them until our geldings are sated. ...' (*SHM*, 93). Here we see Tayang Khan presented as an effete nobleman who has no experience of war and who has only ever amused himself with hunting.

And finally, Tayang's son Guchuluk Khan gives a highly unflattering evaluation of his father. Receiving news via his father that the enemy has a large force assembled, he retorts: '[That] same old woman Tayang. He says these things [because] his heart fails him. Whence came these many Mongqols [of which you speak]? Most of the Mongqols are with Jamuqa, here in our [hands]' (*SHM*, part 194).

After this it all boils down to a situation in which Tayang, refusing to fight out of cowardice, runs from the battlefield, leaving his subjects to their fate. The anonymous author of *The Secret History of the Mongols* clearly shows how dissatisfied in Tayang Khan his close circle is, including his own son. An impression is gained that the Naiman were ready to depose their khan, but the laws of dynastic succession of power at that time would have prevented them doing so. I would even allow myself the bold speculation that Tayang's entourage might have been interested in having Genghis Khan on the Naiman throne – in any case his clan was already part of the Naiman tribal union, albeit relatively minor in significance.

Also supportive of my hypothesis are the actions of Jamukha at that tragic hour for the Naiman, when, finding himself alongside Tayang Khan, he renders his 'sworn brother' Temirshin a service of inestimable value. For example, when Tayang asks him who is fighting alongside Genghis, Jamukha replies – meaning Jebe with Kublai and Jelme with Subutai – 'My sworn brother Temüjin [has] four hounds, raised on human flesh. They have been chained and tied, [but now] they pursue our watchmen. These four hounds [have]

> chisels for snouts and
> awls for tongues.
> With hearts of iron and
> whips for swords,
> eating the dew and
> riding the wind,
> they go.
> On killing days
> they eat the flesh of men.
> On fighting days
> they take men's flesh as their provisions.' (*SHM*, 195)

As for Genghis Khan's brother Qasar, Jamukha speaks as follows: 'Mother Höelün raised one [of] her sons on human flesh.

> He has a body of three fathoms,
> and the appetite of a three-year old ox.
> He wears three layers of armour,
> and [his cart] is pulled by three bulls.
> He can swallow an entire
> man with a quiver,
> and [the quiver] will not [even] touch his throat.' (*SHM*, 195)

Historians today do not have an unambiguous sense of what the relationship was between Genghis Khan and Jamukha. Some have even gone so far as to show that Jamukha captured Genghis Khan in 1186 and then, as soon as Temirshin was proclaimed khan of the Mongol tribes, handed him over to the Chinese as a hostage. Films have even been made with this version of events. Yet the way I see it is that even when they were still very young, the *andas* Temirshin and Jamukha had agreed to work together in matters of attaining power. The practical actions taken by Jamukha support this assumption: Jamukha helps Temirshin rescue his wife Börte from the Merkit; having got into a skirmish with Temirshin (because Temirshin's brother killed Jamukha's brother as a consequence of an ordinary *barymta* raid), Jamukha pursues him into a gorge but does not fight him; Jamukha warns Genghis Khan about the attack being planned on him by the Khereid Wang Khan; Jamukha, finally, gives Genghis invaluable aid in the confrontation with Tayang Khan of the Naiman. It is entirely possible that the author of *The Secret History of the Mongols* created the poetic passage that relates the circumstances of Jamukha's death in order to lend plausibility to the account of their antagonism. In fact they gained power as allies, and it was only power itself, which, as Vissarion Belinsky once said, was second only to pride as the downfall of man, drove them apart.

As for the Naiman, as can be seen from what I mentioned about their relationship to Genghis Khan, simply created the opportunity and circumstances in which a more deserving individual than their kinsman Tayang could take over the leadership of their state, and as a result, go on to create the Mongol Empire.

Let us note another important point. As Mukhtarkan Orazbay indicates (*Naiman memlekti. Qazaqtyn erte tarikhtagy izderi*, Almaty 2007), a major figure in the Naiman khanate, Tatatunga, accepted Genghis Khan's offer and took up the post of what today would be called chancellor of the Mongol empire, and all clerical work relating to the empire was done using the Naiman written language. He taught literacy in this script first to Genghis' brother Qasar, and afterwards all decrees and arrangements of the emperor were issued in Naiman script. Professor Orazbay himself worked for a long time in the Central Committee of the Chinese Communist Party and so gained access to many secret archives; he believes that *The Secret History of the Mongols* was written on an island, Kodege, in the Kherlen river in 1240. This was part of Genghis Khan's summer grazing land and the work would have been written in the language of the Kazakhs in the 13th century using Naiman script.

Mukhtarkan Orazbay also mentions an outstanding military leader from the Naiman, Kitbuqa, who served as mentor and educator to two of Genghis' grandsons by his youngest son Tolui, Hulagu and Kublai. Orazbay shows that the popular story that after Jochi's death it was this Kitbuqa who undertook to notify Genghis of this tragic news by playing him the *dombra* – an allegorical language, if you like, that reached into the heart of the great conqueror with the news of the death of his son, is indeed historical fact and not merely legend, as historians had recently begun to assume. He further mentions, referring to the record of the Taoist monk Qiu Chuji who visited Genghis Khan in Central Asia in the period 1221-1223, that Jochi died not in 1227 but in 1223, and that the monk learned of this death as he was parting with Genghis.

Compare this with the official scholarship, which maintains that both Jochi and his father Genghis Khan died in the year 1227, their deaths separated by three months. If Orazbay is correct, however, then Genghis would have had four years following his son's death in which to return to his homeland – in which case it would be appropriate to search for his place of burial in Mongolia, where the founding clans of the Kazakh peoples lived in the 12th and 13th centuries.

Lastly, Mukhtarkan Orazbay is categorical in his conclusions that Genghis Khan did not send hired assassins to the Saryarka steppe to commit a reprisal on his son Jochi, supposedly for three times not responding to invitations by his father to visit him at his headquarters in southern Kazakhstan. He maintains that Jochi simply never received any such invitation.

The Naiman script, meanwhile, continued to be used for some time in the Mongol empire, such as in this letter, which is a reply by the khan Güyük to the Roman Pope in 1246. A sentence from the letter runs: 'By the strength of God, all the earth, beginning from where the sun rises and ending where it sets, has been granted to us.' Giovanni da Pian del

Carpine, one of the first Europeans to enter the court of the Great Khan, reproduces the text of the letter in his accounts.

The Naiman tribal union began to gain in strength after the 7th century and subsequently absorbed many Kazakh clans into itself. This happened with the Baganal. The latter, which belongs to this day to the large tribal union of the Qiyad and the Nukuz, emerged at some point from the Ergenekon, then, after the 5th century, as is told in the epic tale *Kozy Korpesh i Bayan Sulu*, it was in Tiumen in western Siberia, then travelled further west with the Kori-Koralas to Scandinavia. Later, on its return migration eastward, the tribe reached northern China and Mongolia and lived alongside the Turkic Seir, which formed the basis of the Huns. After the Seir broke into several parts in the mid-7th century, most of its kernel was preserved and subsequently became known as the Naiman, who came to dominate in northern China and Mongolia, and the Baganal, as I mentioned above, entered the Naiman union as *unagan bogol* (slaves in attendance). And thanks only to the personal dignity of Genghis Khan, this clan succeeded in becoming the most important within the Naiman clan union.

It is the greatness of the historic deeds of the Baltaly-Baganal clans that allow me, on the basis of the information currently available, to give them my preference over the other Kazakh clans, the Jalayir, Sirgeli, Tabyn, Tama and Tarakt, who have a similar *tamga* to that of the Baganal – that is, according to the sources, the lineage of our great ancestor Genghis Khan. The word *baganal* in Kazakh means 'pillar-like', 'load-bearing', and it is evident that this clan often provided support to its people.

There can of course be various approaches to solving this problem, such as, for example, on the basis of linguistic analysis of the ethnonym of Genghis Khan's clan. We will examine one of these approaches that is wholly capable of being close to the truth.

The Kazakh Borjigin

With the proud man be proud: he's not the Prophet's father,
With the bashful man be bashful: he's not your slave.
This is how I set out, taking my vows to the road.
Not all who asked could I help; I'm not God,
What is within the powers of a solitary poet?
I did not find answers to every question,
But lied to nobody, although I could have...
Olzhas Suleimenov

According to the 'official' point of view and to the canons of academic scholarship, Genghis Khan descended from the clan of the Qiyad–Borjigin, the long-forgotten name of the Qiyad coming back into use beginning with Khabul Khan, the great-grandfather of Genghis. As for the Borjigin, this name was first given to the offspring of Yesugei, Genghis Khan's father. Let us consider the term *borjigin* for a moment. It is a complex lexical construction containing two roots – *böri*, which in Kazakh means 'wolf', and *jigi*, meaning 'part of the whole'. The lexeme *borjigin* thus semantically means a part of the people that are descended or derived from a wolf. If we recall that, according to a popular legend, the ur-ancestor of the Turkic people was a wolf, then the word *borjigin* clearly means a part of the Turkic people. So, a question arises: to what specific clan of the Turks is this part related?

As we have discussed, the only clans among the Kazakhs whose *tamga* is a wolf symbol are the Naiman clans of the Matai and Sadyr. I therefore suppose that the Borjigin could have belonged to these Naiman clans. It will be useful to recall that the *uran* (war cry) of all Naiman, along with the canonical name 'Qaptagai', is the name 'Matai'.

218

In *Under the wolf's nest* I mentioned that the ethnonym *matai* derived from the Greek *mata*, which means 'mother', 'wet nurse'. The Sea of Azov was once called the Maeotian Lake, because it used to 'feed' its waters through the Cimmerian Bosporus (now the Kerch Strait) into the Euxeinos Pontos (the Black Sea), and the Scythian people who lived around this sea were called the Matai (Maeotae). According to the Bible, Matai (Madai) was a son of Japheth, thus a grandson of the prophet Noah, and his descendants subsequently created the Mitanni nation in Asia Minor (17th century BCE) and Media (8th century BCE) in Western Asia, then governed Babylon for 28 years in the 7th century BCE; and created the Hun empire in northern China in the 3rd century BCE, to which Han China paid tribute.

In modern Kazakh genealogy, one of the descendants of the Matai was from China, a successor of the Hittite Kete, who, arriving in the 11th century from Asia Minor, created the Zhou kingdom in China. As we mentioned earlier, this dynasty collapsed in the 8th century BCE due to internecine fighting and a 'dark age' of multiple kingdoms descended on China. Individual clans of the Zhou dynasty founded the settlement of the Ergenekon in the Altai, then, regaining their strength, began to multiply their numbers. Thus although Rashid ad-Din Hamadani does not mention the Matai among the clans in the exodus from the Ergenekon, they were clearly there, as part of the Koralas or Baya'ut, since later Borte Chino, a descendant of the ancestor wolf, brought them to Burkhan Khaldun. Then it is entirely plausible that Ma'aliq of the Baya'ut, Alan Gua's servant, could have come from the Matai, since, again, the only Kazakh Borjigin with a *tamga* that depicts the wolf ancestor is the Matai. In *Under the wolf's nest* I established the possible relations between the Kazakh clans Botpai (Botbay) and Matai, and since the Koralas were related to the Botpai and migrated away from the Ergenekon at some point, the Botpai and Matai were also there. This view is supported by the fact that the Botpai today are part of the Wusun, who Hamadani maintained were among the groups who left the Ergenekon.

To further support this thesis I would add that in modern Kazakh genealogy the Naiman clans of the Shang and Matai are closely related by blood. The Shang created the first Yin dynasty in China in the 18th century BCE, the legal successor to which was the Zhou dynasty; thus, continuing the tradition of their ancestors, Genghis Khan in his turn created another great empire in the East, with another Turkic dynasty coming to rule China, the Yuan.

Dacians, Dahae, Aday...

Tanysang adaymyn, tanymasang
Kudaymyng
(To my acquaintances I am a member of
the Aday,
but to all others I am the Lord God).

Kazakh saying

As I mentioned above, in *The Secret History of the Mongols* Genghis Khan, having 'unified the people of the felt-walled tents' (*SHM*, 202) in the year 1260, said to Ongur (his cousin, the son of Mungetu-Kiyan who was Yesugei's elder brother): '... you, Önggür, the son of Mönggetü-kiyan, with your Changshi'ut and Baya'ut [men], became one camp for me. You Önggür,
> did not lose your way in the fog,
> did not forsake [us] in the battle.
> When it was wet, we bore the wet together,
> when it was cold, we bore the cold together.' (*SHM*, 213)

When Genghis Khan then asks him what favour he would like in return, Ongur replies: 'If I may choose my favour, [let it be this]: **My Baya'ut kinsmen** are scattered across the tribes. As your favour, allow me to assemble my Baya'ut kinsmen' (my emphasis – K.Z.).

If we eliminate Genghis Khan's Merkit origins, his descent from the Bayad (Baya'ut) can be considered wholly established, and the servant Ma'aliq of the Baya'ut gains the great honour of being the ancestor of Genghis Khan and his people. We are interested, meanwhile, in the descendants of that people in the 21st century. Let us recall that

Tleuberdy Abenay considers the large Kazakh tribe of the Bayuly to be the ethnic successor to the Baya'ut. We can try to substantiate this view.

Ongur's guard were relatives of his from the Changshi'ut and Baya'ut. The first in modern Kazakh genealogy are part of the old Kanju and have the name Shanyshkyly. The Russian orientalist Nikolai Aristov noted that 'The Bayat or Baya'ut clan originated with the Kangly...' (*Zametki ob etnicheskom sostave tiurkskykh plemen i narodnostey*, St Petersburg, 1896). It is known that from the time of the Xiongnu the nation of the Kangju occupied the territory of central and western Kazakhstan from north of Lake Balkhash right to the Aral Sea. Today many Kazakh clans of the Bayuly live in these regions. Moreover the *tamga* of the Shanyshkyly, related to the Baya'ut, is an arrow, and the only clan of the 12 clans of the Bayuly whose *tamga* is an arrow is the Aday. Consequently the Kazakh Aday may be the ethnocultural descendants of Ongur's Baya'ut. My wife's lineage (she is Aday by her father's line) includes a large subgroup called the Mungaly. Some sources, including Rashid ad-Din Hamadani, mention that the Mongols were called the Mugal or Mungal.

Much can be found in the sources about the Aday (also Dahae, Dacians). The Dacians of Europe posed a major threat to the Romans, while their Asian counterparts, the Dahae, established the great Parthian state whose ruler the Roman commander Pompey reverently called the 'king of kings'. I am happy to accept that it could have been this great, warlike people, the Aday, who in the 12th century gave birth to the 'greatest Turk of all times and peoples', as Murad Adji has it, Genghis Khan.

Given the presence of the **'KZ factor'** (see Part 1) that we have established on the territory of Mongolia in the 12th and 13th centuries, there is no doubt that Genghis Khan belonged to the Turkic world. What interests us, however, is what specific relationship he had to a particular clan, including to the modern Kazakh people. Summing up what we have discussed, we can say with a fair measure of certainty that Genghis Khan belonged to one of the following Kazakh clans:

I. The Merkit. This is based on the fact that Genghis Khan's father

Yesugei Baatur took his second wife Hoelun, who had just been married to the Merkit prince Chiledu, as the newlyweds were travelling to their home country, the lands where the Merkit roamed. Temirshin, born afterwards, could thus have been conceived from the Merkit prince Chiledu. It may be noted that today the Merkit are found among the Abak Kerey of the Kazakhs.

II. The Baganal. This possibility arises because the *tamga* of Genghis Khan matches that of the Baganal and because the latter, as we demonstrated earlier, were among the Darlekin Mongols who left the Ergenekon.

Nevertheless, the possibility that Genghis was related to the Sirgeli, Jalayir, Tabyn, Tama, Tarakt or Shanyshkyly cannot be excluded, since their *tamgas* also match that of Genghis Khan.

III. The Matai. This is the only Kazakh clan whose *tamga* symbol is a wolf. The man who brought Genghis Khan's ancestors to Burkhan Khaldun, Borte Chino, was a descendant of the wolf ancestor and the founder of the Borjigin.

IV. The Aday. This version of events is based on the account in *The Secret History of the Mongols*, where the Baya'ut are declared to be the clan of Ongur, Genghis' cousin through his father. The information we have indicates that the ethnocultural descendants of the 13th-century Baya'ut are the Aday, within the tribal union of the Bayuly.

As a researcher I am drawn most to the view that Genghis Khan was from the Matai or the Baganal. Today these clans are part of the Naiman tribal union of the Kazakhs, but in Genghis' day they could consist of two tribal unions. For example, the Baganal were once part of the Kerey, the Balgaly were part of the Kipchak and the Matay formed the framework of the Seir, etc.

V. The Shanyshkyly. Earlier I mentioned the contradiction between Hamadani and *The Secret History of the Mongols* in which the former did not consider Ongur to be the son of Mungetu-Kiyan and thus a cousin of Genghis Khan. This would mean that the Baya'ut were also not related to Genghis Khan. In that case, however, all the laurels of close kinship would pass to the Changshi'ut, who, according to Hamadani, were Genghis Khan's blood relatives by his father's direct line.

Accordingly, the Shanyshkyly clan may lay claim to being related to Genghis Khan if Hamadani is right and *The Secret History of the Mongols* is in error.

By commonly accepted tradition, when he divided his empire Genghis Khan gave his eldest son Jochi, who should have inherited his father's power, the territory known as Ulus Zholshy, which includes all of modern Kazakhstan; and it was to Jochi that he entrusted the clans of his own descent, the Baganal and the Matai, who today live below the Ulytau spur of the Altai and preserve the secrets and testaments of their illustrious son. And who knows, Kalibek Daniyarov may be correct in supposing that the burial vault of the enigmatic Alash Khan, situated alongside the tomb of Jochi Khan at the foot of the Ulytau mountains of central Kazakhstan, may contain the remains of the man whose great actions were the 'terror of the Universe'. And the dust of those remains calls to us, his descendants, to take up a deserving place in this world, one that befits his successors!

* * *

Below are three pages of examples of Naiman writing, kindly lent by Professor Mukhtarkan Orazbay.

Naiman inscription on a stamp used in a letter from Güyük Khan to Pope Innocent IV on the 11th day of the 11th month, 1246

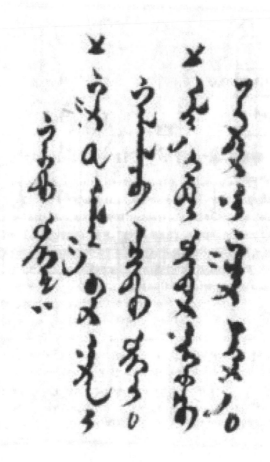

Proverb written in Naiman script, 8th century
You cannot shut out the sun with your hand;
however high the eagle flies, its shadow remains on the ground.

A,E	I,Í,Y	O,U	Ö,Ü	B,P	C,Ç	D	Г	X

L	U,V,V	C,K	M	K,Č	R	S	Ş	Z

Example of Naiman writing of the 8th century, consisting of 7 vowel and 23 consonant sounds, 18 letters

INSTEAD OF AN EPILOGUE

In an article written in the 1960s the Soviet Eurasianist Lev Gumilev wrote: 'It is now three centuries since the problem of a scholarly investigation of the 'Mongol question' first arose, and still there is no solution... How could the Mongols, of whom there were only a little over half a million, have taken over half the world? Something here is not right. It seems that we have missed a certain factor' (*Ritmy Yevrazii*, Moscow, 2004, p. 128).

My investigation has been an attempt to reawaken certain forgotten and overlooked pages of Kazakh history.

The French thinker and commentator Montesquieu displayed a poor opinion of Genghis Khan and his people, but he could not but admit: 'What significance do the conquests of Alexander the Great have compared to the conquests of Genghis Khan? That victorious nation needs only historians to glorify its miraculous deeds... That warlike people, occupied solely with its true glory and certain of eternal victories, had no concern with preserving for posterity the memory of its heroic conquests...'.

In fulfilling my filial duty I have tried to fill in this gap and also, as far as I was able, to correct the errors of our predecessors as mentioned by the great French philosopher. Not being educated as a historian, I have nevertheless been able to grasp this discipline in spirit. I was encouraged and inspired by the words of another French thinker, Pierre de Beaumarchais; after warning the scholar of possible misfortune on the thorny path to knowing the truth, he then gives his blessing to the enterprise: 'The wind that blows out the candle fans the flames in the brazier'.

Leo Tolstoy advises would-be writers, who seek fast success from producing novels: 'If you are able to not write, do not write'. I was unable not to write this book, and now I let go of it, like a grown-up child – may it have its own life and may its fate be a happy one, replete and sought after. Amen.

APPENDIX

MARCO POLO ON THE UIGURS

Man is arranged in surprising ways: he is upset when he loses wealth, but is indifferent to the fact that the days of his life pass away never to return.

Abu al-Faraj

In the mid-8th century power in the khaganate with its centre at Karakorum shifted from the Seir–Kipchak to a tribal union named the Bayirku, which included what are today the Kazakh Naiman, Kerey, Argyn and Turkic groups including the Basmyl, Ediz and others. The khaganate began to be called Uigur, from the old Turkic word *uigur*, meaning 'unity', 'union'. Modern-day Uigurs have no relationship to the creation of that khaganate, however, their ancestors migrated to Turkestan after the power in the khaganate was taken over by Yenisei Kyrgyz. In Turkestan the Uighurs took up strategic positions on the Silk Road. Just as the name and glory of the people of the Mangi El fell to the modern-day Mongols after Genghis Khan had moved with his people to Kazakhstan and Central Asia, and the land left behind by the Mongols as they came into Genghis' homeland was in turn occupied by tribes of Tungus origin, in the same way the modern Uigurs inherited the ethnonym of the great Uigurs, the masters of the Second Turkic Khaganate.

As they changed to a settled way of life the Uigurs assumed a role as intermediaries in trade between China and the West. Creating all the necessary infrastructure, they offered services to aid the passage of caravans and quickly grew wealthy. They used any methods to gain profit; Marco Polo describes the morals of the inhabitants of Uigur oases like this: 'They are very welcoming to foreign guests; the wives are ordered to fulfil all the foreigners' wishes: they go out to attend to their business and do not return home for two or three days, while the visitor does with the wife whatever he wishes and lives at his leisure. The wives love like this in both town and country, and their husbands are not ashamed. The women are beautiful, and cheerful, and like to enjoy themselves.'

Möngke Khan, hearing of similar unworthy morals among his subjects, forbade them such actions on pain of death. The Uigurs, on the other hand equipped the khan with a large embassy with generous endowments, the purpose of which was to convey the message to the effect that they had been bequeathed that way of life by their grandfathers and requested to be allowed to continue living that way. The khan waved them away: 'If you wish to bring shame upon yourselves then go ahead and live your way...' He did not raise the question again. Lev Gumilev later also wrote about the same point.

THE MODERN KYRGYZ AND THEIR ANCESTORS

Fearful is the fire that flares up in the Soul,
dreadful is the enemy the heart treats kindly.
(from the Manas epic of the Kyrgyz)

I would like to mention another nation in particular, one that has managed to preserve its integrity over two millennia. Despite having lost its statehood at various historical junctures, suffering bitter conquest and terrible collapse, it has ultimately risen to the level of the people of a great power. They are the Kyrgyz.

I often visit our brother nation, and when the conversation turns to the past of the two peoples, Kazakh and Kyrgyz, united to a large extent by destiny, I am always struck by their pride in their past. Even while struggling with the current economic difficulties, my Kyrgyz friends and relatives pride themselves on the fact that their nation is older than that of the Kazakhs. Indeed, geographical maps from the 10th-12th centuries of tribes in Central Asia indicate the 'Kyrgyz' in the Yenisei basin; to their west are the Kerey and further west still are the Naiman, while south of them are the Merkit and Khongirad, and beyond that the Tatars and the Chinese. And so on. The name 'Kazakhs', however, does not appear as such, and I have to explain to my friends that the Naiman, Kerey, Merkit and Khongirad are the Kazakhs of today, and that in the 12th century each of these tribes was as important as the tribe of the Kyrgyz. Later these tribes were united under Genghis Khan into a single state known as Mongol or Mangi El, and only later began to call themselves the Kazakhs. But it is rare in history that a people will continue to use the same name that scarcely changes over many centuries – and this rare case is in fact the Kyrgyz. Admittedly, some scope for interpretation is required even here. For example, a brief series of lectures on the history of Kyrgyzstan (V. Voropaeva, D. Dzhunushaliev and V. Ploskikh: *Istoria Otechestva*. 2nd ed., Bishkek: Raritet Info, 2005) states that the first mention of the Kyrgyz is found in a Chinese chronicle which, listing the lands and peoples that have been conquered by the Huns of Modu Chanyu-Matay, refers to the Chunju, Cujshe, Dingling, Gegun and Sinli. The authors state dogmatically that it is an established fact that the Gegun are the Kyrgyz who lived in the eastern Tian Shan.

This is imagination that borders on fantasy! But if from the point of view of lexis such a statement is not indisputable, nevertheless from the point of view of etymology there is a grain of truth in it. The Sinologist Nikita Bichurin, for example, better known perhaps as Father Iakinf, commenting on the description in the ancient Chinese source *Beyshi* (*Sobranie svedeniy o narodakh, obitavshikh v Sredney Azii v drevnie vremena*. Moscow and Leningrad, 1950, vol. 2) of the rout in 93 BCE of the northern Huns by the combined forces of the Chinese, the Dingling, the Xianbei and the southern Huns, and on the fate of the northern Huns who fled westward to what are now central and western Kazakhstan and the small group of Huns that settled in the Tarbagatai area and subsequently established the Chuban, says: 'The northern Chanyu crossed the Gin-Wei-Shan (Tarbagatai) ridge and went west to Kangju; and the weak ones who were unable to follow him, stayed on the northern side of the Kucha. They occupy several thousand li of territory and amount to 200,000 souls. **Their customs and language are the same as the Gaogui,** but their cleanliness is greater – they wash themselves three times per day and only then sit down to eat' (my emphasis – K.Z.).

The Chinese source thus almost identifies the northern Huns with the Gaogui, whom the Kyrgyz authors consider to be the ancestors of the modern Kyrgyz.

It can however be stated accurately that a people was recorded by the Yenisei in the 1st century BCE that began to use the name of the Yenisei Kyrgyz. Gumilev describes the Dingling as a Caucasoid race that lived in southern Siberia from the first millennium BCE and in the first millennium CE. A symbiosis between the Dingling and the Gegun led to this new nation of Yenisei Kyrgyz, since when there has been no mention of the Dingling. These Yenisei Kyrgyz did not become affiliated to the Turkic khaganates but sometimes submitted to them and sometimes maintained an uncompromising stand towards this ethnically related structure. In 840 however they defeated the Uigurs, who had come to power in the Eastern Turkic khaganate. The result was a great-power nation of Yenisei Kyrgyz that lasted briefly until 926, when power in the khaganate shifted to the Naiman–Khitan that had established the Liao dynasty in northern China. Part of the Kyrgyz then returned to their historical homeland, the Minusinsk Hollow, bordered by the Sayan mountains and close to the Yenisei river; in 1207 they voluntarily submitted to Genghis Khan's eldest son Jochi and became part of the Mongol empire. Another part of the Kyrgyz meanwhile migrated south to the Tian Shan mountains south of the Issyk-Kul lake, where they intermixed with the indigenous inhabitants – primarily Wusun, who had migrated from northern China and Mongolia first to the Seven Rivers (south-eastern Kazakhstan) and then, under pressure from the Xianbei and Rouran, moved on to the territory of what is now Kyrgyzstan, a thousand years before the present-day Kyrgyz established their modern nation state.

Meanwhile those of the Kyrgyz that had remained by the Yenisei mixed with the Oirat tribes and formed a new ethnos that is now known as the Buryat. Contrary to the accepted view that the Buryat are Mongoloid, I follow Gumilev in maintaining that they are a Turkic people. In the 19th century Aleksei Levshin wrote of the Kyrgyz as the Burut, and thereby the kinship of the modern Kyrgyz with the Buryat is confirmed in the literature (*Opisanie kirgiz-kazach'ikh ili kirgiz-kaysatskik ord i stepey*, reprint, Almaty, 1996). Meanwhile the Buryat was the name of the tribes that lived in the Tian Shan and by Balkhash and Issyk-Kul lakes, with whom the Wusun may have intermixed when they arrived in the 2nd century BCE from northern China and Mongolia. And these were the indigenous tribes whose symbiosis with the Yenisei Kyrgyz resulted in the nation of the modern-day Kyrgyz. Only one thing is unclear: did the Burut live in the Seven Rivers region at the start of the Common Era and prior to that? Nor is the situation clarified by the 19th-century Kazakh scholar Shoqan Walikhanov, who wrote:

In completing my ethnographic remarks on the Burut and Uysun I consider it necessary to point out that these entirely different peoples did not need to mix. This matter has been examined in their own times by Messrs Levshin, Meyendorf and, with particular passion, Father Iakinf, but up to now nobody has heeded them. Their words have been like a voice crying out in the wilderness; even Humboldt and Ritter could not really understand the matter: they thought that it was the Burut that comprised the Great Kaysak Horde and that this horde should be distinguished from the Little and Middle. But this was a major mistake on the part of these leading figures of scholarship. The Great, Middle and Little Kirgiz-Kaysak Hordes are made up one 'Kazak' people, different to the Kirgiz, **whom the Chinese call the Burut** (my emphasis – K.Z.) and the Russians call barbarian or black. These two peoples differ by language, descent and customs. Even the physiognomy of the Burut is unique, not like the Kaysak...' (cited in Nurbulat Masanov, Zhulduzbek Abylhozhin and Irina Yerofeeva, *Nauchnoe znanie i mifotvorchestvo v sovremennoy istoriografii Kazakhstana*).

Thus if the Chinese called the Yenisei Kyrgyz the Burut, when were they in the Balkhash area? In my view, a significant proportion of the Yenisei Kyrgyz arrived in the Seven Rivers region only after the fall of the Kyrgyz power in 926, i.e. not until the 10th century, and by then, according to data available, the Uysyn had already left the Seven Rivers and reached the Tian Shan and the Pamir mountains. It is probable that not all the Uysyn had gone, however, and these are the people whom Shoqan Walikhanov compares with the Burut. In any case, the symbiosis between the Yenisei Kyrgyz and the Uysyn occurred in the Tien-Shan and the fact that the modern Kyrgyz do not differ from the Kazakhs (Walikhan's 'Kaysaks') in either looks or speech is supportive of my assumption. I therefore believe that the modern Buryat have greater similarity to the Yenisei Kyrgyz, while the Kazakhs and today's Kyrgyz are considered to belong to the six tribes of the Alash for a good reason – they are entirely related.

THE TATARS AND THE TATAR-MONGOL YOKE

Prosperity passes: time continues its flight and once again in a many-winged wave it carries us off to the unknown.
attributed to Shams al-Din al-Samarqandi

The ethnonym 'Tatar' today refers to a Turkic-speaking population that lives between the Volga and Ural rivers, which region accounts for 95% of all Tatars. In addition are the Siberian Tatars (roughly 3%) plus the Tatars of Astrakhan (2%). Also related to the Kazan Tatars are the Crimean and the Lithuanian Tatars. The ethnonym 'Tatar' came to mean this part of the population of Russia in the late 19th and early 20th centuries.

The ethnonym *tatar* was however found in the runic monuments of the Orkhon and the Yenisei as early as the 6th century. The inscriptions on the Kultegin stone, for example, mention the Otyz Tatar as being unfriendly towards the Turkic khaganate of tribes. Descendants of the Otyz Tatar include the Turks, Azerbaijanis, Gagauz, Balkar and Karaim. The Chinese called Tatar everybody who lived north of the Great Wall; they called the White Tatar the Ongud, who are today to be found among Kazakh clans. The Ungit, for example, of the six sons of the Jappas-Bayuly, are derived from the Ongud, and the latter are also found in the separate Karakesek clan among the Alimuly. According to Muhamedzhan Tynyshpaev, the Sirgeli of the Senior *jüz* of Kazakhs are related to the Ongud. Most of the Ongut today live among the Kazakh Tatars. According to Rashid ad-Din Hamadani, the Ongud that lived along the Great Wall of China were numerous and had their own state. Supporting Genghis Khan and voluntarily joining his empire, they went with him to the west. At that time the Bagys clan part of the Ergenekty Naiman from the tribe of the

Saryzhomart joined the Ongud, as did the Sirgeli, as already mentioned. Later the Ongud on Kazakh territory became known as the Waq and were allocated to the *ulus* of Jochi. The Kazakhs of Petropavlovsk, for example, carefully their tradition about their legendary son Er Kokshe of the Waq clan who 'was the Tatar *batyr* and was great of nature, body and strength...' Er Kokshe died in 1420 in a battle between Edige and Qadeer Berdi, one of the sons of Tokhtamysh, khan of the Golden Horde.

The Chinese referred to the Kazakh clans of Naiman, Kerey, Merkit, Jalayir and Khongirad as Black Tatars and the Oirat, Tuvans, Khori-Tumat and other forest tribes as 'wild Tatars'. As we established earlier, the Tatar are descendants of the Volga Bulgars, who are ethnically close to the Kazakh Botbay. Later, in the 14th-15th centuries the Kipchak, Kongirad, Khereid, Qytai (within the Naiman), Tabyn, Bialikshi, Kyrgyz and other Turkic tribes began to penetrate Volga Bulgaria. The Siberian Tatar consist primarily of Kazakh clans such as the Naiman, Khongirad, Kerey, Tabyn, Taz, Qytai (within the Naiman) and also Finno-Ugric groups such as the Istyak, Supra, Bikatin, Uvat, Yurma and others. The Astrakhan Tatars are descendants of the clans of the Golden Horde and are therefore close to Kazakh clans. In numerical terms the majority of the Latvian Tatars are Naiman, Jalayir, Kongirad, Wusun, Baarin and Mansur. Lastly, the Crimean Tatars are predominantly Manghud, Merkit, Qiyad, Kongirad, Wusun, Kipchak, Argyn, Baarin, Shyryn, Mansur and others.

In his 19th-century work 'K voprosu o proiskhozhdenii kirgizskogo naroda' Aleksey Kharuzin wrote that the Tauridan steppe of the Crimean peninsula contained Tatar settlements named after well-known Turkic clans. In the Perekop district, for example, there were Kipchak, Alchin, Wusun, Naiman, Qytan (within the Naiman – K.Z.) and Kerey. The Yevpatoria district was inhabited by Kara-Kipchak, Kurulu-Kipchak, Beldauz-Kipchak, Bay-ogly-Kipchak, Kara-Naiman, Qytai, Kongirad, Uzbeks and Kyrgyz-Kazakhs. In the Feodosia district were Kipchak, Tama, Argyn, Naiman and Qytai. Round Simferopol were Naiman (transcription: Aleksey Kharuzin).

So these are the Crimean Tatars! It turns out that Crimea reproduces many of the Kazakh clans in miniature.

Thus in ethnic terms the Tatars of the Russian Federation consist of the same clans that also exist as Kazakhs. It is notable that the yearbooks of the University of Kazan, *Izvestia ob., arkh., ist., geogr.*, volume 14, issue 3, page 360 state that in 1700 the Kazan Tatars had the same ancestral symbols (*tamgas*) as their counterpart clans among the Kazakhs. So now the question arises: how did this Tatar community come about and why was it given the ethnonym 'Tatar'?

This question has already been partially addressed. Before Genghis Khan the western part of what would later become the Tatar nation, the Volga basin, was formed owing to interrelated but separate parts of the Turkic tribes of the Huns, Alan, Bulgars, Khazars and Goths, which included what are today the Kazakh Argyn, Balgaly, Baltaly, Baganal, Matai, Dughlat, Khongirad, Koralas, Khereid and many clans of the Alshyn.

It is known that the Tatar were enemies of the clan of Genghis Khan; they killed his father, and therefore when Genghis Khan obtained the required strength he brutally avenged the killers for his father: all Tatars were 'levelled with the axle of a cart', that is, all Tatars who were taller in height than the axle of a cart were executed. Later the young Tatar warriors, having grown into men and with outstanding abilities, served in Genghis Khan's avant garde, and that is why the population of the conquered nations uttered the name Tatar with fear. Mention is made in Russian chronicles of the term *tartary* as a symbol of hell. It is not by coincidence that almost all the sources that detail the conquests of Genghis Khan's forces say little about the Mongols but give full attention to the deeds of the Tatars and the Turks.

An example: in his *Livres des merveilles du monde* Marco Polo mentions the Tatars in almost every chapter: 'For a radius of three miles around the city of Karakoron was first captured by the Tatars...'; 'Krerman is an ancient kingdom in Persia itself and was ruled by kings by succession, but since it was conquered by the Tatar...', '... in these lands there are many evil men and bandits, there are killings every day, they fear the Eastern Tatars, their rulers...', 'Persia is a large country, but in the old times it was still larger and more powerful, but now the Tatars have ravaged and plundered it...' 'In the year of our Lord 1255 Hulagu, the great king of the Tatar...', 'In Georgia the king is always called Divnu-Melik, which in French means 'King David'; he is subservient to the Tatars...', etc, etc.

Scholars of the Mongol empire agree that the ethnic origin of the Tatars has not so far been precisely determined. The chronicle *Men-da bey-lu* recounts the words of the ambassador to the Song dynasty of southern China, Zhao Hun, who visited Mongolia in 1221. According to him, Genghis Khan's deputy Muqali called himself a Tatar, although it is known that he was an ethnic Kazakh of the Jalayir. It is therefore possible that the identification 'Tatar' was widely used among the populations under Genghis Khan's rulership alongside the name 'Mongol'.

The warriors of Genghis Khan who went to the Volga once the Golden Horde was founded included Ongud and Manghud that comprised the main part of the Nogai Horde, Baarin and Shyryn; intermixing with tribes that at that time were ethnically Kazakh, they formed the basis of the Kazan, Crimean, Astrakhan and Lithuanian tribes that subsequently became known as 'Tatars'.

Accordingly the Tatar, who before the Common Era lived under the ethnonym of Donghu and later of Kumo Xi (or Tatab) and Ongud, and then came in the 13th century to the West with Genghis Khan, gave their name to the Turkic tribes that were living in the catchments of the Volga, Ural, Don and Kuban rivers.

Of course, to arrive in a new place and give one's name to other peoples who also prize their names is not such a simple matter. Yet the newcomers had the power of the Golden Horde behind them, and also, the arriving Turkic tribes genuinely excelled over the local groups in their 'passionarity' (as Gumilev would say), their fighting spirit and their hunger for statehood. It should be added that over time the population of western Kazakhstan began to replace 'Tatar' with the ethnonym 'Alashyn'. Scholars have strongly opposing views as to the origin of this name. They generally form groups around the term 'Alash' as being a specific synonym for 'Kazakh'. Muhamedzhan Tynyshpaev, for example, considers that it was in western Kazakhstan that the basic core of the future Kazakh nation was formed. One of the twelve clans of the Bayuly tribe is the 'Alasha'. Yet one should not forget that, according to Rashid ad-Din Hamadani, the senior wife of Batu Khan was one Boraqshy-khatun of the Tatar clan 'Alchi'. The base of Batu Khan and his successors was established first by the Ural and later by the Volga, on age-old lands of the Kazakhs of the Junior *jüz*. It may be partially due to this that with time the collective name for the Junior *jüz* of Kazakhs became the ethnonym 'Alshyn', named from the Tatar clan 'Alchi'. This is one of the opinions.

* * *

Soviet-era historiography clung to the term 'the Tatar-Mongol yoke'. It should be pointed out that, firstly, the connection between the yoke and the Mongols is far-fetched, as the name given by Genghis Khan to the people that were united under his flag was not yet known in Rus' in the year 1234. Not one of the sources, describing the westward invasion of the nomads in the 13th century, mentions the Mongols; instead they are referred to throughout as Tatars or Turks. I have already cited particular observations by Marko Polo. The same is true of the writings of Giovanni da Pian del Carpine and William of Rubruck, both of whom visited the headquarters of the Mongol khans in the 13th century.

The Arab historian Ali ibn al-Athir, who died in 1233 and was a direct witness of the invasion, wrote: '... In this year of 617, in the lands of Islam there appeared the Tatar, a large Turkic tribe...' ('Sbornik materialov, otnosyashchikhsia k Zolotoy Orde' in *Istoria Kazakhstana v arabskikh istochnikakh*, Almaty: Dayk Press, 2005, v.1).

Those who went to the West with Genghis Khan, and later with his grandsons Batu and Güyük were not the ancestors of the present-day Mongols but rather the ancestors of the present-day Kazakhs and Tatars, who wandered over these lands and considered them their own.

But did acts of cruelty and mass killings really accompany every conquest? Here is the view of the Russian historian Nikolai Karamzin:

'The khans wanted solely to rule from a distance, without interfering in the affairs of the citizens and demanded only silver and the obedience of the princes...'. Another Russian historian, Vasily Klyuchevsky, continues: 'The khans of the hordes did not impose any of their orders on Rus', being satisfied with tribute, and indeed only poorly grasped the order that prevailed there...'. All these evaluations of the so-called 'Tatar-Mongol yoke' are widely covered in the works of these Russian historians, works such as the *Istoria gosudarstva Rossiyskogo* and *Kurs russkoy istorii*, although mainstream society knows little about them.

Once again let me direct the reader also to Jack Weatherford's *Genghis Khan and the making of the modern world*, which suggests that modern Russia should be grateful to Genghis Khan and his Turkic tribes, thanks to whom Russia and Rus' could have developed into great nations, having previously been mired in internecine wars and factions. Had it not been for Genghis Khan, Russia would in all likelihood have become a province of the Catholic West. The present-day scholar Thomas Barfield (Rus. trans. *Mongolskaia model' kochevoy imperii*, Ulan-Ude, 2004) pointed out that Genghis Khan created a fundamentally new type of state on the border of the great Chinese state. If the previous Turkic states had carried out raids, to put it bluntly, stealing from the settled and prosperous Chinese, then the state created by Genghis Khan broke the existing tribal system and created a centralised political system of government that came to rule over the civilised China, introducing a structure of government and methods of administration that ultimately made it possible to establish the Celestial Kingdom as a single power.

Prince Nikolay Trubetskoy, known for his Eurasianist outlook, accurately defined the place of Russia in the era of the 'Tatar-Mongol yoke' as a province of the great Mongol state that found itself at the very lowest rung of development. Yet the national self-consciousness that was awoken by this 'yoke' and that critically re-examined the 'great idea that possessed an irresistable force of attraction' of Mongol statehood, enabled her to reach to the reality of Russia itself. **Replacing Tengriism with Orthodoxy Christianity, Russia gained the grand idea that later**

brought the Rus' of appanage kingdoms to the rank of a great empire. And for Rus this is the main outcome of the 'Tatar-Mongol yoke'.

As for the Kazakhs, it would be worth recalling that had it not been for Genghis Khan, we would not possess the ninth-largest country in the world by area. Indeed for the very being of a Kazakh nation we are indebted to him. We will not forget this.

LITERATURE AND SOURCES CONSULTED

1. Abramov, D.: *Tysiacheletie vokrug Chernogo moria.* Moscow: Algoritm, 2007.
2. Abu al-Ghazi Bahadur: *Rodoslovnoe slovo tiurkov,* 'Turkestan', TKISO, 1996.
3. Adam of Bremen: *Gesta Hammaburgensis ecclesiae pontificum.* Rus. ed. *Deiania archiepiskov Gamburgskoy tserkvi. Iz ranney istorii shvedskogo naroda i gosudarstva: pervye opisania i zakony.* Moscow, 1999.
4. Adilov, B.: *Dolgaia pesn' argunov ili gunni zagovorili.* Almaty: Olke, 2006.
5. Adji, M.: *Dykhanie Armageddona,* Moscow: Khranitel', 2006.
6. Adji, M.: *Kipchaki – Oguzy* (Moscow: Tipografia 'Novosti', 2001.
7. Adji, M.: *Tiurki i mir: Sokrovennaia istoria.* Moscow: Khranitel', 2004.
8. Akatay, S.: *Naiman khandygy.* Almaty, 2002.
9. Anuchin, V.I.: *Ocherk shamanstva u ieniseyskikh ostiakov,* in Sbornik museia antropologii i etnografii. 2nd ed., St Petersburg, 1914.
10. Aristov, N.A.: *Zametki ob etnicheskom sostave tiurkskykh plemen i narodnostey.* St Petersburg, 1896.
11. Arrian of Nicomedia: *Periplus of the Erythraean Sea.* Rus. ed. see *VDI,* 1939, no. 2.
12. Asadov, F.M.: *Arabskie istochniki o tiurkakh v ranee srednevekov'ie.* Baku: Elm, 1993
13. Baabar, B.: *History of Mongolia.* Ulanbator: Monsudar Publishing, 1999.
14. Baier, B., Birnstein, U., Gehlhoff, B. and Schütt, E.C.: *Neue Chronik der Weltgeschichte.* Gütersloh: Chronik Verlag, 2010.
15. Banzarov, D.: *Ob Oiratakh i Uigursakh.* Kazan, 1849, v.1.
16. Barfield, T.: *Mongolskaia model' kochevoy imperii.* Ulan-Ude, 2004.
17. Barmankunov, M.: *Khrustal'nye mechty tiurkov o kvadranatsii,* Almaty: Bis, 1999.
18. Bartold, V.V.: *Ocherki istorii Semirech'ia*

243

19. Baskakov, N.: *Russkie familii dvorianskogo proiskhozhdenia*. Moscow, 1979.

20. Bayzhumin, Zh.: *Turan: Vzglyad na istoriu chelovecheskogo obshchestva.* – Almaty: Arks, 2012, vols. I – IV.

21. Bazylkhan, B.: *Mongol-Kazakh tol'/Mongolsha-Kazaksha sozdik,* Ulan-Bator: Olgiy, 1984

22. Beletsky, M.: *Zabyty mir shumerov.* Trans. fro Polish, USSR Academy of Sciences, Institute of Oriental Studies. Moscow: Nauka, 1980.

23. Bernshtam, A.N. *Ocherki istorii gunnov,* Leningrad: LGU, 1951.

24. Bernshtam, A.N. *Proiskhozhdenie turok. Problemy istorii dokapitalisticheskogo obshchestva,* 1935, nos. 5-6

25. Bezertinov, R.: *Tengrianstvo – religia tiurkov i mongolov.* Kazan: Slovo, 2004.

26. Bichurin, N.: *Sobranie svedeniy o narodakh, obitavshikh v Sredney Azii v drevnie vremena.* Moscow and Leningrad, 1950, vol. 2.

27. Bremensky, G.: *Slavianskie khroniki.* Moscow, 1960.

28. Bushkov, A.: *Chingiskhan. Neizvestnaia Azia.* Moscow: Olma Media Group, 2007.

29. Bushkov, A.: *Rossia, kotoroy ne bylo. Mirazhi i prizraky.* Moscow: Olma-press, 2004.

30. Bychkov, A.: *Kievskaia Rus'. Strana, kotoroy nikogda ne bylo?* Moscow: Astrel, 2005.

31. Ceram, C.W.: *Götter, Gräber und Gelehrte.* Rus. trans. A.S. Varshavsky, Moscow: Astrel, 2006.

32. D'yakonov, I.M.: *Nauka i zhizn'.* 1989, no. 9

33. Daniyarov, K.: *Al'ternativnaia istoria Kazakhstana.* Almaty, 1998.

34. Daniyarov, K.: *Istoria Alash.* Almaty, 2006.

35. Daniyarov, K.: *Istoria Chingiskhana.* Almaty, 2001.

36. de Sanctis, Gaetano: *Storia dei Romani,* in 4 vols, Rome, 1953–56.

37. Demin, V., Lazarev, Ye. and Slatin, N.: *Drevnee drevnosti: Rossiyskaia prototsivilizatsia.* Moscow: AiF Print, 2004.

38. Dexippus, Publius Herennius, in *VDI,* 1948, no. 1.

39. Domanin, A.: *Mongol'skaia imperia chingizidov. Chingishan i ego*

preemniki. Moscow: Tsentropoligraf, 2005.

40. Drozdov, Yuri: *Tiurkoiazychny period yevropeiskoi istorii.* Moscow: Litera, 2011

41. Fan Wen Lan: *Drevniaia istoria Kitaia.* (Rus. trans. of part of *Modern History of China,* 1947)

42. Garkavts, A.N., compiler and ed.: *Velikaia step' v antichnykh i vizantiyskikh istochnikakh* (collected source texts), Almaty: Baur, 2005.

43. Gimbutas, M.: *Balty. Liudi Iantarnogo moria.* Moscow: Tsentrpoligraf, 2004.

44. Giovanni da Pian del Carpine: *Puteshestvie v Yevraziiskie stepi,* Almaty, 2003

45. Gordon Childe, V.: *The Aryans: a study of Indo-European origins* (Rus. ed. *Ariytsy. Osnovateli yevropeyskoy tsivilizatsii*). Moscow: Tsentrpoligraf, 2010.

46. Grigoriev, V.V.: *O skifskom narode sakakh.* St Petersburg, 1871.

47. Grumm-Grzhimaylo, G.E.: *Zapadnaia Mongolia i Uriankhaysky kray,* vol. 2, Leningrad, 1926.

48. Gumilev, L.: *Chornaia legenda.* Moscow, Airis Press, 2003.

49. Gumilev, L.: *Istoria narodov khunnu.* Moscow: AST, 2004.

50. Gumilev, L.: *Ot Rusi k Rossii.* Moscow, 2004.

51. Gumilev, L.: *Ritmy Yevrazii.* Moscow, 2004.

52. Gumilev, L.: *Tysiachiletia vokrug Kaspia.* Moscow: Ayris-Press, 2003.

53. Hara-Davan, E.: *Chingishan kak polkovodets i ego nasledie. Kul'turno-istorichesky ocherk mongol'skoy imperii 12-14 vekov.* Almaty: KRAMDS – Ahmet Yassaui, 1992.

54. Harenberg, B.: *Khronika chelovechestva.* Moscow, Slovo, 2000.

55. Hippocrates: *On Air, Waters and Places.* Rus. ed. (*O vozdukhe, vodakh i mestnostyakh*) see *VDI,* 1947, no. 1, p. 295.

56. Hoang, M.: *Genghis Khan.* Eng. trans. pub. Saqi Books, 1998.

57. ibn al-Athir, Ali: see 'Sbornik materialov, otnosyashchikhsia k Zolotoy Orde' in *Istoria Kazakhstana v arabskikh istochnikakh,* Almaty: Dayk Press, 2005, v.1.

58. Ismagulov,O.: *Nasledie Kazakhstana ot epokhi bronzy do sovremennosti.* Alma-Ata: 1970.

59. *Istoria Kazakhstana v proizvedeniakh antichnykh avtorov,* Astana: Foliant, 2005.

60. Juvayni, Ata-Melik: *Genghis Khan. Istoria zavoevatelia mira.* Moscow: Magistr-Press, 2004

61. Karamzin, N.: *Istoria gosudarstva Rossiyskogo.* Moscow: Ast, St Petersburg: Kristall, 2003, books 1-3.

62. Kargabaev, M.: *Atlantida kochevnikov.* Karaganda, 2007.

63. Kharuzin, A.: 'K voprosu o proiskhozhdenii kirgizskogo naroda'. *Etnograficheskoe obozrenie,* No. 3, 1895.

64. Khazanov, A.M.: *Kochevniki i vneshny mir.* Almaty, 2002.

65. Kikeshev, N.I.: *Metaistoria. Otkuda my rodom? Mify, gipotezy, fakty.* Moscow: Niola-Press, 2000.

66. Klejn, L.: *Vremya kentavrov. Stepnaia prarodina grekov i ariev.* St Petersburg: Yevrazia, 2010.

67. Klyashtorny, S.: *Istoria Tsentral'noy Azii i pamiatniki runicheskogo pis'ma.* St Petersburg, 2003.

68. Kogan, V. and Dombrovsky-Shalagin, V.: *Kniaz' Riurik i yego potomki. Istoriko-genealogichesky svod.* St Petersburg: Paritet, 2004.

69. Kozha-Ahmet, Hasen: *Zabluzhdenie, dlivsheesia vekami.* Almaty: Bilim, 2013.

70. Kozin, S.: *Sokrovennoe skazanie. Mongol'skaia khronika 1240.* (Stalin's official translation of *The Secret History of the Mongols*). Moscow and Leningrad, 1941, vol. 1. Note that for this English translation, excerpts from *SHM* are taken from Urgunge Onon, trans. & ed, *The Secret History of the Mongols.* London: Routledge Curzon, 2001.

71. Kradin, N.N. and Skrynnikova, T.D.: *Imperia Chingis-hana,* Moscow: Vostochnaya literatura, Russian Academy of Sciences, 2006.

72. Kruchkin, Yu.: *Mongolsko-russky, russko-mongol'sky slovar'.* Moscow: AST: Vostok-Zapad, 2006.

73. Kuanganov, S.: *Ariy-gunn skvoz' veka i prostranstvo: svidetel'stva, toponimy.* Astana: Foliant, 2001.

74. Kudayberdy-uly, Sh.: *Rodoslovnaia tiurkov, kirgizov, kazakhov i khanskikh dinastiy.* Almaty: Zhazushy, 1999.

75. Kulikov, B.: *Arabskie i persidskie istochniki po istorii kypchakov XII-XIV vv.* Alma-Ata, 1987.

76. Laypanov, K.T. and Meziev, I.M.: *O proiskhozhdenie tiurkskikh narodov.* Cherkessk: PUL, 1993, p. 102.

77. Levshin, A.I.: *Opisanie kirgiz-kazach'ikh ili kirgiz-kaysatskik ord i stepey.* Reprint, Almaty, 1996.

78. Mackinder, H.: *The geographical pivot of history.* Paper submitted to Royal Geographical Society, London, 1904

79. Magauin, M.: *Azbuka Kazakhskoy istorii. Dokumental'noe povestvovanie,* Almaty, 1997.

80. Mallory, J.P.: 'Indoievropeiskaia pradrodina', *Vestnik drevney istorii (VDI),* 1997, no. 1, pp. 61-82

81. Man, J.: *Genghis Khan.* London: Bantam, 2005

82. Marco Polo: *Livres des merveilles du monde.* Rus. ed. e.g. Almaty: Kochevnik, 2005.

83. Mary Boyce, M.: *Zoroastrizm: verovanie i obichai.* Moscow: Nauka, 1987 (Rus. ed. of *Zoroastrians: their religious beliefs and practices*).

84. Masanov, N., Abylhozhin, Zh. and Yerofeeva, I.: *Nauchnoe znanie i mifotvorchestvo v sovremennoy istoriografii Kazakhstana.* Almaty: Dayk-Press, 2007.

85. Masson, V.M. and Merpert, Nikolay: 'Voprosy otnositel'noi khronologii Starogo sveta', *Sovremennaya archeologia,* 1958, no. 1.

86. McGovern, W.: *The early empires of Central Asia,* London, 1939

87. Men, J.: *Genghis Khan.* 2nd ed. London: Bantam, 2005.

88. *Mify narodov mira,* v.1, Moscow: Sovietskaia entsikolpedia, 1980

89. Morgan, H.L.: *Ancient society.* (Leningrad ed.), vols. 1-2, 1954.

90. Narymbaeva, A.K.: *Turan – kolybel' drevnikh tsivilizatsiy.* Almaty, 2009

91. Nennius: in *Formy istorichestogo soznania ot pozdney antichnosti do epokhi vozrozhdenia,* Ivanovo, 2000.

92. Obukhov, V.: *Skhvatka shesti imperiy.* Moscow: Veche, 2007.

93. Omarbekov, T. and Kabzhalilov, Kh.: 'O rodovykh znakakh drevnikh

tiurkov i kazakhov' (*Alash*, 2005, no. 1).
94. Omarov, Ye.: *Kratkaia istoria Kazakhskoy tsivilizatsii*. Almaty: Arda, 2005.
95. Pallas, P.S.: *Sobranie istoricheskikh isvestiy o Mongol'skikh narodakh, sochinennoe gospodinom P.S. Pallasom*. St Petersburg, 1766.
96. Parker, E.H.: *A thousand years of the Tatars*, Kazan, 2003; also Ulan Press, 2011
97. Penzev, K.: *Russky Tsar' Baty*. Moscow: Algoritm, 2006.
98. Petukhov, Y. and Vasilieva, N.: *Yevraziyskaia imperia skifov*. Moscow, 2007.
99. Plutarch: Rus. versions in *Izbrannye zhizneopisania*, Moscow: Pravda, 1987.
100. Procopius of Caesarea: *Voyna s gotami*. Moscow, 1950.
101. Rashid ad-Din Hamadani: *Sbornik letopisey*, USSR Academy of Sciences, 1952.
102. Simocatta, Theophylact: *Istoria*, Moscow, 1996
103. Smirnov, K.F. and Kuzminskaya, E.E.: *Proiskhozhdenie indoevropeitsev v svete noveishikh archeologicheskikh otkrytiy*, Moscow: Nauka, 1977
104. Soldatenkova, S.S.: *Drevniaia istoria narodov Vostoka* (Rus. trans. of *Histoire ancienne des peuples de l'Orient*). Moscow, 1895.
105. Strabon Gney Pompey. VDI, 1947, no. 4
106. Struve, V.V. (ed.): *Khrestomatia po istorii Drevnego mira*. Moscow: State educational and pedagogic publishing house of Minpros of RSFSR, vol. 2, 1951
107. Sükhbaatar, O.: *Zaimstvovannye slova v mongol'skom iazyke*, Ulan-Bator, 1997.
108. Suleimenov, O.: *Iazyk pis'ma*. Almaty and Rome, 1998
109. Suleimenov, O.: *Tiurki v doistorii*. Almaty: Atamura, 2002
110. Sultanov, T.: *Podniatie na beloy koshme. Khany Kazakhskikh stepey*. Astana, 2006.
111. *The Anglo-Saxon chronicle*. Trans. Rev. James Ingram. London and Toronto, 1923.
112. Thomsen, V.: 'Deshifrovka orkhonskikh i ieniskeyskikh nadpisey',

Zapisey Vostochnogo otdelenia Russkogo archeologicheskogo obshchestva, v. 8, issues III-IV, St Petersburg, 1894.

113. Thomson, J.O.: *A History of Ancient Geography*, Rus. ed. Moscow, 1953.

114. Tiesenhausen, V.G.: *Sbornik materialov, otnosyashchikhsia k istorii Zolotoy Ordy.* Vol. 1: Izvlechenia iz sochineniy arabskykh. St Petersburg, 1840.

115. Trubetskoy, N.: *Nasledie Chingiskhana.* Moscow: EKSIMO, 2007.

116. Tynyshpaev, M.: *Istoria Kazakhskogo naroda*, Almaty: Sanat, 2002.

117. Utemish-Hadji: *Chingis-Name.* Almaty: Gylym, 1992.

118. Vasiliev, L.S.: *Problemy genezisa kitayskogo gosudarstva*, Moscow: Nauka, 1988.

119. Vladimirtsev, B.Ya.: *Obshchestvenniy stroy mongolov. Mongol'skiy kochevoy feodalizm*, Leningrad, 1934.

120. Voropaeva, V., Dzhunushaliev, D. and Ploskikh, V.: *Istoria Otechestva. Kratkiy kurs lektsiy po istorii Kyrgyzstana.* 2nd ed., Bishkek: Raritet Info, 2005.

121. Walikhanov, Sh.: *Sobranie sochineniy v piati tomakh* (collected works in 5 vols). Alma-Ata, 1984.

122. Wang Tong Ling: *Istoria kitayskoy natsii.* Beynin, 1934

123. Weatherford, J.: *Genghis Khan and the making of the modern world.* New York: Three Rivers Press, new ed. 2005. Citations in this translation are taken from the Kindle edition, Crown Publishing Group.

124. Wei, Juxian: *Issledovania po drevney istorii.* Shanghai, 1937, vol. 3.

125. Yurchenko, A.G.: *Istoricheskaia geografia politicheskogo mifa. Obraz Chingis-khana v mirovoy literature XIII-XV vv*, St Petersburg: Yevrazia, 2006

126. Zakiryanov, K.K.: *Pod znakom volka. Tiurkskaia rapsodia.* Almaty: Altyn baspa, 2012. English/Kazakh version: *Under the wolf's nest. A Turkic rhapsody.* London: Hertfordshire Press, 2012. Zakiryanov, K.K.: Tiurkskaia saga Chingishana. Sokrovennoe skazanie kazakhov. Almaty: Zhibek Zholy, 2008.

127. Zlatkin, I.Ya.: *Istoria Dzhungarskogo khanstva.* Moscow: Nauka, 1983.

Translator's note:
Citations from *The Secret History of the Mongols* in English are taken from Onon, Urgunge, ed.: *The Secret History of the Mongols: The Life and Times of Chinggis Khan*, London: RoutledgeCurzon, 2001.

**Under the Sign of the Wolf: A Turkic Rhapsody
by Kairat Zakiryanov**

Were the origins of Islam, Christianity and the legend of King Arthur all influenced by steppe nomads from Kazakhstan?

Ranging through thousands of years of history, and drawing on sources from Herodotus through to contemporary Kazakh and Russian research, the crucial role in the creation of modern civilisation played by the Turkic people is revealed in this detailed yet highly accessible work.

Professor Kairat Zakiryanov, President of the Kazakh Academy of Sport and Tourism, explains how generations of steppe nomads, including Genghis Khan, have helped shape the language, culture and populations of Asia, Europe, the Middle East and America through migrations taking place over millennia.

After reading Under the Sign of the Wolf: A Turkic Rhapsody you will look again at language and culture, and realise the living histories they represent.

RRP: £17.50
ISBN: 978-0-9574807-2-8

Friendly Steppes: A Silk Road Journey
by Nick Rowan

This is the chronicle of an extraordinary adventure that led Nick Rowan to some of the world's most incredible and hidden places. Intertwined with the magic of 2,000 years of Silk Road history, he recounts his experiences coupled with a remarkable realisation of just what an impact this trade route has had on our society as we know it today. Containing colourful stories, beautiful photography and vivid characters, and wrapped in the local myths and legends told by the people Nick met and who live

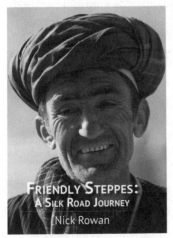

along the route, this is both a travelogue and an education of a part of the world that has remained hidden for hundreds of years.

Friendly Steppes: A Silk Road Journey reveals just how rich the region was both culturally and economically and uncovers countless new friends as Nick travels from Venice through Eastern Europe, Iran, the ancient and modern Central Asia of places like Samarkand, Bishkek and Turkmenbashi, and on to China, along the Silk Roads of today.

RRP:£14.95
ISBN: 978-0-9557549-4-4

The Alphabet Game
by Paul Wilson

With the future of Guidebooks under threat, The Alphabet Game takes you back to the very beginning, back to their earliest incarnations and the gamesmanship that brought them into being. As Evelyn Waugh's Scoop did for Foreign Correspondents the world over, so this novel lifts the lid on Travel Writers for good.

Travelling around the world may appear as easy as A,B,C in the twenty first century, but looks can be deceptive: there is no 'X' for a start. Not since Xidakistan was struck from the map. But post 9/11, with the War on Terror going global, the sovereignty of 'The Valley' is back on the agenda. Could the Xidakis, like their Uzbek and Tajik neighbours, be about to taste the freedom of independence? Will Xidakistan once again take its rightful place in the League of Nations?

The Valley's fate is inextricably linked with that of Graham Ruff, founder of Ruff Guides. In a tale setting sail where Around the World in Eighty Days and Lost Horizon weighed anchor, our not-quite-a-hero suffers all the slings and arrows outrageous fortune can muster, in his pursuit of the golden triangle: The Game, The Guidebook, The Girl.

Wilson tells The Game's story with his usual mix of irreverent wit and historical insight, and in doing so delivers the most telling satire on an American war effort since M*A*S*H.

The Guidebook is Dead? Long Live the Guidebook.

RRP: £14.95
ISBN: 978-0-9927873-2-5

Chants of the Dark Fire
by Zhulduz Baizakova

The author, a former press attaché at the Embassy of the Republic of Kazakhstan, in London, offers with Chants of the Dark Fire a fascinating portrait of, and insight into, life both past and present within this largest of all of the Central Asian states.
The short but colourful career of her grandfather Isa, who dedicated his entire existence to art, provides an ideal tableau for an infectious enthusiasm for the culture of Kazakhstan and Central Asia as a whole.

RRP:£10.00
ISBN: 978-0-9574807-1-1

100 Experiences of KAZAKHSTAN

The original land of the nomads, landlocked Kazakhstan and its expansive steppes present an intriguing border between Europe and Asia. Dispel the notion of oil barons and Borat and be prepared for a warm welcome into a land full of contrasts. A visit to this newly independent country will transport you to a bygone era and discover a country full of wonders and legends. Whether you are searching for the descendants of Genghis Khan who left his mark on this country seven hundred years ago or are looking to discover the futuristic architecture of its capital Astana, visitors cannot fail but be impressed by what they experience. For those seeking adventure, the formidable Altai and Tian Shan mountains provide challenges at all levels. Alternatively, really go off the beaten track and visit Kazakhstan's industrial legacy at Aktau, the Aral Sea or the space launch centre at Baikonur. Bird and animal lovers will gloat over the diversity of species that can be seen from antelopes to flamingos. Above all, whether you are in cosmopolitan Almaty or out in the wilds of Western Kazakstan, you will come across a warm people, proud of the heritage and keen to show you a traditional country that is at the forefront of the region's economic development.

Discovery Magazine's colourful new title, exploring the 100 essential experiences of Kazakhstan covers everything from its cities to culture, horse games to holidays and authors to yurts. Told through personal experiences written by locals, each vignette brings the reader closer to understanding and interacting with one of Central Asia's most intriguing cultures, often missed by transiting travellers keen to reach Uzbekistan and Kyrgyzstan. This publication, filled with stunning photography, brings out the exhilarating flavours of the country's foods, spectacular scenery and warm-hearted people and deservedly leaves you with the urge to return again and visit the next 100 experiences that await you.

RRP: £19.95
ISBN: 978-0-9927873-5-6